For John Barrell

Empire, Barbarism, and Civilisation

The artist William Hodges accompanied Captain Cook on his second voyage to the South Pacific in 1772–5. His extraordinarily vivid images, read against the fascinating journals of Cook and his companions, reveal as much about European cultures and historiography as about the peoples they visited. In this lively and original book, Harriet Guest discusses Hodges's dramatic landscapes and portraits alongside written accounts of the voyages and in the context of the theories of civilisation which shaped European perceptions – theories drawn from the works of philosophers of the Scottish enlightenment such as Adam Smith and John Millar. She argues that the voyagers resorted to diverse or incompatible models of progress in successive encounters with different groups of islanders, and shows how these models also structured metropolitan views of the voyagers and of Hodges's work. This fully illustrated study offers a fresh perspective on eighteenth-century representations of gender, colonialism, and exploration.

HARRIET GUEST is Professor of English in the Centre for Eighteenth Century Studies at the University of York.

Empire, Barbarism, and Civilisation

James Cook, William Hodges, and the
Return to the Pacific

HARRIET GUEST

CAMBRIDGE
UNIVERSITY PRESS

CAMBRIDGE UNIVERSITY PRESS

Cambridge, New York, Melbourne, Madrid, Cape Town, Singapore, São Paulo, Delhi

Cambridge University Press
The Edinburgh Building, Cambridge CB2 8RU, UK

Published in the United States of America by Cambridge University Press, New York

www.cambridge.org
Information on this title: www.cambridge.org/9780521881944

First published 2007

Printed in the United Kingdom at the University Press, Cambridge

A catalogue record for this publication is available from the British Library

ISBN 978-0-521-88194-4 hardback

Contents

List of colour plates	*page*	ix
List of black and white figures		xv
Acknowledgements		xix
Introduction		1
1 The great distinction		28
2 Curiosity and desire		49
3 Curiously marked		68
4 Terms of trade in Tonga and Vanuatu		91
5 New Zealand colonial romance		124
6 Ornament and use in London		149
Epilogue: *The Effects of Peace* and *The Consequences of War* in 1794–1795		169
Notes		199
Bibliography		230
Index		245

Colour plates

Between pages 140 and 141

0.1 William Hodges, *A View of the Monuments of Easter Island* [Rapanui], 1775, oil on panel, 775 × 1,219 mm. National Maritime Museum, London. MoD Art Collection.

0.2 William Hodges, *View of the Province of Oparee* [Pare], *Island of Otaheite, with part of the Island of Eimeo* [Moorea], [1775?], oil on panel, 762 × 1,232 mm. National Maritime Museum, London. MoD Art Collection.

0.3 William Hodges, *Review of the War Galleys at Tahiti*, [c. 1776], oil on panel, 241 × 470 mm. National Maritime Museum, London. MoD Art Collection.

0.4 William Hodges, *The War Boats of the Island of Otaheite* [Tahiti], *and the Society Isles, with a View of Part of the Harbour of Ohameneno* [Haamanino], *in the Island of Ulietea* [Raiatea], *One of the Society Islands*, 1777, oil on canvas, 1,811 × 2,743 mm. National Maritime Museum, London. MoD Art Collection.

1.1 William Hodges, *A View Taken in the Bay of Otaheite Peha* [Vaitepiha], 1776, oil on canvas, 915 × 1,371 mm. National Trust, Anglesey Abbey, Cambridgeshire. ©NTPL/John Hammond.

1.2 William Hodges, *View of Matavai Bay in the Island of Otaheite*, 1776, oil on canvas, 915 × 1,371 mm. Yale Center for British Art, New Haven, Paul Mellon Collection.

1.3 Detail from William Hodges, *A View Taken in the Bay of Otaheite Peha* [Vaitepiha], 1776, oil on canvas, 915 × 1,371 mm. National Trust, Anglesey Abbey, Cambridgeshire.

2.1 William Hodges, *[A] View of Maitavie Bay*, [in the Island of] *Otaheite* [Tahiti], 1776, oil on canvas, 1,371 × 193 mm. National Maritime Museum, London. MoD Art Collection.

2.2 William Hodges, '*Tahiti Revisited*' [the title 'A View taken [in] yᵉ Bay of Oaite peha OTAHEITE' is inscribed on the back of the original canvas], 1776, oil on canvas, 927 × 1,384 mm. National Maritime Museum, London. MoD Art Collection.

2.3   William Hodges, [*View in Tahiti with Waterfall and Girls Bathing*], [1775], oil on panel, 301 × 457 mm. Private collection, England.

2.4   William Hodges, [*Waterfall in Tuauru*], [1775], oil on panel, 762 × 1,235 mm. Copyright 2007 The Kelton Foundation.

2.5   William Hodges, [*A Waterfall in Tahiti*], [1775], oil on panel, 489 × 616 mm. National Maritime Museum, London. MoD Art Collection.

2.6   William Hodges, *Landscape, Ruins, and Figures*, 1790, oil on panel, 950 × 1,325 mm. James Mackinnon.

3.1   Joshua Reynolds, *Portrait of Omai*, c. 1775–6, oil on canvas, 2,362 × 1,448 mm. Sotheby's Picture Library, London.

3.2   William Parry, *Omai, Joseph Banks and Dr. Solander*, 1775–6, oil on canvas, 1,525 × 1,525 mm. Copyright National Portrait Gallery, London / National Museum & Gallery, Cardiff / Captain Cook Memorial Museum, Whitby.

3.3   Benjamin West, *Joseph Banks*, 1771–3, oil on canvas, 2,340 × 1,600 mm. Usher Gallery, Lincoln, courtesy of Lincolnshire County Council, THE COLLECTION, Art and Archaeology in Lincolnshire.

3.4   William Hodges, *Old Maori Man with a Grey Beard*, May 1773, chalk, 542 × 379 mm. National Library of Australia, Canberra. nla.pic-an2720542.

3.5   William Hodges, *Portrait of a Young Maori Man*, June 1773, red chalk, 542 × 375 mm. Mitchell Library, State Library of New South Wales, Sydney.

3.6   William Hodges, *Woman of* NEW ZELAND, [1773–5], red chalk, 544 × 374 mm. National Library of Australia, Canberra. nla.pic-an2717024.

3.7   William Hodges, *Maori Man with Bushy Hair*, May 1773, red chalk, 544 × 375 mm. National Library of Australia, Canberra. nla.pic-an2720564.

3.8   William Hodges, *Portrait of a Maori Chieftain*, October 1773, red chalk, 543 × 374 mm. National Library of Australia, Canberra. nla.pic-an2720518.

4.1   William Hodges, *A View of Cape Stephens in Cook's Straits with Waterspout*, c. 1776, oil on canvas, 1,359 × 1,931 mm. National Maritime Museum, London. MoD Art Collection.

4.2 William Hodges, *Tongatabu or Amsterdam*, [October 1773], watercolour, 375 × 545 mm. National Library of Australia. Rex Nan Kivell Collection. nla.pic-an2720598.

4.3 William Hodges, *The Landing at Mallicolo* [Malakula], *One of the New Hebrides*, [c. 1776], oil on panel, 241 × 457 mm. National Maritime Museum, London.

4.4 William Hodges, *The Landing at Erramanga One of the New Hebrides*, [c. 1776], oil on panel, 229 × 457 mm. National Maritime Museum, London. MoD Art Collection.

4.5 William Hodges, *The Landing at Tanna One of the New Hebrides*, [c. 1775–6], oil on panel, 241 × 457 mm. National Maritime Museum, London.

5.1 William Hodges, *View in Pickersgill Harbour, Dusky Bay, New Zealand*, April 1773, oil on canvas, 654 × 731 mm. National Maritime Museum, London. MoD Art Collection.

5.2 William Hodges, *Waterfall in Dusky Bay, April 1773*, 1775, oil on canvas, 1,359 × 1,930 mm. National Maritime Museum, London. MoD Art Collection.

5.3 William Hodges, [*Waterfall in Dusky Bay with a Maori Canoe. II*], [c. 1776], oil on panel, 273 × 356 mm. National Maritime Museum, London. MoD Art Collection.

5.4 William Hodges, [*A Maori Woman, Carrying a Child*], [April 1773], red chalk, 170 × 87 mm. British Museum, Department of Prints and Drawings, London. 201.c.5, no. 283. © Copyright The Trustees of The British Museum.

5.5 William Hodges, [*A Maori Man Holding a Hatchet*], [April 1773], red chalk, 221 × 76 mm. British Museum, Department of Prints and Drawings, London. 201.c.5, no. 282. © Copyright The Trustees of The British Museum.

5.6 William Hodges, *A View in Dusky Bay, New Zealand*, 1773, oil on circular wooden panel, 660 mm diam., 810 × 795 × 64 mm. Auckland Art Gallery Toi o Tamaki, purchased 1961.

6.1 Joshua Reynolds, *Head of Omai*, ?1775, 603 × 527 mm. Yale University Art Gallery.

6.2 William Hodges, *Omai*, between August 1775 and June 1776, oil on oval panel, 240 × 200 mm. Royal College of Surgeons, London.

6.3 John Webber, *Portrait of Captain James Cook*, 1776–80, oil on canvas, 1,095 × 695 mm. Museum of New Zealand Te Papa Tongarewa, Wellington (1960-0013-1).

6.4   John Webber, *Portrait of Captain James Cook R. N.*, 1782, oil on canvas, 1,140 × 910 mm. National Portrait Gallery, Canberra. Purchased by the Commonwealth Government with the generous assistance of Robert Oatley and John Schaeffer 2000.

6.5   William Hodges, *Captain James Cook*, c. 1775, oil on canvas, 762 × 635 mm. National Maritime Museum, London.

6.6   Nathaniel Dance, *James Cook*, 1775–6, oil on canvas. 1,270 × 1,016 mm. National Maritime Museum, London. Greenwich Hospital Collection.

6.7   John Hamilton Mortimer, [*Captain James Cook, Sir Joseph Banks, Lord Sandwich, Dr Daniel Solander and Dr John Hawkesworth*] ?1771, oil on canvas, 1,200 × 1,660 mm. National Library of Australia Canberra, nla.pic-an7351768.

7.1   Thomas Medland after William Hodges, *The Effects of Peace*, 1794, aquatint engraving, 760 × 510 mm. National Maritime Museum, London.

7.2   Thomas Medland after William Hodges, *The Consequences of War*, 1794, aquatint engraving, 760 × 510 mm. National Maritime Museum, London.

7.3   James Gillray, *Presentation of the Mahometan Credentials – or – The Final Resource of French Atheists*, London, published by H. Humphrey, 26 December 1793. BMC no. 8356. Courtesy of The Lewis Walpole Library, Yale University.

7.4   [I. Cruikshank], *A Peep at the Plenipo – !!!*, London, published by S. W. Fores, 1 January 1794. BMC no. 8423. Courtesy of The Lewis Walpole Library, Yale University.

7.5   Daniel Orme after Mather Brown, *The Attack on Famars*, London, 1796. © Copyright The Trustees of The British Museum.

7.6   Mather Brown, *Lord Howe on the Deck of the 'Queen Charlotte'*, 1794, oil on canvas, 2,591 × 3,658 mm. National Maritime Museum, London.

7.7   I. Cruikshank, *LORD HOWE They Run, or the British Tars Giving the Carmignols a Dressing on Memorable 1st of June 1794*, London, published by S. W. Fores, 25 June 1794. BMC no. 8471. Courtesy of The Lewis Walpole Library, Yale University.

7.8   Philippe-Jacques de Loutherbourg, *The Battle of the First of June, 1794*, 1795, oil on canvas, 2,665 × 3,735 mm. National Maritime Museum, London, Greenwich Hospital Collection. BHC0470.

7.9 James Gillray, *The Genius of France Triumphant, or – B R I T A N N I A petitioning for P E A C E, – Vide, The Proposals of Opposition*, London, published by H. Humphrey, 2 February 1795. BMC no. 8614. Courtesy of The Lewis Walpole Library, Yale University.

7.10 I. Cruikshank, *French Happiness/English Misery*, published by S. W. Fores, January 1793. BMC no. 8288. Courtesy of The Lewis Walpole Library, Yale University.

7.11 James Gillray, *Fatigues of the Campaign in Flanders*, London, published by H. Humphrey, 20 May 1793. BMC no. 8327. Courtesy of The Lewis Walpole Library, Yale University.

Black and white figures

0.1 James Cook, *A Chart of the Southern Hemisphere; Shewing the Tracks of Some of the Most Distinguished Navigators*, in James Cook, *A Voyage Towards the South Pole* (London: Strahan and Cadell, 1777), I, pl. I. National Library of Australia, Canberra, nla.map-nk2456–15. *page 2*

0.2 William Woollett after William Hodges, *Monuments in Easter Island*, in Cook, *Voyage* (1777), I, pl. X, engraving, 240 × 390 mm. National Library of Australia, Canberra, nla.pic-an7682817–1. 4

0.3 Adapted from a detail of C. Cooper, *Pacific Ocean on Mercator's Projection* (London: Sherwood, Neely and Jones, 1 Nov. 1809), from John Smith, *A System of Modern Geography, or, the Natural and Political History of the Present State of the World* (London: Sherwood, 1811). 8

0.4 William Woollett after William Hodges, *The Fleet of Otaheite Assembled at Oparee*, in Cook, *Voyage* (1777), I, pl. LXI. National Library of Australia, Canberra, nla.pic-an7682805. 16

1.1 Titian, *Diana and Actaeon*, c. 1556–9, oil on canvas, 1,880 × 2,030 mm. Duke of Sutherland Collection, on loan to the National Gallery of Scotland. 37

2.1 William Hodges, George Romney, and Sawrey Gilpin, *Jaques and the Wounded Stag in the Forest of Arden*, 1789, oil on canvas, 92.1 × 1,232 mm. Yale Center for British Art, Paul Mellon Fund. 64

2.2 Richard Wilson, *Solitude*, 1762, oil on canvas, 1,003 × 1,251 mm. City and County of Swansea: Glynn Vivian Art Gallery Collection. 65

3.1 Joshua Reynolds, *Members of the Society of Dilettanti*, 1779, oil on canvas, 1,968 × 1,422 mm. Brooks's Club, London, reproduced by kind permission of the Society of Dilettanti. 77

3.2 Sydney Parkinson, *Black Stains in the Skin called Tattoo*, 1769, pen and ink, top left 273 × 184 mm, top right 273 × 184 mm,

bottom left 286 × 229 mm, bottom right 149 × 120 mm.
British Library Add. MS 23920, fol. 66(a–d).   82

3.3   Herman Spöring, *Black Stains on the Skin called Tattoo*, 1769,
      pencil, top left 102 × 104 mm, top right 118 × 121 mm,
      bottom left 102 × 45 mm, bottom right 76 × 99 mm. British
      Library Add. MS 23920, fol. 67 (a–d).   83

3.4   Sydney Parkinson, *Portrait of a New Zeland Man* 1769, pen
      and ink wash, 394 × 298 mm. British Library Add MS 23920,
      fol. 54 (a).   84

3.5   Artist unknown, plate from [John Marra], *Journal of the
      Resolution's Voyage* (London: F. Newbury, 1775), 31 × 63 mm.
      National Library of Australia, Canberra.   85

3.6   T. Chambers after Sydney Parkinson, *The Head of a Chief of
      New Zealand, the Face Curiously Tataow'd, or Marked according
      to their Manner*, from Sydney Parkinson, *A Journal of a Voyage
      to the South Seas* (London, 1784), pl. 16, opposite p. 90,
      251 × 184 mm. Rex Nan Kivell Collection, National Library of
      Australia, Canberra, nla.pic-an8391494.   87

4.1   James Cook, *Chart of the Friendly Isles*, in Cook, *Voyage*
      (1777), I, pl. XIV. National Library of Australia, Canberra,
      aus-nk5677-1-s16x.   92

4.2   J. K. Sherwin after William Hodges, *The Landing at
      Middleburgh one of the Friendly Islands*, in Cook, *Voyage*
      (1777), II, pl. LIV (fp. 192), 275 × 515 mm. National Library
      of Australia, Canberra, nla.pic-an7691871.   94

4.3   William Hodges, *Tonga Tabu or Amsterdam*, [June 1774–], pen
      and indian ink wash, 619 × 1,172 mm. British Library,
      London, Add. MS 15743, fol. 2.   96

4.4   J. K. Sherwin after William Hodges, *The Landing at Tanna,
      One of the New Hebrides*, in Cook, *Voyage* (1777), II, pl. LIX
      (fp. 54), 235 × 473 mm. National Library of Australia,
      Canberra, nla.pic-an7691862.   98

4.5   J. K. Sherwin after William Hodges, *The Landing at
      Erramanga, One of the New Hebrides*, in Cook, *Voyage* (1777),
      II, pl. LXII (fp. 46). National Library of Australia, Canberra,
      nla.pic-an7691847-1.   100

4.6   J. Basire after William Hodges, *The Landing at Mallicolo, One
      of the New Hebrides*, in Cook, *Voyage* (1777), II, pl. LX (fp. 30).
      National Library of Australia, nla.pic-an7691873.   101

4.7 William Hodges, *[A Party of Maori in a Canoe]*, [June 1773–],
     pen and indian ink wash, with tints of watercolour, 375 × 545
     mm. La Trobe Library, State Library of Victoria, Melbourne.   102

4.8 Detail from James Cook, *Chart of Discoveries Made in the
     South Pacific Ocean*, in Cook, *Voyage* (1777), II, pl. III.
     National Library of Australia, Canberra, aus-nk5677-2-s4x.   114

5.1 James Cook, *Chart of New Zealand, Explored in 1769 and 1770*,
     in Cook, *Voyage* (1773), II: 283. National Library of Australia,
     Canberra, FERG 7243.   125

5.2 John Rutherford, from an original drawing taken in 1828,
     frontispiece to James Drummond, ed., *John Rutherford the
     White Chief: A Story of Adventure in New Zealand*
     (Christchurch: Whitcombe and Tombs Ltd, n.d.).   128

6.1 Bernard Baron with William Hogarth after Hogarth, *Marriage
     A-la-mode*, III: *The Inspection* (London: Hogarth, April 1745),
     385 × 465 mm. Private collection.   150

6.2 Royce after Dodd, *Omai's Public Entry on his First Landing at
     Otaheite*, print from [John Rickman], *Journal of Captain
     Cook's Last Voyage* (London, Newbery, 1781), opposite 136.   162

6.3 Detail from John Flaxman after William Hodges, Wedgwood
     plaque bearing portrait of Cook (c. 1779–80), blue and white
     jasper ware, 240 × 180 mm. Alexander Turnbull Library,
     Wellington, New Zealand, ref. G-681.   167

7.1 Thornton after Richard Westall, 'William Hodges Esqr. R. A.
     landscape painter to the Prince of Wales', *Literary and
     Biographical Magazine*, June 1792. Private collection.   172

7.2 *Key to the Print from the Great Picture of Lord Howe's Victory
     Exhibiting at Orme's Gallery, Old Bond Street*, London,
     D. Orme, 1795, NMM PA17781.   188

7.3 I. Cruikshank, *The BRITISH NEPTUNE Riding Triumphant,
     or the Carmignols Dancing to the Tune of RULE BRITANNIA*,
     London, published by S. W. Fores, 16 June 1794. BMC no.
     8469. National Maritime Museum, London, PAG8504.   190

7.4 T. Medland after Robert Cleveley, *The End of the Battle*,
     London, A. Poggi, 1795, NMM PAH7876.   191

7.5 D. Orme after M. Brown, *Lord Howe on the Deck of the 'Queen
     Charlotte'*, London, D. Orme, 1795, NMM PAH7879.   192

7.6 James Gillray, *The Blessings of PEACE / The Curses of WAR*,
     London, 12 January 1795. Private collection.   194

Acknowledgements

This book has been a good many years in the making, and in the course of writing and rethinking and revising I have learnt from help and advice, given directly or indirectly but always generously, from many friends and colleagues. I would particularly like to thank Stephen Daniels, Markman Ellis, Charles Greig, Andrew Hemingway, Cora Kaplan, Iain McCalman, Felicity Nussbaum, Jane Rendall, Neil Rennie, Michael Rosenthal, Simon Schaffer, Vanessa Smith, Kathleen Wilson, and Shamoon Zamir. I remember with gratitude that Tony Tanner encouraged this research in its initial stages, and first introduced me to Nick Thomas, whose profound and extensive knowledge of Oceania and its history has done so much to illuminate this field of study. I have enjoyed the opportunity to work with Nigel Rigby, Geoff Quilley, and Margarette Lincoln at the National Maritime Museum, and I am also grateful to the staff of the Yale Center for British Art in New Haven, the National Humanities Center in North Carolina, and the ANU's Humanities Research Centre. The book has benefited from the helpful comments and questions of audiences at numerous research seminars and conferences, including those held at the universities of Auckland, Cambridge, Carleton, Kent, Leeds, Plymouth, Sussex, Sydney, Tasmania, Wayne State, Wellington, and Winchester, as well as at Queen Mary, London, Centre de Recherche en Histoire des Sciences et des Techniques, La Villette, Paris, the Courtauld Institute, the Huntington Library, the School of Prehistory and Anthropology Research Seminar on Colonialism at ANU, and the Institute of Historical Research in London.

Colour reproductions were made possible by generous grants from the Paul Mellon Centre for Studies in British Art and the Leavis Fund of the University of York. For their help with the processes of obtaining rights and reproductions I am grateful to Giulia Bartram of the British Museum's Department of Prints and Drawings, Jennifer Broomhead of the State Library of New South Wales, Barbara Brownlie of the Alexander Turnbull Library, Julie Bush of the Lincoln Museum, Marcus de Chevrieux of the Kelton Foundation, Shona Corner of the National Galleries of Scotland, Jenny Crispin of the Hunterian Museum, Jane Cunningham of the Courtauld Institute, Sue Daly of Sotheby's, Virginia Ennor of the British

Museum Picture Library, Lynn Flower of the Map Collection of the National Library of Australia, Melissa Gold Fournier of the Yale Center for British Art, Georgina French of the Bridgeman Art Library, Gerard Hayes of the La Trobe Picture Collection, Geoffrey Heath of the Auckland Art Gallery Toi o Tamaki, Anna Henderson at Exeter University Press, Bruce Howlett of the Australian National Portrait Gallery, Richard Kelton, James Mackinnon, Heather Mathie of the Alexander Turnbull Library, Doug McCarthy of the National Maritime Museum, Joanna Moore of the Museum of New Zealand Te Papa Tongarewa, Helen Pecheniuk of the National Library of Australia, Charles Sebag-Montefiore of the Society of Dilettanti, Evelyn Smith of the Glynn Vivian Art Gallery, Kathi Spinks of the State Library of New South Wales, Arabella Stewart of the National Trust Photo Library, Helen Trompeteler of the London National Portrait Gallery, and Susan Odell Walker of the Lewis Walpole Library. I am also grateful for the support of Linda Bree and Maartje Scheltens at Cambridge University Press.

My family have contributed to this project in all sorts of ways, from scrambling around the confined spaces of the *Endeavour* replica, to bravely enduring the insects of Botany Bay. This book is dedicated to John Barrell, who has been an unfailing source of encouragement about my ventures into the South Seas.

Introduction

I

On 13 March 1774 James Cook moored off Easter Island (now known as Rapanui). His ships, the *Resolution* and *Adventure*, had left Plymouth twenty months earlier, and had spent the best part of 1773 weaving their way among the islands of the South Pacific before becoming separated in fog in the southern Indian Ocean. Cook had then taken the *Resolution* deep into the Antarctic Circle, repeatedly venturing as far south as he thought it 'possible for man to go' in search of the elusive southern continent (see fig. 0.1).[1] The men were exhausted and scurvy-ridden, but Cook nevertheless determined to begin another sweep of the South Seas, and felt able to claim that 'they rejoiced at the prospect of [the voyage] being prolonged another year'.[2] He sailed north to Rapanui, where a canoe came out to welcome the voyagers with a great bunch of ripe bananas, at the sight of which the 'sudden emotions of joy in every countenance . . . are scarcely to be described; they can only be felt by people in the same wretched condition with ourselves'.[3]

The *Resolution* left Rapanui on the night of the 16th. William Hodges, the voyage artist, had little opportunity to sketch the islanders – though a man succeeded in stealing his hat – but he produced drawings of a man and of one of the very few women they met, which were engraved for Cook's published account of the voyage. He also sketched the remarkable statues that dominated the landscape and fascinated successive European voyagers, and later painted them in his extraordinary *View of the Monuments of Easter Island* (plate 0.1). In their comprehensive three-volume study of *The Art of Captain Cook's Voyages*, Rüdiger Joppien and Bernard Smith note that the painting 'possesses many of the qualities of a reflective and carefully composed composition', though they argue that 'the lack of studied foreground staffage, the absence of classicizing and literary elements, which become a feature of Hodges's larger post-voyage paintings' indicate that he did not work it up on his return, and there are no records of its having been exhibited in his lifetime.[4] Joppien Smith and describe the painting as a pendant to Hodges's *View of the Province of Oparee* (Pare, in Tahiti, plate 0.2), which uses a panel of the same size, and is characterised by a similar use of

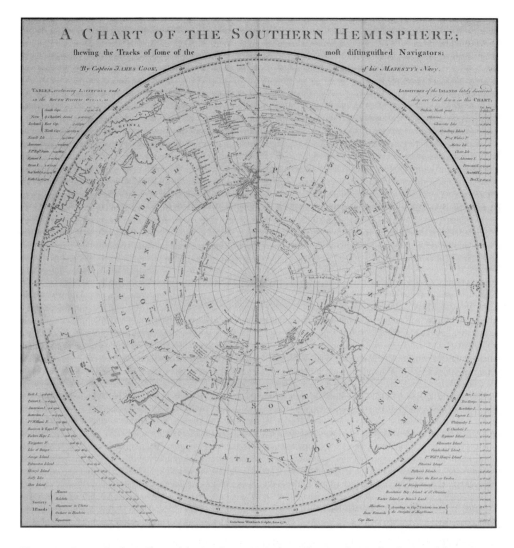

Figure 0.1 James Cook, *A Chart of the Southern Hemisphere; Shewing the Tracks of Some of the Most Distinguished Navigators*, in James Cook, *A Voyage Towards the South Pole* (London: Strahan and Cadell, 1777), I, pl. I

thick and liquid paint, and by careful attention to the qualities of light and weather. In this latter picture, the canoe, abruptly abutting the edge of the picture space in the foreground, and the two turbanned islanders seated in it, share something of the dramatic effect of the statues looming up in the Rapanui image. But the Tahitian view of limpid turquoise waters, touched with the colours of the sunset that suffuses the sky, accentuates by contrast the harshness and aridity of the almost barren rocks of Rapanui. It suggests a sensual pleasure echoed in the reclining, apparently indolent figures of the islanders who face the viewer, inviting recognition, in contrast to the forbiddingly hard uprights of the monuments gazing enigmatically out to sea, their features only obliquely visible, and shaded by the storm clouds that lower over Rapanui.

The view of Easter Island can be read in a number of different but overlapping contexts. Bernard Smith, in *European Vision and the South Pacific* (2nd edn. 1985), sees it primarily as 'an essay in the depiction of light and weather', and points out that the 'squally weather conditions depicted by Hodges . . . occurred only once during the visit' – on 16 March, the day the *Resolution* sailed.[5] But Hodges's landscape is not obviously an attempt to record the immediate circumstances of the *Resolution*'s visit. The people of the island are represented only in the distance, where they can demonstrate neither their friendliness nor the propensity for pilfering that plagued the voyagers. The sweet tropical fruits and fresh food which the islanders made available to the desperate crew despite their evident scarcity are not suggested. The foreboding clouds may indicate the conditions of 16 March, but they are as appropriate to Hodges's interest in representing the history and manners of the islanders as to a preoccupation with light and weather. Like the skull and bones prominently displayed at the foot of the stone figures, they confirm that the image alludes to the Europeans' philosophical reflections on the culture of the island, rather than to the narrative of the events of the voyage. Both painting and engraving can best be understood in the context of the voyagers' perceptions of the monuments as vestiges of the island's 'former Grandeur', indications of the islanders' rapid and recent decline from 'former great felicity, & opulence'.

Johann Forster, the voyage's naturalist, noted signs of the islanders' earlier 'more happy State' in their statues and wells, and in evidence that the population had once been more numerous, and he speculatively attributed their decline to various causes – war, disease, natural disaster – as well as to the explanation Europeans found so persuasive in narratives of their own progress and decline – 'too great luxury'.[6] Forster and other journalists on the voyage understood the condition of the island as though it were a stage in the moralised narrative of cyclical progress and decline that structured European historiography. It was this reading of the island that the engraving of the monuments produced for Cook's published account of the voyage, which William Woollett appears to have based on another sketch, emphasised, in the echo (pointed out by Smith) of Richard Wilson's *Et in Arcadia Ego* (1755) (fig. 0.2). The voyagers also understood the condition of the islanders in relation to their assessments of other Pacific cultures. The pairing of the views of Pare and Rapanui draws on their

Figure 0.2 William Woollett after William Hodges, *Monuments in Easter Island*, in Cook, *Voyage* (1777), 1, pl. x, engraving, 240 × 390 mm

perception of the affinity between the islands, which led Cook to reflect that

it is extraordinary that the same Nation should have spread themselves over all the islands of this Vast Ocean from New Zealand to this Island which is almost a fourth part of the circumference of the Globe, many of them at this time have no other knowledge of each other than what is recorded in antiquated tradition and have by length of time become as it were different Nations.[7]

Europeans perceived Tahiti as both culturally and physically welcoming, receptive to their presence, and at Easter Island detected similarities in customs and language and in the physiognomy of the people, whose 'Features did not seem to differ materially from those of Europeans'. But this island did not seem inviting.[8] Cook commented that its 'ilconveniences' – 'little refreshments, no safe anchorage, no wood for fuel, no fresh water but what must be got by a great deal of trouble and Labour' – were such that 'nothing but necessity will induce any one to touch at this isle'.[9]

The monuments nevertheless indicate a historical depth in the civilisation of the island, and the voyagers are keen to show that their perception of this, both in their understanding of the functions of the statues and of their relation to ancestor figures they had seen elsewhere in the Pacific, is more profound than that of earlier European visitors. In particular, they focus on the inadequacies of the account of the Dutch explorer Jacob Roggeveen, who had visited the island in 1722, and whose speculations they are all eager to debunk and correct. Hodges's image of a forbidding and inhospitable landscape on which the great figures of the ancestors turn their backs, in apparent indifference, beneath a darkening sky, casts Easter Island as a scene in a historical narrative of the progressive civilisation of Tahiti and the relative decline of Rapanui that would have indicated the historicity of the islands themselves, and confirmed the universality of the European historiographic model of cyclical progress, decline, and fall. The painting provides evidence of the superiority of understanding that Cook and his men believed was emerging from their voyage, in contrast to earlier European ventures in the South Seas.

For Bernard Smith, in *European Vision*, the painting is an important example of Hodges's 'fearless attempts to break with neo-classical formulas and to paint with a natural vision'. He argues that the painting is marked by Hodges's attention to particular weather conditions, whereas in the engraving prepared for the published account of the voyage 'the neo-classical and literary element is considerably stronger', and the painting is thus an important step towards 'the triumph of romanticism and science in the

nineteenth-century world of values'.[10] W. J. T. Mitchell has criticised the predominance in Smith's thesis of 'a progressive Whig narrative that overcomes
all contradictions in the conquering of the Pacific by science, reason, and
naturalistic representation'.[11] Mitchell's generalised account oversimplifies
Smith's argument, but the narrative of Romantic conversion, of the heroic
struggle to discard the conventions of the past and embrace the immediacy
of 'natural vision', certainly identifies Smith's seminal work with the historical moment of its production in the late 1950s. My own work is indebted
rather to Smith's emphasis on the need to understand European encounters
with the people and landscapes of the South Pacific as more or less shaped
by the cultural baggage they carried with them, but where Smith focused
on the demands of a picturesque aesthetic and scientific topography I am
primarily concerned with the voyagers' more or less explicit attempts to
theorise cultural differences, with historical moments which expose fundamental and significant tensions, fractures, in the way they conceive of the
islanders' cultures and their own.

Cook's three voyages of 1768–80 span the period in Britain of the Wilkite
riots and war with the American colonies – a period of major reassessment
and reconfiguration of British national and imperial identity. The second
voyage of 1772–5, with which this book is largely concerned, was planned
and undertaken during years when the conduct and status of the East India
Company was troubling the consciences of polite London society as well as
parliament, when concern at the inhumanity of the plantation system in the
West Indies was becoming increasingly audible, and when unrest in North
America was beginning to test the limits of British imperial power.[12] In the
various records, in words and images, of the voyage, encounters between
islanders and voyagers prompt reflections on the progress and nature of
civilisation in the metropolis as well as in the island cultures of the South
Pacific. The challenge of representing the natural landscapes of the islands
is bound up with the challenge their cultures pose to European conceptions
of social order and hierarchy.

II

J. C. Beaglehole commented that the second voyage 'was not very much
longer than the first, but for variety of experience it transcends most other
voyages ever made'.[13] A glance at the map showing the track of the three
voyages immediately demonstrates how closely this voyage in particular was
focused on the South Pacific itself, as the *Resolution* repeatedly returned to

tropical island groups between forays among the ice floes of the Antarctic. On leaving England, Cook looped round the west coast of Africa to the Cape, and south to the Antarctic Circle, round through Queen Charlotte Sound, to the Tuamotus, Tahiti, and the Tongan archipelago, back to New Zealand, and deep into Antarctic regions again. The voyage made a second sweep, in 1774, from Easter Island, through the Marquesas, back to Tahiti and Tonga, across to Vanuatu, south to New Zealand again, and then round Cape Horn to South Georgia and the Cape of Good Hope, and back to England. Islands previously unsighted, or only glimpsed and speculatively noted by European expeditions, were meticulously charted, and the voyagers gained a second sight of places which at least some of them were beginning to feel they knew well as a result of earlier visits, and of the publications resulting from them (fig. 0.3).[14]

It is difficult to generalise about the men who took part in Cook's second voyage: some had visited the Pacific before, with Cook in 1769, or with Wallis in 1767; some had experience of long voyages to the East or West Indies, or North America; a significant proportion of them were not English.[15] But they do seem to have shared a sense of increasing familiarity with islands that Europeans had visited before, and particularly parts of Tahiti and New Zealand; and to have felt that their knowledge of the cultures they encountered acquired new depth and detail as a result of the geographical breadth of experience of the second voyage, and the length of their sojourns at some islands. For some, belief in the depth of their knowledge of some cultures meant that they could now afford to recognise and acknowledge the limitations of their capacity to hear or understand those they encountered. James Boswell's respect for the authenticity of Cook's perceptions was confirmed when the navigator 'candidly confessed' that he and his men 'could not be certain of any information they got, or supposed they got, except as to objects falling under the observation of the senses; their knowledge of the language was so imperfect they required the aid of their senses, and anything which they learned about religion, government, or traditions might be quite erroneous'.[16] The second voyage, with its repeated traverses of the South Seas, produced philosophical accounts of encounters between cultures; narratives distinguished by their self-reflective thoughtfulness and spirit of enquiry rather than by the excitement of first contact or the impatience of increasing disappointment or disillusion.

Cook's voyages were enormously important achievements for Britain in the late eighteenth century. National confidence, still weakened by the aftermath of the seven years war, and further shaken by the advent and progress of the American war, was bolstered by accounts of the voyages, and tales

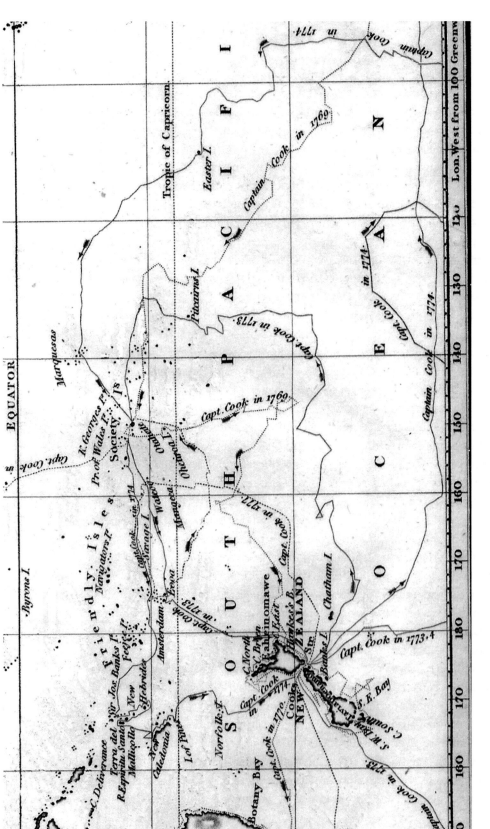

Figure 0.3 Adapted from a detail of C. Cooper, *Pacific Ocean on Mercator's Projection* (London: Sherwood, Neely and Jones, 1 Nov. 1809), from John Smith, *A System of Modern Geography; or, the Natural and Political History of the Present State of the World* (London: Sherwood, 1811).

of daring ventures to waters and coasts previously uncharted by European explorers.[17] When news of Cook's death reached England early in 1780, the King wept, and newspapers up and down the country spoke of the event as a public tragedy – matter for general mourning that was diluted with and soon overwhelmed by national self-congratulation for Cook's successes. The *Derby Mercury*, for example, followed the London press in reporting Cook's death with a skilful blend of pathos and pride: 'The unhappy Murder of that famous Circumnavigator', it urged, 'is not only a national loss, but a Misfortune in which all Europe must naturally feel themselves deeply interested.'[18]

From the late 1770s, and with increasing energy after his death, Cook's extraordinary achievements were repeatedly celebrated, though they could also be difficult to quantify. The *Annual Register* for 1777, for example, acknowledged in a review of the authorised narrative of the second voyage that the expedition's 'great object' had been 'to determine a nullity' – the absence of a great southern continent in the South Pacific – and that it 'must therefore be deficient in that glare, which the opposite result would have afforded'. The third voyage went on to dispel hopes of the North-West Passage. Perhaps because these results were difficult to imagine positively, Cook's posthumous reputation tended to focus on celebrations of his character almost at the expense of his achievements. David Samwell, who travelled with Cook as surgeon on the third voyage, insisted that the 'character of Captain Cook will be best exemplified by the services he has performed', and then portrayed the man revealed by his actions as a sublime, almost Christ-like hero, whose 'qualities rendered him the animating spirit of the expedition: in every situation, he stood unrivalled and alone; on him all eyes were turned; he was our leading-star, which at its setting, left us involved in darkness and despair.'[19] Representations of Cook as martyr were complemented by images that apotheosised him: the idea of Cook as godlike hero and martyr went hand in hand with the perception in his three voyages of a satisfying narrative structure of heroic endeavour, exceptional adventure, and tragic resolution.[20]

Kathleen Wilson has observed that 'After decades of war and the celebration of leaders whose fame rested on more militaristic and sanguinary acts performed in the service of their country, Cook represented not only an alternative masculinity, but also a new kind of national hero, one who demonstrated both English pluck and humanity, sense and sensibility, to best advantage.'[21] The posthumous character of Cook as hero, the dedicated servant of humanity to whom 'the rights of man were sacred', and proselyte of European principles of domestic affection, 'chasten'd love', and 'parental duty', was, for his European audience, an important achievement of his voyages.[22] But perhaps the most significant products or end results for that audience were the various records, textual and visual, of the voyages. Accounts of Cook's voyages were eagerly devoured by British readers. Reports of them were received second or third hand as travellers they encountered returned to European ports from far-flung quarters of the world, and printed in metropolitan and provincial newspapers. Perhaps with more first-hand authenticity, unofficial accounts written by or at least attributed to the voyagers themselves streamed from the presses in books, pamphlets, and periodicals in the years following the return of Cook's ships. John Hawkesworth's authorised account of the first voyage, loosely based on the journals of Cook and Banks, aroused considerable controversy for its representations of sexual behaviour, and its comments on the role of providence in the progress of the voyage, but it sold extremely well and was very widely read. It was published in June 1773, and Cook did not see a copy of it until his return to the Cape in March 1775, but the careful preparation and correction of his journal of the second voyage indicates that he was well aware of the importance of publication as, for much of the British and European public, the most tangible and immediate result of his endeavours. His journal of the second voyage is a good deal more discursive and reflective than his journal of the first had been. Along with the publications of the Forsters and other voyagers, as well as Hodges's paintings, the authorised account of the second voyage, handsomely illustrated with engravings from Hodges's work, provided material for philosophical theories of human history, as well as a mass of data to satisfy scientific enquirers, and food for the avid speculative curiosity of the reading and viewing public.

III

Those who accompanied Cook on his second circumnavigation were well aware that the voyage had the potential to offer great rewards; to yield 'discoveries, which cannot fail of crowning, their employers at least, with immortal honour', as well as to advance their own careers or build their fortunes.[23] Crew members eagerly collected natural and artificial curiosities, which they knew would find a ready market on their return. The 'experimental gentlemen' attached to the expedition, whether they were instructed to collect flora and fauna, to observe people and manners, to conduct astronomical investigations, or to paint landscapes, intended to emulate and exceed the achievements of the earlier Pacific voyages of Byron (1764–6), Wallis (1766–8), and Cook himself on his first voyage with Joseph Banks and his team (1768–71), and of course to demonstrate the superiority of the British venture to those of European competitors. Johann Reinhold Forster, admired for his brilliance, avoided for his cantankerousness, accompanied the voyage as senior natural historian and philosopher, aided by his son George. Johann Forster's *Observations Made during a Voyage round the World* (1778) confirmed the significance of the voyage to European enlightenment ethnography and philosophy, and George Forster's account of the voyage, published in 1777, was, as Nigel Leask has argued, 'in many ways a milestone for romantic period travel writing, establishing the principles which would increasingly be demanded from scientific travel writers over the next half-century'.[24]

A brief outline of the Forsters' careers may help to suggest the importance of the voyage to European intellectual life, and to situate their remarkable publications. Johann Forster came from Danzig, in West Prussia, and initially trained in theology. He successfully combined his devotion to scholarship with his duties as a pastor in the region of Danzig for twelve years, until, in 1765, he left to undertake a survey of the Volga for Catherine II. In 1766, he travelled to London, where he became actively involved in the Royal Society, the Society of Antiquaries, and the Society for the Encouragement of Arts, Manufactures, and Commerce. He was elected a fellow of the Royal Society in 1772. He made important friendships with Thomas Pennant and Daines Barrington, and it was Barrington who later recommended him for the voyage to the South Pacific. From 1767 to 1769, he worked as tutor in modern languages and natural history at the Warrington Academy, the centre which nurtured many of the most prominent dissenting liberal intellectuals of the period. He translated a number of travel accounts and important works of Linnean natural history, and in 1772 published his translation of Bougainville's *Voyage autour du monde*. Following the voyage with Cook he returned to Germany in 1780 to take up a chair at Halle university. His son, Johann George Forster, was eighteen years old when he embarked with Cook in 1772. Before the voyage, he had assisted his father with his translations, and on their return, George Forster worked with his father's journals, and probably to some extent with his active collaboration, on the book that was to become *A Voyage round the World* (1777). George Forster went on to a distinguished career in Germany as an intellectual and academic, engaging in debate with Immanuel Kant, and travelling with Alexander von Humboldt. He became one of the leading Jacobins in Mainz, and died in Paris early in 1794.[25]

Johann Forster explained in the Preface to his *Observations* that he saw the voyage to the South Pacific as an opportunity for practical philosophy:

The History of Mankind has often been attempted; many writers have described the manners and characters of individuals, but few have traced the history of mankind in general, considered as one large body. What is extant on that head in the French and English languages, contains either slight sketches and fragments, or systems formed in the closet or at least in the bosom of a nation highly civilized, and therefore in many respects degenerated from its original simplicity.

His work, on the other hand, based on his first-hand experience, was enriched by 'the opportunity of contemplating mankind in . . . its various stages from that of the most wretched savages, removed but in the first degree from absolute animality, to the more polished and civilized inhabitants of the Friendly and Society Isles'.[26] This opportunity was the basis for the superiority of his work, but he insists on its place within that existing genre; he defines his work as a contribution to the ongoing business of compiling or constructing the philosophical 'History of Mankind'. The voyagers conceive of their project firmly in the context of European notions of historiography and progress.

This historicised and textualised context structures the chart of relative assessments of island cultures Forster included in his *Observations*. He wrote that

The happy inhabitants of the tropical islands in the South-Sea, occupy a rank in the class of human beings, which is by no means so despicable, as might, at first sight, be imagined; and the Taheiteans and their neighbours in the Society-islands, may claim the highest rank among these nations. They are certainly, for many reasons, superior to the cannibals in New-Zeeland, and still higher above the rambling, poor inhabitants, of New-Holland, and the most unhappy wretches of Tierra del Fuego. In the same proportion the people at Tanna, and Mallicollo, exceed those at New-Caledonia; the inhabitants at the Marquesas, stand higher than the people of the Friendly-islands, and these must yield to the Taheiteans, as every circumstance concurs to confirm their high rank.[27]

The chart delineates a cultural map characterised by both precision and strategic vagueness. It initially establishes an authoritative and unambiguous ranking of island cultures, where the most centrally tropical islanders clearly trump the temperate or the more peripherally tropical, but it also blurs comparative assessments of people within the tropics, so that Forster does not here assert any clear relative ranking of, say, the Tannese in relation to the Tongans (Cook's Friendly islanders) or the Tahitians. Forster goes on to discuss, in the section these sentences introduce, what he takes to be some of the key indications of relative civility, the 'Principles, Moral Ideas, Manners, Refinement, Luxury, and the Condition of Women among the Nations in the South-Sea-Isles'.[28] Though occasionally that hesitation or uncertainty that marks his initial chart re-emerges, much of the discussion suggests his confidence in the value of this assessment exercise, and in the analytical tools or discursive categories available to him.

Forster's list of the categories and concepts by which the progress of civilisation was to be judged was, by the time he was writing, familiar enough. The journalists of Cook's voyages articulated their sense of the diversity of the islands and island groups they encountered in the South Pacific in discourses which permeated educated British culture of this period, discourses often derived directly or indirectly from the Scottish enlightenment. They attempted to apprehend their experiences of island cultures by enmeshing them in complex networks of historical narratives, on commerce, on sexuality and gender difference, on political organisation, population size, climate, religious belief, and racial heirarchy, which were perceived to be the most adequate and appropriate means of conceptualising modern European social diversity and of assessing the relative progress of recorded civilisations. The plurality and specificity of the island cultures of Oceania, however, frequently tested these conceptual tools of exploration. The discursive map produced by voyagers' attempts to represent the islands, through journals, images, and collections of natural and artificial curiosities, was spotted with unexpected blots and blanks. A striking example is provided by Johann Forster's reflections on Maori cannibalism, where the moral discourse in which he condemns their supposedly 'inhuman appetites' collides with his thesis that the practice 'prepares the way for a more humane and benevolent scene' in the context of enlightenment narratives of the progress of civilisation.[29] Every island group produces encounters and experiences that snag the smooth seine of description and analysis that the European voyagers projected, and the attempt to plot discursive or hierarchical relations between the island groups exposed gaping flaws in the discursive network that supported Europeans' conceptions of their own modernity.

The work of William Hodges is central to what might be described as the philosophical project of the voyage. Many of his voyage paintings, and particularly the grander canvases, record historical events, documenting, for example, the parade of the war boats of Tahiti, which Cook and his companions witnessed with appropriate awe at Pare in Tahiti in late April and May of 1774, or portraying the Europeans landing on the beaches of some of the eastern islands. But these images are not only contributions to the linear narrative of the voyage, and they are not easy to assimilate to the ongoing adventure story of Cook's heroism, or the morality tale of his increasing irascibility. They are, much more evidently and inescapably, images in which the elaborately theorised conventions of high art mesh with the conflicting demands of natural history for the accurate representation of climate, topography, flora and fauna, and with the challenge which the cultures of the South Pacific posed to the values and preconceptions which, with varying degrees of explicitness, informed the expectations and apprehensions of the voyagers.

IV

Hodges produced a number of sketches of the war canoes which the voyagers saw assembled on 26 April, and in smaller numbers on 14 May 1774, and these images provide some indication of the ways in which his work during and after the voyage functioned in a complex relation to textual accounts of the voyage as well as to the circumstances for its display; and the extent to which it mediated between metropolitan concerns and the experiences of the voyagers. His small oil painting of the *Review of the War Galleys at Tahiti* (plate 0.3) provided the basis for William Woollett's engraving which accompanied Cook's account of the May review, and he also worked up the subject for his grand painting of *The War Boats of the Island of Otaheite*, exhibited at the Royal Academy in 1777 (plate 0.4). The subject demanded careful and repeated attention not only because it presented a colourful spectacle, 'one of the most magnificent sights which it is possible to be entertained with in the South Sea'.[30] For mariners from a nation which prided itself on naval supremacy, and devoted a considerable proportion of its expenditure to maintaining it, naval strength was a key indication of the progressive nature of Tahitian society.[31] George Forster commented that 'All our former ideas of the power and affluence of this island were so greatly surpassed by this magnificent scene, that we were perfectly left in admiration.' He made the review of the Tahitian fleet the basis for a detailed comparison with the 'united efforts of Greece against Troy', and concluded that the similarity between the two civilisations extended to their manners, 'domestic character', and 'political constitution.' The spectacle of the fleet confirmed his sense that Tahitian culture could best be understood through its relation to 'a similar state of civilization' drawn from European historiography, and increased his respect for the islanders' achievements.[32]

The fleet assembled on 14 April consisted of 'one hundred and fifty-nine great double war-canoes, from fifty to ninety feet long betwixt stem and stern', accompanied by seventy smaller canoes, and the Europeans were much struck by the numbers required to man the vessels. George Forster noted that 'The immense number of people . . . assembled together was, in fact, more surprising than the splendor of the whole shew. Upon a very moderate calculation, there could not be less than fifteen hundred warriors, and four thousand paddlers, besides those who were in the provision boats, and the prodigious crowds on the shore.' On learning that the fleet had been drawn from a single district, Forster deduced that the population of the island as a whole must total 120,000 on 'a most moderate computation'.[33] In his published account, Cook used the occasion to estimate a total population of 204,000, and concluded that 'There cannot be a greater proof of the richness and fertility of Otaheite (not forty leagues in circuit) than its supporting such a number of inhabitants.'[34] These estimates of the size of the island's population were probably exaggerated,[35] but they would certainly have impressed British readers, accustomed to consider population as directly 'connected with national wealth' (as did Cook) and dependent on the nation's ability to maintain the 'liberty and personal security' of its members.[36] Woollett's engraving (fig. 0.4) after Hodges's small oil shows the great Tahitian canoes crowding the bay in a vista of upright prows reminiscent of representations of the Thames as the source of Britain's commercial and imperial wealth, where, in James Thomson's famous description, 'Like a long wintry Forest, Groves of Masts / Shot up their Spires.'[37] The image works in conjunction with Cook's narrative and observations, which provide its immediate context, as well as with Forster's reflections, to provide an idea of Tahitian culture as both exotic and capable of commanding respect in comparison with the achievements of Europeans.

The larger oil painting produced for display at the Academy is very different. The canoes here are an impressive spectacle, but they are not fully manned, and the image is not crowded with people or signs of the massed fleet. Joppien and Smith point out that this is to some extent a matter of Hodges's respect for the 'time-hallowed principles of classical composition', but they also suggest that it makes the 'dominant accent' of the painting the feathered head-dress of the warrior, which George Forster, in his *Voyage*, had represented as 'resembling that glory of light with which our painters commonly ornament the heads of angels and saints'.[38] This is an image of the South Pacific as an exotic place of 'magnificent sights', and casts Hodges as an artist to whom the 'public are indebted . . . for giving them some idea of scenes which they before knew little of', as one critic put it.[39] The

Figure 0.4 William Woollett after William Hodges, *The Fleet of Otaheite assembled at Oparee*, in Cook, *Voyage* (1777), I, pl. LXI

Royal Academy exhibition opened on 24 April 1777. Cook's account of the voyage, handsomely illustrated with engravings from Hodges's work, was available from 30 April 1777. George Forster's account of the voyage had been published on 17 March 1777, but perhaps because of its lack of engravings, sales were slow, and it did not have the impact of Cook's enormously successful volumes. Johann Forster's *Observations* were not published until mid-1778.[40] The Academy picture worked to stimulate interest in the South Seas as a site of exotic spectacle, and to direct attention to the lavish official publication, but it did not directly draw on or complicate the text. The contrast between the small painting engraved for the published account, and the grand image prepared for the Academy, suggests that Hodges was acutely alert to the implications of the circumstances in which his work would be seen.

The Academy painting may allude to George Forster's *Voyage*, as Joppien and Smith suggest. The group of figures on the shore in the foreground suggest biblical rather than classical comparisons, and the admiration and awe which the voyagers experienced when they saw the fleet at Pare is here displaced on to them. The smaller painting presents a more crowded and challenging image, which engages much more directly with the reflections of Cook and Forster on naval strength and population size. Until his return to London, Johann Forster expected to have at least a significant hand in the composition of the official history of the voyage, for which Hodges was also preparing his work. Though the Forsters' volumes were, in the end, published separately, it is clear that Hodges worked closely with the Forsters during the voyage, and frequently accompanied them in their expeditions on different islands.[41] His work participated in the philosophical projects of Cook and the Forsters, either directly alluding to their accounts, and suggesting alternative conceptions of island culture, or indicating ways in which the deeper knowledge and range of experience gained on the second voyage might revise or add to earlier accounts or preconceptions of the islands – particularly in images such as the views of Matavai Bay and Vaitepeha, discussed in my first chapter, or the Academy image of the war boats at Pare, which anticipated the publication of Cook's account.

V

William Hodges's life and work have been ably documented by Isabel Combs Stuebe, and, more recently, in *William Hodges, 1744–1797: The Art of Exploration* (2004), a collection of essays on Hodges's work in Britain, India, and the South Seas edited by Geoff Quilley and John Bonehill, and published to accompany the major exhibition of Hodges's work at the National Maritime Museum in 2004.[42] The son of a respectable London smith, Hodges first studied painting at Shipley's School before entering the studio of Richard Wilson, the prominent landscape painter, as an articled apprentice in 1758. Hodges's distinctive style of landscape painting was formed during the seven years he spent with Wilson, and the influence of his master is strongly apparent in his later work. After he left Wilson's studio, he produced a number of landscapes of British rural scenes (exhibited at the Society of Artists and elsewhere in London) in which the compositions are, Stuebe notes, 'reminiscent of Canaletto'.[43] In May 1772 Sir Joseph Banks and his party withdrew from participation in Cook's second voyage, following a disagreement between Cook and Banks over alterations to the *Resolution* – adaptations which Banks thought necessary to his project, but which in the opinions of Cook and other sailors made the ship unseaworthy. Hodges, then a rising artist of twenty-seven, was called on to replace Johann Zoffany, who had been intended by Banks to serve as artist to the voyage. Following his return from the South Pacific, Hodges was paid £250 a year by the Admiralty to work his Oceanic sketches up into paintings, and to supervise the production of engravings for Cook's published account of the voyage.

Between 1780 and 1784, Hodges travelled in northern India, attracting the remunerative patronage of Warren Hastings from 1781. Hodges was the first professional British landscape painter to work in India, and his travels resulted in numerous paintings and sketches, as well as in his major publications, *Travels in India* (1793), and the forty-eight large aquatints published as *Select Views in India* (1785–8). In 1787 he published two large engravings of *The Tomb of Emperor Shere Shah at Sasseram* and *The Tomb of the Emperor Akbar at Secundrii*, as well as *A Dissertation on the Prototypes of Architecture, Hindoo, Moorish, and Gothic.* Hodges returned to England a comparatively wealthy man, and continued to enjoy Hastings's patronage for the Indian scenes he produced in the later 1780s. His landscapes of this period portrayed northern India as a scene of progressive cultivation nurtured under the benevolent influence of Hastings's governorship.[44] In 1786 Hodges was elected an associate member of the Royal Academy, where he exhibited Indian scenes as well as European landscapes. He also painted landscapes based on his travels in northern Europe in 1788, and to St Petersburg in the early 1790s. In the winter of 1794–5, Hodges mounted an ambitious one-man show at Orme's Gallery in Old Bond Street. The exhibition was not a success, and closed prematurely following damning comments from the Duke of York. Hodges then gave up painting, and retired with his family to Brixham in Devon, opening a bank in Dartmouth in partnership with Thomas Gretton. The bank failed in the financial crisis of 1797, and Hodges died in circumstances which led some of his contemporaries to suspect suicide.

Hodges's landscape painting, critics agree, is everywhere marked by the influence of his seven-year apprenticeship in Richard Wilson's studio. In the biographical sketch of Wilson which he published in the *European Magazine* in 1790, Hodges attributed to him 'a style of painting as near perfection as perhaps . . . is possible'. He acknowledged criticisms of Wilson's negligence of detail or finish in a manner clearly intended to rebound on his master's detractors:

There are persons who object to Mr. Wilson's pictures not being sufficiently finished in the foregrounds; and it must be admitted, that to look very near them, they are not so highly finished as many Dutch works we see; but they at all times agree with the whole: That was his great wish and constant aim; when That was accomplished, he left his picture. He did not possess the phlegmatic industry to labor upon the down of a thistle.[45]

Throughout his career, Hodges struggled with the notion of 'accuracy' as a key value in visual representation. He wrote to his friend the poet William Hayley in 1793:

Allow me to say that . . . truth is the basis of every work of mine – and through the various countries I have passed my endeavors have invariably aimed, to give the manners of mankind in the varied shades from the Savage in the wilds to the highly civilized in the palace. I cannot but own I have sometimes secretly quarrelled with the World for allowing me the Character of a man of Genius in the display of fanciful representations than that of accurate observation.[46]

But critics repeatedly commented on what they saw as the 'unfinished' nature of his landscapes, apparently referring primarily to the manner of applying paint that he had learnt from Wilson. Hodges's apprenticeship did not teach him to view his work as a lens for the 'accurate' transmission of material reality, but led him to strive for a notion of truth centring on the representation of the 'manners of mankind', of something much more closely bound up with contested cultural values adapted from the vision Wilson's landscapes had earlier attributed to the land-owning elite.[47] The *Morning Post* commented, in its review of Hodges's *The Abbey, From the Romance of the Forest*, exhibited at the Royal Academy in 1794, that 'This Artist's forte seems to be the conception of grand and poetic scenery; where the minor excellencies of execution and detail are unattended to in the broad expansion of the *idea*.'[48] The idea to which Hodges's work repeatedly returned was that ambition to depict the 'varied shades from the Savage . . . to the highly civilized'. This ambition is a central focus of this book. It was for Hodges, like his shipmates, informed directly or indirectly by narratives on the nature of modern society and of the progress of civilisation which were articulated most fully and most influentially by the theorists of the Scottish enlightenment, but which were also elaborated on in the theories of art expounded by men such as Sir Joshua Reynolds and James Barry in the lectures they produced for the Royal Academy, as well as in the diverse writings of, for example, James Boswell, William Cowper, and Mary Wollstonecraft.

VI

The chapters that make up this book are organised loosely to follow the trajectory of Cook's second sweep across the Pacific in 1774, but I have not attempted to discuss each island group in turn, and the discussion frequently returns to the reception of the voyagers and their writings in London, and dips south to compare the representation of tropical islands with accounts of New Zealand. Similarly, though the main focus of the book is on the second voyage of 1772–5, and on the opportunities this voyage offered for reflective re-encounters between Europeans and islanders, I have frequently drawn on accounts of the first and third voyages, as well as on Hodges's writing on India. This is not an attempt to tell again the story of the second voyage, and nor is it a narrative of Hodges's career as an artist.[49] This book narrates a cumulative process of exploration and analysis through the discussion of particular moments which expose the difficulties and uncertainties of constructing an imperial vision in the South Pacific.

The first three chapters all focus largely on accounts of what Europeans called the Society Islands, or on the reception of those accounts and images in the metropolis – accounts which I suggest complicate any simple notion of an opposition between the civilised and the exotic. Each chapter is concerned primarily with what is internally problematic in voyagers' representations of island cultures when those texts and images are considered in the context of European theories of civilisation or national identity, theories which are part of the cultural baggage the voyagers took with them, and which frame (and to some extent determine) their attempts to meet the conceptual challenge which South Pacific cultures posed to them. I am interested in the extent to which the voyagers' encounters with island cultures expose in their conception of their own position a fragility or uncertainty, a receptivity to changed possibilities, created by the competing and sometimes conflicting demands of their own culture. These chapters explore this first in accounts of Cook's visits to the Society Islands, and then through the discursive mapping of other island groups in relation those islands, which European voyagers perceived as the most hospitable of the cultures they encountered, as well as the most readily understood. Cook and his fellow journalists conceived of the different island cultures they encountered through their similarity or difference to Tahiti, in an accretional logic similar to that which structures this book.

Chapters 1 and 2 are concerned with Cook's return to Tahiti in 1773. Chapter 1 explores the interaction of gender and exoticism in William Hodges's account of his arrival in Madras in 1780, and then uses Hodges's large landscape, *A View Taken in the Bay of Otaheite Peha* (1776), with its prominent figures of Tahitian women bathing, as the focus for a consideration of the way the representation of women may accommodate the doubled modes of perception European visitors brought to the islands of the South Pacific. I argue that the contested 'accuracy' of Hodges's portrayal of the island is marked by the competing demands of, on one hand, a discourse which constitutes the civilised man as one capable of taking comprehensive, generalising views (in contrast to the supposed immersion of the savage in the local and particular), and, on the other, the privileging of detail as the characteristic of modern experimental knowledge and curiosity. Chapter 2 discusses perceptions of the status of women in the islands in the context of the enlightenment belief that the treatment of women is the key index of relative civilisation, and in particular of the arguments of the Scottish enlightenment theorists (such as John Millar and Henry Home, Lord Kames) concerned to historicise sexual desire as a cause and symptom of the progress of civilisation.

Chapter 3 considers the significance of tattoos in portraits of Mai (more frequently known as Omai), the Raiatean islander brought to London by Cook in 1774, and goes on to discuss the tattoos of islanders and sailors in the context of theories of ornament as characteristic of the taste of women and savages. This chapter develops the discussion of gender on which the first two chapters focused to consider the changing character of British cultural conceptions of genteel or civilised masculinity in relation to exotic manliness. I use Joshua Reynolds's Discourses on art to show how a notion of civilised masculinity as ideally trans-national, detached and capable of a kind of dispassionate cultural relativism, is complicated by a more modern sense of national identity, shown in attachment to a version of modern dress and ornamental detail. Sailors adapted for themselves the tattoos which distinguished elite groups of warriors in the Society Islands, acknowledging a parallel with their own identity as an esoteric masculine group. The Society Islanders, however, are imagined as comparatively civilised and feminised in contrast to what Europeans saw as the manly and fractious barbarism of the New Zealanders, whose cryptically marked skins are perceived to be analogous to the incoherence of their society. The chapter discusses portraits of Mai by Reynolds and Parry, and drawings of tattooed islanders by Hodges, Parkinson, and others.

In Chapter 4, the focus of the argument shifts as the geographical range of my discussion extends to the more westerly islands of Tonga and Vanuatu (which Cook named the New Hebrides). William Hodges represented these islands in a series of four landing scenes; *Landing at Mallicollo* [Malakula], *Landing at Erramanga* [Erromango], *Landing at Tanna*, and *Landing at Middleburgh* [Eua] *One of the Friendly Islands*. The chapter first discusses the engraving of the *Landing at Middleburgh*, and uses the controversy over the 'accuracy' of its representation to exemplify the difficulty the voyagers encountered in attempting to conceive of Tongan society in the terms they had found appropriate to the Society Islands and New Zealand. As the voyages extended westward across the tropics, voyagers begin to assess the cultures they encounter in terms of the islanders' capacity for industry or invention, of what is seen as their aptitude for improvement, rather than in the context of the notions of public spirit and social cohesion that had dominated their admiration for Tahiti and their more troubled appraisal of New Zealand. The Tongans were perceived as skilful traders possessing a degree and kind of social organisation that impressed the Europeans with a sense of their own vulnerability. The capacity for improvement they were seen to display left sailors unsure of the basis for their own assumed superiority. The Tongans were treated with respect, or even fear, because of their ability to play on the weaknesses and appetites of the voyagers. I go on to consider Hodges's representations of landings in the New Hebrides, and discuss the widely divergent estimates of the islanders produced by Cook and the two Forsters to show how competing models of the progress of civilisation divided their views.

After completing his survey of the tropical islands, Cook returned to New Zealand, where he first heard news of the deaths of ten men of the crew of the *Adventurer* after its separation from his ship the *Resolution*. Chapter 5 discusses Hodges's representations of New Zealand in the context of the account of the death and consumption of the *Adventurer*'s crewmen given in John Rickman's unauthorised publication on the third voyage. Rickman's account is embedded in the tale of a romance between a sailor and a Maori woman in which historical event appears to be interwoven with fantasy. This tale is discussed as a colonial romance of reciprocity, following Mary Louise Pratt and Peter Hulme, and provides the opportunity to discuss the voyagers' perceptions of New Zealand as a potential site for colonisation; a project which in metropolitan perceptions is closely bound up with dismay at the war with America, and the notion that Cook's venture promises, or threatens, a new kind of imperial ambition. Chapter 6 returns to the subject of Mai's experiences in London and on his return to the South Pacific, and considers the different conceptions of Britain's imperial role that are involved in the reception in London of the islander and of Cook himself. The chapter contrasts the ornamental and anachronistic role attributed to Mai, with the professional dedication celebrated in the portrayal of Cook as 'a new kind of hero for a new time', as Bernard Smith put it. The chapter returns to the subject of Britain's conception of itself as a colonial power, and considers how that role is played out in representations of Cook and Mai.

My last chapter offers a coda or epilogue to the career of William Hodges, and focuses on his last exhibition, which opened in London in 1794. The paintings central to the show were Hodges's grand canvases of *The Effects of Peace* and *The Consequences of War* – images which he represented as the fruition of his desire to elevate the genre of landscape painting and imbue it with some of the social and moral consequence of history paint-ing. The Duke of York, who visited the exhibition in January 1795, was scandalised by what he took to be the democratical tendencies of these paintings, and his outrage seems to have resulted in the premature clos-ing of the exhibition, rapidly followed by Hodges's decision to abandon painting and leave London. Hodges died not long after, and the paintings disappeared, though engravings from them came to light in the summer of 2004. My essay uses the evidence of newspapers and journals to recon-struct in detail the circumstances for Hodges's exhibition, and argues that the lofty ambitions of his grand canvases were recast by events to give his images a degree of political urgency and controversial edge he could not have foreseen. But I conclude that the visual language of Hodges's land-scapes had, certainly from the voyage years, a moral and political resonance which could not safely be secured to the service of a single argument or discourse, but reflected the complex nature of national and imperial cultures of modernity.

The events I am concerned with in this epilogue are obviously distinct in time and space from those I discuss in the main body of the book, but they provide a fitting conclusion because they examine the fate in London of the aesthetic ideals and ambitions which had informed Hodges's voyage paintings. Hodges's work was, as I have mentioned, shaped by his apprenticeship in the studio of Richard Wilson. David Solkin has argued that Wilson's work was wedded to what was by the end of the eighteenth century a nostalgic notion of the British social order dominated by the landed gentry. Wilson's 'self-image and artistic approach', Solkin wrote, 'were inseparably bound to a certain notion of culture, one might even say of human civilisation, which was slowly but inexorably disintegrating around him, together with the particular kind of society that had nurtured those values for so long'. He concludes that though Wilson's patrons among the gentry were able to adapt and change, 'Wilson got left behind.'[50] Hodges explicitly embraced the ambition to represent in landscape a certain cultural truth about human civilisation and its progress, and though what informed Hodges's work were enlightenment theories of progress which attempted to build a commercial ethic on the foundation of classical notions of civil society, rather than the patrician mythology of Wilson's patrons, the explicitly moralised images central to his exhibition of 1794 were, like Wilson's, out of step with the divided and antagonistic political cultures created by the war with France. Hodges, like Wilson, has until recently been forgotten as a result.

VII

The progress of Cook's ships across the three voyages, and the increasing intimacy and violence of encounters between islanders and Europeans, has been most recently and authoritatively charted by Anne Salmond, in *The Trial of the Cannibal Dog: Captain Cook in the South Seas* (2003), and Nicholas Thomas in *Discoveries: The Voyages of Captain Cook* (2003). Both Salmond and Thomas revise earlier accounts in the prominence they give to reconstructions (necessarily speculative, but persuasive) of islanders' views of encounters with Cook and his men, and both are interested in the blurring of boundaries between islanders and voyagers. Salmond suggests that by the third voyage 'Cook's sailors (or some of them) were no longer purely "European", and Cook himself became increasingly de-Anglicised and unfamiliar:

the Tahitians called Cook "Tute"', and "He was now known as "Toote" on board his ships, a passionate, unpredictable character".[51] Thomas also discusses the implications of the judgement made by the midshipman, George Gilbert, that in the course of the third voyage Cook's behaviour was 'rather unbecoming of a European', observing that his attitude to punishment perhaps 'became too unpleasantly like the callous brutality that marked some chiefs' treatment of some common men'.[52] Like Salmond, Thomas suggests that Cook came to feel stronger affective ties to the Polynesian chiefs with whom he exchanged names and enjoyed relationships of mutual respect than he did to European values, leading his compatriots on more than one occasion to 'think that he placed the interest of a native chief ahead of theirs'.[53] The following chapters can be read in the context of these narratives on the progressive complexity or confusion of European self-conceptions. They explore a similar sense of the permeability and even fragility of European and specifically British identity; but I consider this primarily in the context of the way the British thought of themselves, and assessed their own progress as a society, rather than in relation to the personal character of Cook or the course of his voyages.

The chapters that make up this book draw on both visual and written records to explore the self-reflexiveness that characterised enlightenment culture and historiography. But this is not a history of the kinds of impulsive passions and desires that Jonathan Lamb discusses in his *Preserving the Self in the South Seas, 1680–1840* (2001). Lamb explains that his focus is the notion of a self that 'is not constituted by reflection, interpellation, or language', though it is revealed in rhetorical tropes, such as the litotes Lamb lists, and that enable him to trace, for example, the 'mounting bewilderment in [Cook's] mind'.[54] I am interested primarily in what the various texts and images produced as a result of the voyages tell us about the apprehension of cultural difference in the process of imperial expansion in the South Seas – in the uncertainties and hesitations produced in the discourses of Cook and his companions by the different civilisations they encountered (however misunderstood) and the problems they posed to the voyagers' preconceptions of the islanders and of themselves. These, I think, afford a greater degree of insight into the impact of cultural encounters in the South Pacific on European self-conceptions and habits of thought.

To focus on European representations of Oceanic people is problematic, because this practice involves the danger that the significances of the voyagers' presence to those they wished to observe are effaced, that the subject positions of the islanders at that time are silenced. J. G. A. Pocock points out that there is a real sense in which the most important encounter made by Europeans in the Age of Enlightenment was the encounter with themselves, with their pasts and their own historicity, so that it was into these highly sophisticated and even self-critical schemes of historiography that they sought to integrate, or gave up trying to integrate, the cultures with which they came into contact.

European self-consciousness, he suggests, is shaped by this sense of its own historicity, by what I have referred to as discursive mapmaking, where the discourses of historiography are understood to articulate 'a sequence of moral and cultural transformations, concerning each one of which the consciousness must reach contestable judgements because the consciousness was itself historically generated'. People who appeared peripheral or invisible to this Eurocentric history, and whose presence perhaps implicitly denied its pertinence or exposed its limits, could not readily be perceived to be endowed with the consciousness it generated; they could not easily be audible to Europeans as subjects.[55] But the European historiographies of the period before the French Revolution which Pocock discusses are characterised by an openness to contestation, a capacity for self-criticism, that may distinguish them from their more explicitly colonialist and racist nineteenth-century successors and find an echo in more recent attempts to address the historicity of European self-consciousness.

If the problems and limitations of Eurocentric historiography constrain our ability to recognise different subjectivities in or through the texts of the Cook voyages, it may nevertheless be worthwhile to attempt to understand how the colonising discourses of the past worked, to participate in what Paul Gilroy describes as Foucault's 'tentative extension of the idea of a *critical* self-inventory into the political field . . . in a commentary upon the Enlightenment'. Gilroy has in mind Foucault's comment that: 'the critical ontology of ourselves has to be . . . conceived as an attitude, an ethos, a philosophical life in which the critique of what we are is at one and the same time the historical analysis of the limits that are imposed on us and an experiment with the possibility of going beyond them'. Gilroy, arguing for the reconfiguration of debates about modernity to address the history of the African diaspora, suggests that 'the modern subject may be located in historically specific and unavoidably complex configurations of individualisation and embodiment', which may mean that the 'distinctiveness of the modern self might reside in its being a necessarily fractured or compound entity'.[56] If the Cook voyages are now available as a collection of texts and artefacts all of which are articulated in the context of Eurocentric history and modernity, they are nonetheless about encounter, about the way the 'prior assumptions' of European explorers were contested or changed, their smooth discursive continuity fractured or disclosed as fragmented by events they could not always predict or integrate unproblematically into their historiography. The fractures or discontinuities these historically specific encounters expose may be characteristic of the modern self, and of the self-reflexive enlightenment historiography that contributes to its production and generation, and they may help us to analyse the 'limits that are imposed on us', and to 'experiment with the possibility of going beyond them'.

1 | The great distinction

I

In 1780, five years after his circumnavigation with Cook, William Hodges travelled to India. He had already made the representation of unfamiliar landscapes and foreign peoples his speciality, and was known and celebrated for his large canvases of scenes in the South Pacific, and he consolidated this reputation when he became the first European professional landscape painter to portray the interior of northern India. In 1793 he published an account of his *Travels in India,* a journal of his observations and experiences that would, he wrote, 'enable me to explain to my friends a number of drawings which I had made during my residence in India'. There he described his first perception of the coast, the sight of the English town of Fort St George (Madras), and the climactic moment at which he felt the excitement of encounter with the foreign:

> Some time before the ship arrives at her anchoring ground, she is hailed by the boats of the country filled with people of business, who come in crowds on board. This is the moment in which an European feels the great distinction between Asia and his own country. The rustling of fine linen, and the general hum of unusual conversation, presents to his mind for a moment the idea of an assembly of females. When he ascends upon the deck, he is struck with the long muslin dresses, and black faces adorned with very large gold ear-rings and white turbans. The first salutation he receives from these strangers is by bending their bodies very low, touching the deck with the back of the hand, and the forehead three times.

The difference of this country, the great distinction that the European feels, is not predominantly for Hodges a matter of the colours and contours of the landscape, the strangeness or incongruity of the architecture, although he notes that these 'present a combination totally new' to the English eye. The novelty of this view, and the strangeness of the climate to one 'accustomed to the sight of rolling masses of clouds floating in a damp atmosphere', are remarkable and pleasing. But 'the moment' at which the great distinction is felt is for him that of encounter with people who rustle and hum in alien and inarticulate conversation, people who are incomprehensible but evidently not alarming, curious but not threatening. Their strangeness, the difference of dress, colour, and language, seems to the spectator to present an essential and momentous distinction that he understands in terms of gender: for a moment he entertains not the *metaphor* but the *idea* of an assembly of females.[1]

The primacy of gender in Hodges's account of his initial perception of the difference between Europe and Asia is hardly surprising. European travellers repeatedly employ discourses of gender in this context in the seventeenth and eighteenth centuries, and these work to mark the spectacular unfamiliarity of dress, of physical build, and to conceal what might otherwise appear to be discrepancies or inconsistencies in European observations.[2] Hodges goes on to unfold his apprehension of Asia into a sequence of sights and sounds more particular to Madras, and to complicate his identification of the great distinction with that of gender. He writes:

The natives first seen in India by an European voyager, are Hindoos, the original inhabitants of the Peninsula. In this part of India they are delicately framed, their hands in particular are more like those of tender females; and do not appear to be, what is considered a proper proportion to the rest of the person, which is usually above the middle size. Correspondent to this delicacy of appearance are their manners, mild, tranquil, and sedulously attentive: in this last respect they are indeed remarkable, as they never interrupt any person who is speaking, but wait patiently until he has concluded; and then answer with the most perfect respect and composure.[3]

It is in particular the hands of the Hindu people of business that seem to the European spectator to be '*like* those of tender females'. Their gender is no longer an idea presented to his mind in a startling apprehension of difference, but a simile produced by his detailed powers of observation. These people are above middle size, but the simile is implicitly appropriated to the description of their 'delicacy of appearance', and alluded to in the account of their mode of conversation. The Hindu merchants 'never interrupt', but listen sedulously, and answer with composure, and it is their implied gender that makes it unnecessary for the narrator to explain why this is 'indeed remarkable' – their attention is remarkable, he suggests, both because it marks the feminine docility of their manners, in contrast to the impatience of European men, and because it contrasts with the garrulous chatter that had first impressed him with the idea of an 'assembly of females'.

The importance of this idea in Hodges's narrative is apparent in a range of the issues his account raises – his perception of the differences between the Hindu and Muslim peoples, his conception of their religion, their 'stage' of civilisation, his construction of them as a curious and cryptic spectacle passing before his knowing gaze. But its immediate implications, in the opening chapter of the *Travels*, have more to do with the position of the English in Madras in the early 1780s. It is worth noting that in the writings of Hodges's near-contemporaries, for example, in William Robertson's *Historical Disquisition concerning Ancient India* (1791), or in the writings of Sir William Jones, the 'soft and voluptuous' nature of the Hindu people, expressed in their poetry, or manifested in religious practices appropriate to 'the extreme sensibility both of their mental and corporeal frame', is itself the focus of interest. But in Hodges's account of Madras, his allusions, both implicit and explicit, to their spectacular femininity do not take it to be symptomatic of their historical or national character, though later in his narrative it does acquire this significance. The femininity that is attributed to the Hindu people of Madras works, rather, to emphasize the immediate and striking 'first impression' that they make 'upon an entire stranger', an impression that precludes the possibility of profound analysis or historical depth.[4]

The gendered construction of the Hindu business people, and later of the indigenous population of Madras, indicates that they are passive, attentive, responsive in their relations with Europeans, and allows the spectator to elide or gloss over the question of what they are responsive to, what European activities demand their sedulous attention. In that first passage that I quoted, the transition from the perception of these people as merchants, engaged in business, to the description of their obeisances, is smoothed by the reference to their strange femaleness, a startling idea that makes it unnecessary to acknowledge the problematic combination of military and commercial power wielded by the British in Madras. The spectacular strangeness of what he observes obscures the difficulties of the spectator's own position in relation to that British power – his dependence on the licence and patronage extended by the East India Company, juxtaposed with his repeated claims to independent perception and impartial judgement.[5]

The femininity of these 'original inhabitants', in this context, does not appear to be itself the object of the spectator's curious interest. It seems to indicate the lack of any historical or characteristic depth, to mark the great distinction that confronts him as essentially natural, and beyond change or investigation. He focuses on it perhaps in order not to look elsewhere, rather than because it gratifies his curiosity. Hodges writes:

The appearance of the natives is exceedingly varied, some are wholly naked, and others so clothed, that nothing but the face and neck is to be discovered; besides this, the European is struck at first with many other objects, such as women carried on men's shoulders on pallankeens, and men riding on horseback clothed in linen dresses like women: which, united with the very different face of the country from all he had ever seen or conceived of, excite the strongest emotions of surprise!

It is impossible to describe the enthusiasm with which I felt myself actuated on this occasion; all that I saw filled my mind with expectations of what was yet unseen. I prepared therefore eagerly for a tour through the country.

The spectator is struck by the variety he sees, by what he seems to regard as transgressions of gender roles, but this is not enough. The people are not the face of the country, and the face is not the concealed identity. Madras and its people seem here to be like the partly clothed attendants of some classical deity, who direct the Englishman's curious eye, not to their own concealed nakedness, but to that of a figure yet unseen. The spectator wants to look through, look beyond, to the interior of the continent, and not to be detained by that initial apprehension of the coastal border with its great distinction.[6]

The first few pages of Hodges's *Travels in India* establish the importance of notions of gender in constructing the relations of the European spectator and narrator to the peoples he observes; and they also demonstrate that the idea of the Hindu crowd as a feminine spectacle, which the narrator initially finds surprising and striking, quickly yields to his enthusiastic eagerness to see something else, beyond. The feminisation of the Hindu people makes them visibly spectacular to the narrator, but it also seems to make them hardly worth contemplating, as though they were too visible to be worthy of his gaze, to gratify his curiosity, in comparison with the 'yet unseen'. Hodges is eager to get beyond Madras, to explore the interior, perhaps because, in his account, the recognition and identification of the people there seems overdetermined. Madras, he points out, 'was formed by the English' in the mid-seventeenth century, and since the wars of 1748–52 they 'may be considered as Sovereigns' there. But their presence does not have the interest of the exotic, and is for him 'more like a tale of enchantment than a reality'. Their dominance over the local Hindu population seems absolute, though vaguely defined, and hostility, in the form of the 'torrent' of war, comes from an enemy perceived to have 'over-run' the country beyond.[7]

The Hindu people of Madras, he implies, are insubstantial, and somehow without depth, in their feminised submission. He comments that there is little here 'to illustrate the history or characters of the original inhabitants': their feminised presence, in the absence of tangible historical evidence, reveals to the European eye 'no Characters at all'.[8] Instead, it manifests their subordination and responsiveness, and the identification of that in terms of gender elides the distinctions between the various forms of their disadvantage, and effaces the differences between the positions of subordination accorded them in relations of commerce, or military government, or religious and cultural discrimination. Because the distinction of gender may accommodate and describe all of these, it tends to homogenize their different implications, and to blur any conflicts between them. It is perhaps this attribute that makes gendered identification of primary importance in Hodges's account, but not itself the focus of interest. Instead it functions like a lens that enables the spectator to perceive or ignore further and apparently more complex objects of knowledge.[9]

In Hodges's account of Madras, notions of gender describe the perceived relation between the population and the residues of its historical culture. They describe the visible strangeness of the people, rendered merely spectacular in the absence of indications of historical depth and substance, and gloss over the relationship between the perceived status of the 'original inhabitants', the licensed independence of the spectator, and the imperial and commercial ambitions of the British. Difference of gender was also a privileged notion in representations of the South Seas – both in Hodges's paintings, and in the writings of his fellow travellers. Johann Reinhold Forster's comment on the men of Tahiti – that the 'outlines of their bodies are . . . beautifully feminine' – is broadly representative of the way Europeans saw them. The predominance of this notion of difference as a means of describing the distinction between the European spectator and what he observes works to emphasise similarities, parallels, between European perceptions of the peoples of Oceania and of Asia. Central to this book is the thesis that gendered discourses are in this period both flexible and complex in their implications in ways that proved invaluable to the work of developing and representing British commercial and imperial ambitions.[10]

II

I will explore, in this chapter, some of the implications of the gendered construction of European perceptions of the exotic, and suggest some of the ways in which we might understand these to be engaged in Hodges's paintings. My discussion will focus on one painting, because I think that the interaction of gender and exoticism in that one image will best introduce the distinctive nature of the relation between these discursive categories in the late decades of the eighteenth century. This is Hodges's painting of *A View Taken in the Bay of Otaheite Peha* [Vaitepiha] (plate 1.1). It was probably produced in 1775–6, and intended to be exhibited with the pendant *View of Matavai Bay in the Island of Otaheite* (plate 1.2).[11] Both paintings suggest the fertile abundance of vegetation, the physical or sensual ease, that made the idea of Tahiti an image of Paradise to Europeans. The apparent leisure of the women in the foreground of *Otaheite Peha*, and the indolence of the men in the foreground of *Matavai Bay*, reinforce the conception of the island as a place where, in Forster's words, 'the living' is 'easy & cheap'. The image of Vaitepiha, in particular, appeals to that idea of Tahiti that exercised a powerful attraction for the imagination of European men – a place where man might sweat in pleasure and not labour, a place which justified the conflation of the exotic and erotic.

In the image of Matavai Bay, there is a similar luxuriance of foliage, of dripping paint, emphasized by the liquid expanse of water in the foreground, the oily plasticity of the sails and rigging. But the painting presents the waters that encircle the island as a masculine space, in contrast to the femininity of the interior landscape. The Tahitian men in their canoes may in a sense be feminised by their indolent physicality, or because the aggressive finery of the warriors in the middle distance exemplifies that idea of exotic effeminacy that William Blake alluded to when he commented that 'Savages are Fops & Fribbles more than any other Men.' But the pairing of this image with that of Vaitepiha nevertheless confronts the European gaze with a striking contrast between manly boldness and feminine leisure.[12]

The contrast between the paintings points up the importance of gender in distinguishing the different social spaces that the landscapes represent. But for contemporary critics the contrast contained within each of these compositions, in the manner in which they were painted, seems to have been more remarkable. Contemporary responses to Hodges's work repeatedly comment on what they saw as the disparity between the topographical intentions of his images, their aim of making unfamiliar scenes known, and the apparent lack of accuracy and negligent concern for the known features of the landscape implied by Hodges's generous use of broad brush strokes and liquid paint. A reviewer commented on the Pacific landscapes exhibited at the Royal Academy in 1777:

The public are indebted to this artist for giving them some idea of scenes Which they before knew little of. It is rather surprising however, that a man of Mr. Hodges's genius should adopt such a ragged mode of colouring; his pictures all appear as if they were unfinished, and as if the colours were laid on the canvas with a skewer.

These reservations are echoed by other eighteenth-century critics.[13] Hodges himself, however, believed that his work was distinguished by his genius for what he called 'accurate observation'. He argued, in his later writing, that 'every thing has a particular character', which he implied that the artist must discover and disclose if his work is to have any 'pretensions to reputation as characteristical' of the nation that is being portrayed. He concluded that pictures achieve their highest value when they are 'connected with the history of the various countries, and . . . faithfully represent the manners of mankind'.[14] His success in achieving these aims may have been apparent to some of his contemporaries: Sir William Jones praised his aquatint *Views of India* for 'correct delineations', and they served as patterns and sources for artists working in India until well into the nineteenth century. More ambiguously, perhaps, Sir Joshua Reynolds referred to his representations of Asiatic buildings with approval in his thirteenth Discourse, and commented that he produced the 'best landskips' in the Academy exhibition of 1786.[15]

The relation in Hodges's work between accurate observation and boldness, between particular character and ragged colouring, was controversial, and I suggest that the features of his work that could arouse this debate can most fruitfully be understood in the context of the role notions of gender played in constructing European conceptions of the exotic in the late eighteenth century. I can best demonstrate that relation by discussing Hodges's *View Taken in the Bay of Otaheite Peha* in a little more detail. The prominence and boldness of the figures of the two women in the landscape are immediately striking. The vivid pinkness and inflated form of the bathing woman in the centre, and the bluish-pink skin colour of the seated woman on the right, give them prominence in contrast to the greens, blues, and yellows of the landscape. Their position in the foreground of the painting throws them into relief, and emphasises their presence, to a degree that is unusual in Hodges's work. The figures of the women function as focal points for the landscape beyond, their familiar forms providing a point of reference that makes its unfamiliar and almost fantastic contours knowable, and drawing their own exotic interest from their place within it. But if the figures of the women make the scene somehow recognisable, they do so because the image draws on several different and perhaps incompatible conventions: on theories about primitive and exotic societies as well as on images of economic and sensual paradises. Joppien and Smith suggest that this landscape represented a challenge to the way Cook wished to see the Tahitians portrayed after his second voyage. Cook had been dismayed by the emphasis on the apparently promiscuous sexual behaviour of the islanders in accounts of his first voyage, and wished to redress the balance in the account of his second. He asked for all reference to what he called 'the Amours of my people' to be expurgated, so that the edited and published account would be 'unexceptionable to the nicest readers'.[16] But Hodges's painting, I think, points up the pressures that made this chastening ambition unworkable. In the painting of Vaitepiha the representation of exotic sexuality provides a focus for what is difficult or contradictory about the relationship between the discourses which structure European visions of the South Pacific.

Perhaps the most obviously troubling aspect of the idea of the South Seas as it is represented in these paintings is the apparent ease of the inhabitants. For they enjoy a desirable but apparently unearned leisure and plenty that implicitly question the values of industry and progress; the need for endeavour, resolution, and adventure. The manner in which that troubling ease is represented in this pair of paintings both emphasises and conceals this problem. On the one hand, the prominent position of the women in the landscape, and the implications of their gender, may work to lend a moral gloss to the idea of a natural paradise. It was a commonplace of enlightenment social theory that the position of women is the index to the degree of civilisation achieved in any society, and their position, their behaviour and treatment, was judged according to what might be described as a bourgeois pastoral fantasy of the gendered apportioning of labour and ease. The leisure of women in the second half of the eighteenth century is understood in this context as a sign, a product and reward, of the labour of men. European explorers are insistently disapproving in their accounts of anything visible, recognisable, as female labour in the societies they observe, because they take it to be evidence of the degeneracy and tyranny of the men of that society.[17] On the other hand, however, the leisure apparently enjoyed by women may not be a sign of a society emerging into civilisation from what Europeans saw as a primitive and barbarian state. For it may not indicate that the women are engaged in the easy consumption of whatever the men in the pendant canvas may have fished up or fought for. The indolence of the men might indicate that they enjoy a barbarous ease purchased as a result of the women's servitude, or the commodification of their sexuality. That ambivalence, about whether the women's leisure indicates an earned and moralised ease, or sexual abandon, is central to the way these images represent Tahiti as the object of the European spectator's curiosity and desire.

The different ways in which the representation of the women's leisure, and its relation to the luxuriant landscape of the island, might be understood point obliquely towards the mixed and contested purposes of European exploration. The view of Vaitepiha invites comparison with the subgenre of scenes of young women bathing, scenes which cast the European spectator both as the unintrusive admirer of women's secluded freedoms, and as Actaeon, only secured from animality by the composing frame, the self-conscious distancing and deferral of the pleasures he views. In Hodges's painting, the need for that distance is emphasised by the dissolution of the form of the bathing woman in the water that supports her: in order for her to achieve coherence, to become integrated into corporeality, the spectator must stand well away from the picture, and see her within the landscape and the frame, he must recognise her exotic distance as the condition of her desirability. The subordination of the figure to the unity of the landscape as a whole invites at the same time as it anaesthetises curiosity and desire; it licenses these by assimilating and diffusing them to the compositional whole that offers to transcend physicality, to displace the pursuit of it on to the chaste idea of the whole landscape. The painting applies the conventions for the representation of a golden age that is erotic because it is innocent to the landscapes explored in the South Pacific: it exploits the deferred sensual promise of the exotic to represent the landscape and climate of Tahiti, the composition of the painting, as the necessary condition, and perhaps the diffused but comprehensive object, of desire. The bathing woman, viewed in this context, confirms the desirable salubrity of climate that dominates Hodges's smaller oil sketches, and that climate in turn confirms the innocence of the leisure that the Tahitian women enjoy.[18]

The lack of finish with which the bathing woman is painted helps to give the spectator an idea of scenes he before knew little of, because it fences innocence with a protective, enforced distance. But it was not only because of its climate that Tahiti appeared to offer the attractions of Paradise to European explorers and armchair travellers. Though its pleasures could be understood as those of classical Arcadias, they were also immediate, and material. In this painting, the ambivalent relation between these different notions of the kind of Paradise Tahiti offered can be seen in the contrasting and perhaps incongruous representation of the two women in the foreground. The seated woman forms through her gesture a sub-group with the figure of the *tii,* the carved image to her right, and both are painted with a degree of detail and finish that is conspicuously lacking in the central, bathing woman (plate 1.3).[19] The seated woman and *tii* invite a curious and close inspection that is at odds with the distance needed to make sense of the form of the woman in the water. The posture of the woman alludes to that of Diana, in Titian's *Diana and Actaeon* (fig. 1.1). The angle of her arm picks up the gesture with which Titian's goddess attempts to protect her

Figure 1.1 Titian, *Diana and Actaeon*, c. 1556–9, oil on canvas, 1,880 × 2,030 mm

modesty, a gesture repeated by the nymph in the centre of Titian's painting; and that allusion is underscored by the lack of any narrative explanation for the apparent modesty of the Tahitian woman in Hodges's image, for there is no obvious intruder or voyeur within this composition.

Viewed from a distance, the figure of the *tii* assumes the familiar proportions of Priapus, and, by virtue of that classical allusion in its form, it may legitimise whatever sexual abandon the figures of the women might suggest. In a letter ostensibly written by Lord Lyttelton in the 1770s, the notoriously dissolute aristocrat discussed his collection of drawings and paintings of nude women and boys, and commented that while most of these had to be kept in his private dressing-room, scenes involving sacrifices to Priapus could be prominently displayed in the library, perhaps because the figure seemed to dispel the prurience provoked by what was described as his 'inanimate Seraglio'.[20] For Priapus's phallic form guarantees the heterosexuality of his worshippers, as well as the satisfaction of their desires within the social landscape of the painting. But the detailed representation of the *tii* invites scrutiny, which confirms its difference from the more familiar classical idea of Priapus. It invites a close inspection that discloses, to the right of the image, the elevated *tupapau*.[21] These two exotic curiosities, close together at the margin of the painting, are reminiscent of the kind of occasional and collectable objects which attracted virtuosi as well as scientists to the South Pacific. They fulfil a function similar to that of the curiosities and memorabilia from Cook's first voyage that surround Joseph Banks in Benjamin West's portrait (plate 3.3). The riches of Banks's collection, drawn from a dispersed variety of cultures, are organised to display his cosmopolitanism, their exotically random incoherence, as well as to indicate authenticity, the first-hand and intimate experience that informs knowledge. The representation of these exotic *things* locates the sign of authenticity in material detail, removed from any indication of the more generalised effects of climate or topography.[22]

The *tii* in this painting alludes to two different possible contexts, two sets of meanings which may not be entirely incompatible or exclusive, but which do, I think, create a tension for the spectator. The figure may be Priapic, and indicate the association of the image with a familiar subgenre which emphasises the subordination and containment of women within the landscape. Or it may be a sign of the exotic in something curious and potentially collectable, like the things in the portrait of Banks. The knowledgeable spectator who understands the *tii* as the representation of a deceased ancestor, as published accounts of the voyage suggested, might also be sufficiently well informed to recognise the *tupapau* behind it as an elevated stage bearing a corpse. The figure of the *tii* in juxtaposition with the *tupapau* may call attention to what Europeans considered the dark and morbid superstitions associated with the intricacies of exotic cultures and lurking in the details of the painting. Grouped with this image, the finished and quite elaborately detailed form of the seated woman poses a strong contrast to the diffusive and vague outline of the bather. The representation of her tattoos invites the curious attention that detects the presence of the *tupapau* on the right, and it locates the exotic as the reward of that attention, rather than in the grasp of the landscape as a whole. That curious exoticism of detail exercises a fascination that detracts from the sensual pleasure conjured by the bathing woman enveloped, half-submerged in the landscape. For my discussion has

suggested that when the women are perceived in subordination to the landscape, their leisure a function of its luxuriant climate, they are susceptible
to a humanising appropriation that casts them as the innocent objects of
the spectator's Actaeon-like gaze. But the exotic inscription of this woman's
tattooing may in a sense dehumanise her, because it isolates her from the
landscape and makes her an object of curiosity.

Joshua Reynolds, in his seventh Discourse, argued that 'All . . . fashions are
very innocent', because they have the sanction of custom, but he excluded
from this pale 'some of the practices at Otaheite', which were 'painful, or
destructive of health'. Accounts of the Tahitians had dwelt on the apparent
painfulness of the tattooing operation, and Reynolds's comments locate it
in a different register of exoticism from that which celebrates the healthy
climate, the beauty, and innocence of the islanders. In this register, the exotic
is identified with what Reynolds called 'circumstances of minuteness and
particularity', which, he observed, 'frequently seem to give an air of truth
to a piece, and to interest the spectator in an extraordinary manner'.[23] This
different register invites curious investigation, but the idea of exoticism that
it represents encourages the spectator to peer into the canvas with a kind
of distasteful fastidiousness. This idea of the exotic precludes the distance
that was necessary to bring into focus the loose form of the bathing woman,
diffused into the richness of the landscape.

III

The representation of the two women in the foreground of Hodges's painting employs incongruous visual languages, incongruous because they make
potentially incompatible demands on the position of the spectator, and
imply different relations between the discourses of gender and the exotic. I
have suggested that the problem that the relation between them poses illuminates the sense in which that reviewer whom I quoted earlier felt that
Hodges's work did offer an 'idea of scenes Which [the public] before knew
little of', though it was an idea that they gained by looking through, looking
beyond, the paint on the surface before them. For what Hodges meant by
the capacity for 'accurate observation' on which he prided himself may have
more to do with the way his painting demonstrates this doubled focus, than
with the desire to produce the sort of cluttered but flat fidelity to human
and material detail that other artists of the exotic, some armed with camera
obscura, achieved in this period.[24] This is not only a matter of reconciling the
representation of detail with what Hodges described, in writing of the work

of his master Richard Wilson, as the 'broad bold and manly execution' of the whole. For this is a disjunction that indicates problems in the way primitive and exotic societies were understood in the late eighteenth century.[25] What Europeans want from images of Tahiti, what made the idea of the place so attractive to them, may inform the combination of qualities that Hodges's image demonstrates, and I will now turn to some contemporary discussions of Tahiti which illuminate the nature of the disjunction that characterises this image, and also suggest that it can nevertheless be perceived to soothe rather than unsettle the spectator's eye.

The islanders of the South Pacific were frequently perceived in terms of their similarity or difference to those classical or barbarian societies familiar to the educated European. The voyagers themselves made lengthy comparisons between the Tahitians and, usually, the ancient Greeks, and essayists discussed the resemblance of South Pacific customs to those of the Greeks and Romans, the North American Indians, the Goths, and the ancient Hebrews. Vicesimus Knox, lucubrating on the custom of human and animal sacrifice, concluded that: 'I cannot but be struck with the wonderful similarity observable in the manners and superstitions of savage men throughout the world, and in all ages.' In contrast to this perception of wonderful homogeneity, the barbarian or savage peoples observed by Europeans were thought not to perceive similarities between themselves and other groups. Barbarous and savage people were understood to be incapable of generalising their ideas, and to be 'miserably deficient', in the words of Henry Home, Lord Kames, in the two mental powers necessary to reasoning – 'the power of invention, and that of perceiving relations'. William Robertson wrote, of the 'rude and barbarous times' through which he believed every country passed, that:

When the intellectual powers are just beginning to unfold, and their first feeble exertions are directed towards a few objects of primary necessity and use; when the faculties of the mind are so limited as not to have formed general or abstract ideas; when language is so barren as to be destitute of names to distinguish any thing not perceivable by some of the senses; it is preposterous to expect that men should be capable of tracing the relation between effects and their causes; or to suppose that they should rise from the contemplation of the former to the discovery of the latter, and form just conceptions of one Supreme Being, as the Creator and Governor of the universe.

One of the distinguishing constituents of barbarism, as these comments indicate, was that barbarous peoples were thought to be limited, imprisoned, by a disconnected specificity – of place, superstitious belief, language – that excluded general ideas and just conceptions. It was this feature, for example, that Cook alluded to when he traced unacceptable barbaric behaviour, like cannibalism, to its root cause in the alienation or isolation of one primitive group from another, and in the failure or refusal, therefore, to acknowledge common human features, common humanity.[26]

This contrast between the diverse specificities that constitute barbarian society and thought, and the grasp of wonderful similarity which distinguishes the civilised, is based in the ideological construction of two contrasting subjects; of a barbarian or a civilised observer whose capacity to systematise what he sees in the context of general ideas is the index of his place and power in the social and natural hierarchy. But in the later decades of the eighteenth century the contrast between these two modes of perception is more complex than that distribution of talents would suggest. The massive scholarly investment in archaeological and anthropological research, the perceived need to unearth the authentic materiality of cultures historically or geographically remote from those of Europe, appropriated to learned thought the absorption in specificity which had previously defined the objects of knowledge. So, for example, the accounts of Cook's second voyage produced by the naturalists Anders Sparrman and Johann Forster both made much of their distance from the comprehensive theories of moral philosophers, a distance substantiated by the detailed and specific nature of their knowledge, its intimate and empirical dependence upon particular things. The preface to Sparrman's account asserted that 'every authentic and well-written book of voyages and travels is, in fact, a treatise of experimental philosophy'. It was the mark of its authenticity that it should contain 'the best materials for the purpose of building . . . systems', but should not develop those systems itself. Forster's book demonstrated a similar commitment to the local and particular. His theories on the 'various stages' of mankind's development were supported by the proximity of his detailed *Observations . . . on Physical Geography*, and *Natural History*.[27] Their accounts organised and systematised their data, but they were nevertheless characterised by an absorption in diverse materials, a respect for the isolation and simplicity of the particular example, that indicated an instability in the contrast I described between barbarian and civilised observers.

That contrast was reinforced by the purposive selectivity that the natural philosopher exercised in presenting the 'best materials'. The 'treatise of experimental philosophy' described or implied relations of cause and effect which it was imagined to be beyond the capacity of the barbarian to trace, and the teleological project that informed those relations was essential to their authenticity and authority, as Robertson's conclusions indicated. But it nevertheless remains the case that in late eighteenth-century conceptions of knowledge, and most acutely in theories of art, the status of empirical research appeared problematically servile and lowly. Joshua Reynolds wrote that the landscape painter 'applies himself to the imagination, not to the curiosity, and works not for the Virtuoso or the Naturalist', and a similar sense of the lowliness of empirical curiosity in the context of heroic art informed James Barry's argument, that art arises

from the disappointment of the human mind, sated, disgusted, and tired with the monotony of real persons and things which this world affords . . . In proportion to the serenity and goodness of the mind, it naturally turns away from such a state of things, in search of some other more grateful and consoling; and it has a natural horror of those atheistical cavils, which would malignantly deprive it of all other resource, by mercilessly chaining it down to the scene before it.

What Barry objects to is the particular state of the scene before the mind, a state that he perceives as miserable in its imperfection; but he also suggests that the mechanical condition of mind that is 'chained down to the specific properties of natural objects' may be atheistical in its opposition to ideal truth, and may therefore not be capable of entertaining those purposive projects that end in general ideas, and 'just conceptions' of the first cause.[28]

John Wesley's comments on the published account of Cook's first voyage provide an interesting example of some of the implications of this instability in the opposition between the barbarian and the civilised. He wrote in his journal for 17 January 1774:

Meeting with a celebrated book, a volume of Captain Cook's Voyages, I sat down to read it with huge expectation. But how was I disappointed. I observed, 1. Things absolutely incredible: 'A nation without any curiosity.' And what is stranger still, (I fear, related with no good design) 'Without any sense of shame! Men and women coupling together in the face of the sun, and in the sight of scores of people! Men whose skin, cheeks, and lips are white as milk.' Hume or Voltaire might believe this: but I cannot. I observed, 2. Things absolutely impossible . . . A native of Otaheite is said to understand the language of an island eleven hundred miles distant from it in latitude; besides I know not how many hundreds in longitude! So that I cannot but rank this Narrative with that of Robinson Cruso; and account Tupia [the Raiatean who acted as a guide and interpreter] to be, in several respects, a-kin to his man Friday.

Wesley's huge expectation and disappointment, I think, are informed by that discursive opposition, though his remarks also indicate its instability and redefinition. He expects that physical, sexual behaviour should be common – the face of the sun, the sight of scores of people, should induce a universal and perhaps instinctive response – while intellectual behaviour, the articulation or understanding of language, should, his disbelief implies, indicate the social or topographical place and identity of the subject. In the barbarian, therefore, language should be limited in its specificity, it should express only the particular circumstances in which the islander is thought to be absorbed. Like the Indian in Pope's *Essay on Man*, who is represented as believing that his dog, bottle, and wife will be found in heaven, the conceptions of the islander should be dictated by his immediate experience.[29]

Wesley's reaction to the transgression of this social or natural hierarchy complicates the opposition between civilised and barbarian subjects. For the discovery that the sexual behaviour of the islanders does not resemble what he considers to be common and natural leads Wesley to reflect on their physical similarity to Europeans – he remarks that the men's complexions are white as milk, to underscore his alarmed disbelief. His response to their apparent lack of sexual shame suggests that this, rather than any intellectual capacity, should be fundamental to recognisably human subjectivity and interiority: if they had not behaved in this disturbing way, he implies that he would have been able to credit them, on the basis of the invisibility of their sexual activities and the visibility of their milky complexions, with a natural human capacity for moral or social shame, and therefore with a subjectivity at least potentially civilised. As it is, the sign that they possess something resembling the systematic and abstract rationality of a civilised subject – their capacity to use a language which is apparently not tied to their immediate material circumstances – seems to him proof that they are 'akin to . . . man Friday', that they are fictive, and are, not civilised, but the possessions and servants, the subjects, of those who are: *his* man Friday.[30]

Wesley's brief comments register the shift from a construction of exotic barbarism in which the local particularity of language is a privileged constituent, to a construction which privileges what is social and specular, and which recognises the regulation of sexuality as the prime indication of moral personality. His remarks demonstrate, in a conveniently concise form, the appropriation of humanist, universal value to the bourgeois construction of subjectivity in terms of a socially regulated and moralised interiority, and they indicate that the coherence of the interior and the social is manifested in sexual behaviour. Discussions of the South Sea islanders in the later decades of the eighteenth century return repeatedly, insistently, to the problematic issue of their sexuality, to the relation between the exotic and the erotic that

troubles Hodges's painting, and this insistence marks the instabilities of the
opposition between the civilised and the barbarian, in the ideological context of bourgeois humanism.[31] Wesley's comments exemplify a more general
discursive redefinition of the concept of the barbarian, which acknowledges the importance of his visible and intellectual attachment to a specific
locality – the sense in which the barbarian is understood to be somehow
more thoroughly and definitively indigenous, more distinctively native and
enchorial – but which privileges his unacceptably exotic sexual behaviour
as the determining constituent of his barbarous condition. This displaces
and diffuses the force of the opposition between a civilised, intuitive comprehension of the whole, and barbarian absorption in detail.

This redefinition does not dissolve that opposition, but it means that
the barbarian can be identified, *either* by local and particular containment,
confinement, by the inability to generalise or form coherent theories, *or*
by libidinous abandon, by characteristically exotic sexuality. The second,
libidinal identity is opposed to middle-class conceptions of the social subject,
rather than to the perhaps more abstract ideal of the civilised man. The
interest in material detail, in phenomena defined by their specific locality,
that distinguished the work of naturalists like Forster, is contrasted to the
barbarian's failure to moralise his desires, his lack of curiosity and shame,
and this opposition conceals the problematic nature of the comparison
between their attachment to epistemological discontinuities, materials and
not systems, and his. It is worth noting that in Wesley's remarks barbaric
sexuality is associated with shamelessness but not with curiosity, not with
the 'turn for experiment . . . and disposition to enquire' that characterised
both the endeavours of enlightened scientists and the reception of their
works.[32] Thus the discursive gendering and eroticisation of the peoples of
the South Seas works to accommodate instabilities and incoherencies in
the ideological construction of bourgeois humanism. For emphasis on the
sexual constituent of barbarism redefines its opposition to the civilised,
and masks the tensions or contradictions involved in the appropriation of
humanist attributes to the bourgeois subject.

The privileging of exotic sexuality masks the discrepancy between contrasting ideological constructions of knowledge; between, on the one hand,
the conception of civilised and civilising knowledge, in which particulars
are given form and meaning by their relation to the whole that is grasped in
an intuitive act of comprehension, and, on the other, the construction of a
more bourgeois concept of knowledge as achieved in the progressive acquisition of diverse material facts. It glosses over the tension between the project
of adventuring into an unknown new world, which has to be discovered

and appropriated piecemeal, and the idea of enlarging the map of the known world, assimilating, drawing in, the details supposed to be implicit in its design.[33] It points up and calls attention to the contrast between the amorality of barbarism, which is the object of curious fascination or chaste disapproval, and the moralised European subject. It can perform these demanding functions because, as Hodges's painting suggests, the object of erotic fantasy is constructed as diverse and formless, without chaste definition or containment except in so far as it is distanced and deferred, but at the same time it is, as Reynolds noted, the 'smaller objects' that 'serve to catch the sense', it is the curious attraction of detail that lends material and sensual substance to fantasy.[34] These two exotic registers find their focus, their expression, in the eroticised and feminised body of the barbarian.

This process, where the complex relation between different European notions of cultural difference and of the purpose of exploration finds a focus in representations of gender and the exotic, is perhaps most clearly demonstrated in Forster's *Observations made During a Voyage round the World* (1778). I have already mentioned that Forster bases the authority for his lengthy disquisitions on '*Ethic Philosophy*' in the detailed empirical investigation of physical geography and natural history, and his remarks on the 'various stages' of mankind bear witness to the dominance of that rationalist methodology. In his account of the South Sea islanders, he stresses that a man 'born in a civilized nation' cannot envy the 'state of intoxication' – with its implications of physical and moral degeneracy – which the 'savage or barbarian', living in an hospitable climate, independent of social regulations, mistakes for happiness.[35] But in Tahiti he believes he observes a society developing from barbarism into early civilisation, free from the vices which corrupt its later and more fully formed stages; a society which is not only the appropriate object of moral disapprobation and empirically fastidious curiosity.

The affection, and even admiration, that he feels for these people seems almost to take him by surprise, and to be experienced in spite of his methodology, with its implications of moral distance and distaste. The experience seems to force on him a kind of sentimental paternalism that is at odds with the principles of his work. He writes that:

I felt for many of them emotions, which were not so far distant from paternal affection and complacency, as might be expected, when we recollect the great difference of our manners and our way of thinking. But I found likewise . . . what a great and venerable blessing benevolence is . . . when this best gift of heaven sits enthroned in the heart, fills the soul with gracious sensations, and prompts all our faculties to expressions of good nature and kindness: then only does it connect all mankind as it were into one family; youths of different nations become brethren, and the older people of one nation, find children in the offspring of the other.

Forster's feelings of benevolence, the gracious sensations of his soul, work to connect and assimilate the islanders to the family of mankind. In that family structure, of course, he assumes the position of the paternal head and enjoys the enthronement of his own virtuous superiority to the Tahitians, whom he implies are childlike in their 'natural levity' and inattention. But while this all-embracing affection and complacency do establish the distance between the mature civilised man and those who are emerging from barbarous adolescence into civilised youth, they do not insist on the contrast between his self-conscious morality and their perceived amorality or degeneracy.[36]

In later decades of the eighteenth century, however, as I have already suggested, this kind of benevolent paternalist humanism is adopted to the service of precisely that distinction. Forster's discussion engages in this process of redefinition through situating this paternalist vision in the more immediate context of the bourgeois ideal of the domestic family. He writes, of the family unit, which he believes is the source of the civilising development he traces in Tahitian society, that the 'father seemed to be the soul which animated the whole body of the family by his superior wisdom, benevolence and experience'. That difference between the soulful father and the bodily family, only animated by his 'gracious sensations', inscribes the generosity of Forster's paternalist vision with the distinction essential to his rationalist project.[37] Forster debates at some length in the course of his argument the controversial question of race: he considers, on the one hand, the theory, notoriously associated with Lord Monboddo, that the race of humanity extends to include orang-utangs, and on the other the theory that the race is divided into distinct species, which exclude those who are not European from kindred with those who are. And his refutation of both of these theories is based in a bourgeois concept of familial and marital relations. So that, in refutation of the first, more extensive theory, he asserts that it does not deserve serious argument; he writes:

I appeal to an argument taken from the better half of our species, the fair sex; we all assent to the description which Adam gives of his partner: a creature

> *So lovely fair,*
> *That what seem'd fair in all the world, seem'd now*
> *Mean, or in her summ'd up, in her contain'd,*
> *And in her looks; which from that time infus'd*
> *Sweetness into his heart, unfelt before,*

And into all things from her air inspir'd,
The spirit of love, and amorous delight.
Grace was in all her steps; heav'n in her eye,
In every gesture dignity and love.

I cannot think that a man looking up to this inimitable masterpiece, could be tempted to compare it with an ugly, loathsome ouran-outang!

The human family, for Forster, is circumscribed by ties of desire, like those bonding Adam to Eve, and he emphasises the grounding of his argument in physical immediacy when he concludes that should any man persist in the first argument, 'may none but ouran-outangs vouchsafe and admit his embraces'.[38]

The importance that Forster gives to sexual desire as the key characteristic of the common human species is moralised, as it was in Wesley, by the regulations implicit in that discourse, which identifies the body as what needs government, and is spiritually inanimate or amoral, ignorant and not wise, innocent and not experienced, feminine and not paternal, desired and not desiring. He complains, only a few pages earlier, that

We are united in societies, where the constant intercourse with foreigners, makes it next to impossible to preserve the purity of races without mixture, and pity it is, that the guiles of art and deceit are so great in one sex, and curiosity, levity, and lewd-ness, are so common in the other, in our enlightened and highly-civilised societies, that they contribute still more to make the preservation of races precarious. This depravation prevailed so far, that even OMAI became the object of concupiscence of some females of rank.[39]

It is hardly surprising to find that it is not female sexuality or curiosity that define the extent or the boundaries of the human species, that for European women of rank to desire an exotic man is evidence of depravity. But for European men to see in the women of the South Seas something conformable to the desirable outline of Milton's Eve is at once less than serious, and the expression of the paternalist impulse.[40]

In Forster's *Observations*, his insistence that the bodies of the Tahi-tians, whatever their sex, are 'beautifully feminine' conceals any disjunction between the different ways they are perceived, for it provides a means of glossing over discontinuities in European perception and self-conception. On the one hand, the comprehensive views of the civilised man indicate his paternal maturity, whereas the mercurial volatility and discontinuity of perception that characterise the barbarian subject define him as childlike and feminine. On the other hand, the distinction between the moralised bourgeois subject and the amoral barbarian defines the first in terms of his capacity for expectant curiosity or desire, and the second as the appropriate feminised object of that desire. In Hodges's *View of Otaheite Peha* I have suggested that the interplay of detail and abstraction, of precise delineation that demands close inspection, and diffusion that can best be viewed from a distance, might best be understood in the context of the troubled status of the European project of colonial and commercial expansion in the South Pacific. It images the centrality of gender difference to the divided nature of European conceptions of the great distinction, and points to the tensions and uncertainties that run through European visual and textual representations of Cook's second voyage.

Reflecting on the significance of navigation to the cultures of northern Europe, Johann Forster commented in 1784 that

voyages made for the gratification of curiosity and for the extension of commerce, seem to have greatly contributed to the promotion of knowledge, and to the introduction of milder manners and customs into society. For it is highly cultivated nations only, that explore distant countries and nations for the sake of commerce, in like manner as seeking them for the gratification of curiosity, pre-supposes a still higher degree of cultivation and refinement.[1]

Cook's second voyage to the South Pacific was ostensibly undertaken, above all, for the gratification of curiosity. The French ambassador reported that, in the space of a brief meeting, Lord Sandwich, the First Lord of the Admiralty, assured him more than twenty times over that curiosity was the only motive for the expensive and hazardous circumnavigation. Curiosity was one of the characteristics that people without civilisation were thought to lack. George Forster observed, for example, that the people encountered at Christmas Sound, Tierra del Fuego, responded to the extraordinary phenomenon of the European ship 'seemingly without the smallest degree of curiosity'. This perception was important to his conclusion that they followed 'a mode of life . . . nearer to that of brutes, than that of any other nation', and were characterised by 'the strangest compound of stupidity, indifference, and inactivity'.[2] In contrast, the impartial or indiscriminate avidity of curiosity was seen as a hallmark of high civilisation. Sandwich's assurances about British expansion in the South Pacific assert the political innocence of the venture. They imply that curiosity and civilisation are intertwined, and guarantee the disinterestedness of what might seem to be the most blatantly acquisitive moves of European powers in their competition for extensive commercial empires in other continents and distant seas.[3]

Curiosity was central to Johann Forster's project in the South Pacific – and materially so, for the disputed value and status of natural and artificial curiosities was continually at issue in his transactions with the islanders and with the officers, gentlemen, and crew of Cook's ships. The journals of Forster and his fellow travellers narrate numerous anecdotes of the natural philosopher's vexed and anxious attempts to distinguish the exchanges that stocked his cabinets from those of his companions. His commerce in philosophical curiosities was embarrassed by proximity to trade in provisions, to sexual commerce, to appropriations by islanders and voyagers that were seen to involve no legitimating direct exchange and so were identified as theft, and to the energetic trade between Europeans and islanders in objects that seemed to have no curiosity or use value at all. Forster's collections were important to his philosophical enquiries, to the status he would be able to claim for himself as a theorist and empirical investigator on his return to Europe, and he may also have anticipated that they would be a useful resource in times of financial hardship. His acquisitions, like the ambitious ventures of the British Admiralty, claim a curious status that seems ambivalently both to confirm their disinterestedness, their distance from competitive strife, and to imply their energetic immersion in the fray of commercial and personal interests.[4]

The ship's astronomer William Wales struck at the heart of Forster's conception of himself and his philosophical endeavour when he published the claim that 'there can be no good reason given why the seamen should not be as fond of curiosities as himself'. Wales asserted that Forster's acquisitive enthusiasm had encouraged the seamen to trade in curiosities for which they knew he would pay well, and that the libidinal appetites of the Forsters, like those of most of the voyagers, had involved them in sexual commerce with the islanders. What is most revealing about Wales's attack is his insistent harping on the frailty of the distinctions between kinds of investigation and modes of exchange on which Forster's *Observations* were based. Wales's aspersions muddy Forster's claim to a curiosity that 'pre-supposes a still higher degree of cultivation and refinement' than 'commercial views' imply, for they indicate that Forster's avidity can be yoked and even identified with those wants and desires from which he was most anxious to free his civilised and enlightened philosophy. Forster's acquisitive hunger, Wales asserted, had competed with the officially sanctioned trade in provisions for the ship, had been no different from what the philosopher represented as the idle curiosity and profiteering of the seamen, and had even hindered the progress of scientific experiment. The philosopher's attempts to distinguish his own civilised enquiry had in Wales's view falsely 'involved the whole ship's company, officers and men, in one universal censure of *ignorance, brutality, cruelty, wantonness,* and *barbarity*'.[5]

Forster's work as a natural philosopher in the South Pacific was conducted in a context in which curiosity, with its ambivalent implications of personal avidity and professional purity, was constantly shadowed by the speculative form of commerce. As Forster's reflections on the art of navigation implied, curiosity depended for its advancement on commerce. However, enlightened and professional or philosophical curiosity – curiosity freed from those implications of sexual and material desire that continually threaten to taint its propriety – was nevertheless defined by a hostility or distance from commercial views. That distance was necessary to the philosopher's claim that his perceptions were marked by a 'higher degree of cultivation and refinement'. This ambivalent relation between commerce and curiosity was central, I suggest, to the uneasiness with which Forster and his fellow voyagers reflected on European expansion in the South Pacific and its implications for both islanders and Europeans. This chapter will look at the implications of this unease for the representation of women in Johann Forster's journals and published *Observations*, and in some of Hodges's Tahitian landscapes.

William Hodges produced two versions of the pair of paintings of Vaitepiha and Matavai Bay which I discussed in Chapter 1. The versions which he produced for the Admiralty (now in the National Maritime Museum) are probably later, and the changes to the second, larger image of Matavai Bay indicate the importance of women to reflections on the Europeans' presence (plates 2.1 and 2.2). Joppien and Smith have pointed out that the first image of Matavai Bay 'presents Tahitian society in its pristine independence, untouched by European contact', whereas the second is 'a depiction of civilization and its benefits extended to the savages of the South Seas'.[6] The two versions of the scene present before-and-after scenes where the Tahitian war boats central to the first are replaced by the *Resolution* and *Adventure* in the second, and where the white tent on the promontory also indicates successful working relations between islanders and voyagers.

The changes between the first and second image significantly alter the relation of the scene to the image of Vaitepiha. *Tahiti Revisited*, the Admiralty version of the Vaitepiha landscape, is smaller than the second image of Matavai Bay, and there is no suggestion that it was intended to be hung with it. In the earlier pairing, the inland view of women bathing in apparent idleness contrasted with the seascape populated by men. In the first Matavai Bay, manly activities are suggested by the head-dress of the warrior in the middle distance, and the fowl and fruits gathered in the foreground. In contrast to the leisure of the women, these might seem signs of busy masculine productivity, but in relation to European notions of industry, they are signs of natural plenty and relative ease. The extraordinarily luminous and vivid reds, oranges, and yellows suffusing the sky and water, the use of thick impasto, and the fluid definition of the men's bodies combine to suggest the tropical brilliance and sensual ease which the voyagers so admired as characteristic of Tahiti. In the later image, the use of colour is markedly more restrained. The warrior in his distinctive costume has disappeared, and the reclining figure of the seated man in the foreground has shifted into the shade of the sail, his prominent position now occupied by a bare-breasted mother and child. The woman's features are obscured by the shadow of her hat, while her torso, catching the light, turns to face the viewer's gaze, positioned for display in a manner reminiscent of Titian's *Venus Anadyomene* (1520–5), or of eighteenth-century allegorical representations of Plenty.[7] The bathing women in *Tahiti Revisited*, on the other hand, are less obviously posed for display than they had been in the earlier canvas. The body of the girl in the water is more modestly concealed, and the presence of the third woman, apparently chatting with the seated and tattooed woman, provides a social narrative to explain her posture, and perhaps make it seem more casual or mundane. The image is not modified as dramatically as the view of Matavai Bay, but it is in this later version more securely located in the familiar subgenre of scenes of women bathing, absorbed in each other's company and unaware of any watcher.

The differences between the two images of Matavai Bay suggest that the presence of the British ships modified the gendered economy of the island. In the later image, the Europeans appear to be trading with the islanders gathered around their ships, and this scene of peaceful exchange is represented past or through the foreground figure of the woman, as though delicately to suggest the relation between sexual and commercial desire that exercised Forster. But here that relationship is not shadowed with unease, and her presence may suggest a more positive narrative in which the European ships bring interlinked blessings of civilisation and commerce which enhance the domestic security and social status of the island women. Her prominence works almost to domesticate the picture space, to confirm the apparent ease and fluency of the reciprocal relationship between islanders and voyagers, and to suggest that the fertile richness of the island and its culture can readily afford whatever trade the Europeans may desire.

II

There is a marked difference between Forster's journals and his published *Observations* in the representation of relations between islanders and voyagers. The journals had only a limited circulation, and in them Forster clearly felt able to write more openly about both his controversial and some-times provocative reactions to his fellow voyagers, and his anxieties about the islanders, and in particular about the commerce between island women and sailors:

The Women in *Otahaitee*, especially those of the better sort, are all inclined to grow fat, & some old ones are very unwieldy: this makes that even the youngest have a very relaxed habit of body, their flesh is flabby, & if you add to this the tawny, sallow, yellow complexion, they can by no means so much be praised for their handsomeness: & what makes these Women most insupportable to me, is their character of most accomplished Jilts: they know from experience that all the Europeans that have hitherto touched at their Isle, are fond of women; & therefore they avail themselves of this foible & coquet with every Man they see, & all this only to obtain some trifling presents of beads, nails, red & Silk handkerchiefs, etc. etc. & on the other hand they are very small in person, seldom is a woman of a moderate stature to be seen among these Isles, & they look when compared with the Men, as a race of dwarfs.[8]

Forster's notes on the manners and character of the island women suggest a fastidious attention to detail, but were also marked by uncertainty. His com-ments on the women of Tahiti expressed distaste, but there was also perhaps some hesitation in the way his remarks glanced from their physical to their moral character, and then focused on the trivial returns they expected for their pains. He commented earlier on the neighbouring island of Raiatea that 'Their women coquet in the most impudent manner, & shew uncom-mon fondness for Foreigners, but are all Jilts & coax the Foreigners out of any thing they can get: & will not comply to sleep with them, unless they be common prostitutes, or the bribe very great & tempting.'[9] His criticism of the sexual morals of the Raiatean women, and implicitly of the Tahitians, is confused, on the one hand valorising chastity, and on the other the terms of fair trade, on which these jilting islanders default.

In the entry on Tahiti, Forster contrasted the island women unfavourably with the women of the Tongan islands, whose 'fine brisk full & lively Eyes deserve the attention of the best Connoisseurs'.[10] But though he invoked principles of aesthetic judgement and connoisseurship his response implied something more visceral, as he indirectly acknowledged in his assertion that none of these island women stand comparison with 'our European fair ones'.

The bloom of their complexions, the vermillion of their lips, the roses on their cheeks & the lily bosom ecclipses all at once the beauty of these women. If I may mention in this depraved age the innocence & chastity of our Brittish maids, their improved minds & all the other accomplishments they so commonly are masters of, & all the virtues, which so early are instilled into their minds; not the least remembrance is left of all the charms of these copper beauties; all Ideas of them must be effaced from the mind of each of their warmest Admirers & force from them due hommage to Virtue, Elegance & beauty so superlatively united in Britannia's fair Daughters.[11]

Initially the comparison appeals again to imagined standards of connoisseurship, favouring red and white over the racial otherness of 'copper beauties'. But these standards then appear inadequate, and the argument becomes uncertain. Forster suggests that the 'warmest Admirers' of the island women have moral reformation foisted on them, whether they like it or not, and find themselves reluctantly compelled to acknowledge the superiority of 'Britannia's fair Daughters'. But this reformation depends on their willingness to weigh in the balance the virtues of chastity and educational improvement – virtues which he concedes are out of step with the depravity of advanced civilisation.

Forster's concern about the propriety of commercial relations with islanders is most apparent in his comments on transactions with Maori at Queen Charlotte Sound in May 1773. On this his second visit Cook was appalled by the eagerness of some Maori men to 'oblige their Wives and Daughters to prostitute themselves whether they will or no'. He understood this new behaviour directly as 'the consequences of a commerce with Europeans and what is still more to our Shame civilized Christians . . . we interduce among them wants and perhaps diseases which they never before knew'.[12] George Forster's account of the voyage, which drew extensively on his father's journals, departed from Cook's version of events in asserting that the men offered their reluctant daughters and sisters, but not their wives. He observed that 'Whether the members of a civilized society, who could act such a brutal part, or the barbarians who could force their own women to submit to such indignity, deserve the greatest abhorrence, is a question not easily to be decided.' Like Cook, he concluded that the islanders had become 'debased' because 'we created new wants by shewing them iron-tools; for the possession of which they do not hesitate to commit an action that, in our eyes, deprives them of the very shadow of sensibility'.[13]

Johann Forster's journal is more particular, adding the significant detail that this behaviour was not general but limited to the male relations of two women, but he also represents the 'indelicacy hardly credible' of these island men as motivated by their desire for iron tools. He points out that the people of Dusky Bay, in the South Island of New Zealand 'had nobler Sentiments' than those of Queen Charlotte Sound, which were shown in the willingness with which they 'made us presents of their own accord', and in the behaviour of the girl they encountered there, who 'had likewise principles of honour & virtue; she never suffered any indecency or familiarity'. At Queen Charlotte Sound, in contrast, the islanders 'were very impudent in asking & severally stole some trifles as hankerchiefs, lamps, fourhourglasses, knives etc.'. He observed that the women would exchange sexual favours for 'a Shirt, a bottle, a handkerchief or some other such trifle' once their fathers or husbands had been placated with the offering of an iron nail.[14]

Forster reflected more generally on the effects of European commerce with the islanders when it was discovered that Maori women at Queen Charlotte Sound were infected with venereal disease. He wrote that 'They have acquired nothing or next to nothing, by the Commerce & intercourse of our Ships crews, even the prizes of this libidinous intercourse with our young Sailors is so trifling *viz.* a Nail or a Shirt, that nothing is capable to compensate in the slightest manner the great injury done to their Society.' Forster represents the 'poor Natives of New Zeeland' as the victims of a rapacious sexual passion implicitly linked to commercial avarice. He suggests that the 'brutal passion' of sexual desire, which 'breaks through all social ties, extinguishes all principles of true honour, virtue & humanity', is incidental to or symptomatic of the 'principles of lust, avarice & ambition', which he implies animate commercial and imperial expansion. Reflecting on the potential scourge that intercourse with Europeans has introduced, he argues:

Had the Man, who first infected the Female on this Isle, immediately after fulfilling his brutal lust, stabbed the object of his temporary passion, he would certainly deserve to be detested & abhorred as a most consummate villain: but if we consider the fatal consequences, which must now attend his connexion with that woman, & the general devastation his communicated evil must cause, I cannot help thinking, that howsoever detestable the murder of such a poor wretch must be, it would be a real benefit to the whole community & preserve a harmless brave & numerous Nation from all the horrors of being poisoned from their very infancy, of fetching infection in the embraces of love, & of instilling the same venom in the tender embryo that is to be the result of love & the object of paternal piety & tenderness.[15]

The disease that is for Forster the sign of the evils of European exploitation here becomes the prime source of the horrors that threaten this 'harmless brave & numerous Nation'. All the evils he anticipates from commercial intercourse with Europeans become embodied in the figure of the first infected woman. Her sacrificial murder, he implies, might even have redeemed relations within the New Zealand family, which he more usually represents as characterised by a lamentable and barbarous lack of feeling, especially marked in the treatment of women.

III

In Forster's journals, the women of Tahiti and New Zealand were represented as bound up in the processes of commercial exchange. They provided a fig-ure for the corruptions and vices that the Forsters believed intercourse with Europeans had introduced to the societies of the Pacific. I have suggested that it may have been the intimate but difficult relation between commer-cial and sexual exchange that prompted the odd movement in the journals between veneration for some women, and antipathy for others. In the *Obser-vations*, however, Forster was more concerned to emphasise the positive role of island women. In his accounts of the people of what Cook called the Friendly Islands and the Society Islands, and in particular of Tahiti, Forster stressed the active contribution of women to the relatively advanced state of civilization that he identified. He gave an unusually positive inflection to a commonplace of the period in his assertion that 'the rank assigned to WOMEN in domestic society, among the various nations, has so great an influence upon their civilization and morality' (258). In his argument the condition of women was not merely the *index* to the degree of civilisation achieved in any society, as it was for most social and political theorists. The rank of women exerted influence on the degree of civilisation that nations achieved.

Forster's assessment of the role of women at Tahiti was based in enlight-enment theories about women, but he was clearly also concerned to develop these theories and adapt them to his novel experiences. He explained that 'the Society, the Friendly Isles, and the Marquesas' had to be recognised to have progressed 'one remove above barbarians' because the island women exerted a civilising influence and had gained 'a greater equality': their condition indi-cated but also somehow produced the characteristics of civilisation. Forster commented on their rank that 'if, from no other reason, from this alone' the progressive state of these societies could be recognised. He observed that 'the more the women are esteemed in a nation, and enjoy an equality of rights with the men, the more it appears that the original harshness of manners is softened, the more the people are capable of tender feelings, mutual attachment, and social virtues, which naturally lead them towards the blessings of civilization' (260). He asserted that 'the female sex has . . . softened the manners of their countrymen' (261), emphasising the activity of women as the agents of social change. It is in the context of this emphasis on women's agency that his insistence on the notion of 'equality of rights' is best understood. The language of rights implied a political dimension to the process of social change that women effected. That implication was also apparent in Forster's observation that the charms of the island women had secured them 'a just and moderate influence in domestic and even public affairs' (260).

Forster's argument here alluded to the thesis John Millar had advanced in the detailed discussion of the condition of women in his *The Origin of the Distinction of Ranks* (1771). Like most theorists of the period, Millar represented the progress of commercial civilisation in Europe as double-edged– the signs of improvement were for him inevitably also the symptoms of incipient corruption and decline – and this uneasy conjunction of improvement and decline was clearly apparent in the implications of that progress for women. In advanced and affluent civilisations, women had a greater, more visible importance in polite society. But these 'improvements, in the state and accomplishments of the women' ultimately endangered women's importance, because they removed those restraints and obstacles that Millar saw as necessary to the cultivation of romantic passion, and made women exclusively or only 'subservient to the purposes of animal enjoyment'. The social prominence of women in opulent civilisations, Millar concluded, was incompatible both with their own interests and 'with the general interest of society'. Millar's argument represented the condition of women – and indeed of civilisation – as more unambiguously admirable and desirable in the stage of progress that immediately preceded the achievement of opulence. In that stage, the interests of women were largely confined to 'the members of their own family', and they were instructed principally in what was 'thought conducive to the ornament of private life' or the 'practice of all the domestic virtues'.[16]

In *The Origin of the Distinction of Ranks*, the condition of women acted as an index or figure for the condition of civilisation. Wherever commercial prosperity was perceived to be overstepping the thin line that divided it from 'luxury and refinement', women came to embody and excite the vices of unbridled desire – passions that resembled Forster's 'principles of lust, avarice & ambition'.[17] The degenerate condition of women indicated the perversion of those passions that, in their moralised and contained form, had been the motors of commercial progress. This use of women as figures for the uneasy moral implications of commercial success was comparable with the function ascribed to them in Forster's journals. In the *Observations*, however, where the rank of women was explicitly linked with the achievement of civilisation, the public role of women worked physically and morally to lead or seduce men into desiring 'the blessings of civilization' (260).

In part the importance that Forster attached to the position of women in Tahitian society had to do with their domestic and familial roles, and with what he perceived as the practice of virtuous monogamy. He argued that monogamy was prevalent on Tahiti because marital partners could be changed at will, and he claimed that 'the beginning of their civil society is founded on paternal authority, and is of the patriarchal kind. The husband and wife of his bosom, whom love unites by the silken ties of matrimony, form the first society' (223).[18] In that 'first society,' women disciplined their children. They exercised a maternal authority perceived to be denied them in, for example, New Zealand, where Europeans thought women were treated with barbarous tyranny because male children were taught 'to hold their mothers in contempt, contrary to all our principles of morality'.[19] The bonds of feeling within the Tahitian family, in contrast, manifested that civilising softness that Forster believed women promoted. The hearts of the Society Islanders, Forster wrote, 'are capable . . . of the most tender connexions, of which, in our mixed and degenerating societies, we have very few instances; perhaps none at all, where such a disinterested, generous love, or such an enthusiasm of passion forms the basis of the tender connexion' (222).

Forster's argument did not suggest, however, that the domestic family unit was the only or the most important arena for the exercise of feminine influence. In accounting for the tendency of peoples to degenerate from their civilised origins as a result of migration, he suggested that the family unit could be antagonistic to the development of society. Groups of migrants 'are deprived of the charms and choice of society, which is confined to the few individuals of a family' (197). Confined to their families, they became 'strangers to social feelings, and still more so to social virtues' (198), and were incapable either of preserving and transmitting the knowledge they had once had, or of inventing improvements. In North America, for example, Forster argued that the predominance of the family over potentially more extensive social groupings was the 'true cause of the debasement and degeneracy' (207) that was perceived to characterise the savage stage of civil development. The fact that he saw the Tahitian family as the 'first society' rather than as a 'few individuals' was evidence of the softening powers of women, but the strength of bonds of feeling within the family did not necessarily lead to improvement or manifest the civilising powers of women. Improvement was rather the effect of the softer attachments and social feelings women have produced *between* families. For the authority women exercise within the Tahitian family was not limited to that arena. Despite his perception of Tahitian society as a sort of mixture of the feudal and patriarchal models, he attributed considerable authority to women in both the public and private life of the Society Islands: 'The married women have . . . a great respect shewn to them, and their influence is great in all public and private affairs; and as soon as the heir of a family is born, the father in a certain manner loses his importance' (254). The influence of women within the family was represented as continuous with a much more extensive and public authority, and it was perhaps as a result of that continuity that the family was seen as the first society.

The civilising influence of women in the Society Islands, as well as their role in public affairs, were connected more directly in Forster's argument with the qualities he believed women acquired as a result of their oppression in nations that have not yet become civilised – qualities that 'may perhaps prepare' barbarous men 'for the first dawnings of civilization' (259). Forster, like most theorists of the period, asserted that among peoples categorised as savage and barbarous, women were treated as drudges and beasts of burden, and regarded as the property of their husbands. But Forster departed from the familiar theoretical model in his argument that

this very oppression, and the more delicate frame of [the women's] bodies, together with the finer and more irritable texture of their nerves, have contributed more towards the improvement and perfection of their intellectual faculties, than of those of the males. The various objects surrounding them make quicker and more vivid impressions on the sense of the females, because their nerves are finer and more irritable; this makes them more inclined to imitation, and more quick in observing the properties and relations of things; their memory is more faithful in retaining them; and their faculties thereby become more capable of comparing them, and of abstracting general ideas from their perceptions. (259)

As a result of these qualities, he suggested, women were capable of producing 'new improvements' and of controlling their passions into 'cooler reflexion' (259). The absence of the first of these capacities was one of the principal characteristics of savagery, and the lack of the second was critical in distinguishing barbarism from civilisation. Women here were not only the indices of the degree of civilisation achieved by their nations, but the forerunners of that progress, apparently acting in advance of and out of step with the men. The women achieved this position, in Forster's argument, because their oppression had cultivated in them cognitive abilities similar to those that British theorists understood as the product of liberal education. These women were able to compare their perceptions and abstract general ideas from them. Forster's account of the qualities the oppression of women had produced suggested that if the women of Tahiti did 'enjoy an equality of rights with the men' (260) it may have been because they were perceived to possess similar intellectual abilities.

The positive representation of the condition of women in the Society Islands in Forster's *Observations* is not by any means consistently maintained, but it is an important strand of his argument, and it does throw into relief the extent to which he perceived in the society of the islanders a kind of inverted image of European civilisations – an ideal projection marked by the absence of commercial prosperity with its attendant corruptions. In his introductory remarks on Tahiti, he wrote that there 'the inhabitants are hitherto fortunate enough to have none of the artificial wants, which luxury, avarice, and ambition have introduced among Europeans' (146). He argued that marriage and reproduction were unproblematic, and a matter of 'pleasing expectation' to Tahitians, and contrasted their happiness with 'the many wants of our civilized state, the labours we must undergo in supplying these wants . . . and the many difficulties preceding and attendant on our marriages' (146–7).

The connection between the 'many wants' promoted in a commercial culture and sexual desire was most fully theorised in the 1770s by John Millar and by Henry Home, Lord Kames, in his *Sketches of the History of Man* (1774). But those theorists argued that sexual desire only became more than a transient brute appetite because of the leisure that civilised prosperity afforded, and that its refinement into romantic passion and companionate affection depended upon the 'many difficulties' produced by inequalities of wealth, divergent occupational interests, and competition in commercial society. Mary Wollstonecraft, for example, alluded to this theory in her comment that

Nothing can be more absurd than the ridicule of the critic, that the heroine of his mock-tragedy was in love with the very man whom she ought least to have loved; he could not have given a better reason. How can passion gain strength any other way? In Otaheite, love cannot be known, where the obstacles to irritate an indiscriminate appetite, and sublimate the simple sensations of desire till they mount to passion, are never known. There a man or woman cannot love the very person they ought not to have loved – nor does jealousy ever fan the flame.[20]

Wollstonecraft had read Forster's *Observations*, and cited his discussion of polygamy in her *Vindication of the Rights of Woman* (1792).[21] But here she endorsed, perhaps mockingly, the argument that romantic love is fostered by the enforced deferral of its gratification.

Forster's argument resembled those of Millar and Kames in the close connection it assumed between the wants promoted by commercial culture and the 'difficulties of marriage' that created.[22] But though Forster represented the virtues of Tahitian society as those of an early or pre-commercial state, he also maintained that it was possible for most of the Tahitians to enjoy the pleasures of love in the absence of the difficulties created by the complex organisation of the advanced societies of Europe. He praised, as I have mentioned, the 'disinterested, generous love' and 'enthusiasm of passion' that characterised the domestic manners of the Tahitians, and he did not suggest that their pleasures were diminished because 'love, and all its concomitant, and most mysterious endearments, enjoyments, and consequences' had never 'been stamped in these happy isles with a notion of turpitude' (244). Despite the absence of shame, Forster claimed that the women of the Society Islands exhibited natural modesty.[23] They inhabited an ideal pre-commercial state while apparently enjoying what theorists represented as the sentimental and emotional maturity characterising commercial civilisations.

IV

The bathing women of Hodges's landscape of Vaitepiha had probably first appeared in what seems to be an earlier as well as smaller oil sketch of a waterfall, probably in the Tuauru valley of Tahiti (plate 2.3).[24] Here the body of the woman in the water is yet more vaguely defined than in the first landscape of Vaitepiha, merely a disturbance of the light on the water; and her seated and comparatively fleshly companion has no tattoos on her buttocks. The women are sheltered within a deep valley, whose walls, topped with shrubbery and palms, enclose the image, leaving space for only a small patch of sky. George Forster, who recommended the valley to Hodges as a subject, observed that the 'fine cascade . . . made the scene more lively, which in itself was dark, wild, and romantic'. In comparison with the more open and extensive views of Vaitepiha, this is a deeply secluded, inward-looking space, its 'dark, wild, and romantic' privacy secure from any casual intrusion. George Forster noted that the Tuauru valley became 'more and more confined by mountains, so that we found it difficult to proceed, having been obliged to cross the river near fifty times. At last we came to the same place where Mr. Banks was obliged to stop in his excursion. We found it equally impossible to proceed.'[25] The valley or gorge Hodges painted is almost as far into the hidden interior as was accessible to the voyagers. This is an image of the island at its most private and inaccessible, and perhaps the inviting strangeness of the scene makes the representation of buttock tattoos, as synecdochic signs of the exotic and erotic appeal of the island, superfluous.

The remote seclusion of the scene also makes it even more strongly reminiscent than were the two views of Vaitepiha of the Titianesque subgenre of scenes of bathing women caught unawares, to which many British artists of the period, including Gainsborough, Turner, and Wheatley, contributed, and which Michael Rosenthal discussed as peculiarly modern in his essay of 1992.[26] This juxtaposes or even overlays the romantic wildness of the scene with a known and familiar topos, and situates what might be perceived as their anachronistic or ahistorical exoticism in relation to European modernity. It approximates the nudity of Tahitian women who were imagined to know no shame to that of European women, whose bodies are imagined to be visible only as a result of subterfuge or accident. As a result the image is characterised by a curious tension between the familiar and the exotically romantic, the intimate and the withheld.

The seated bathing woman appeared again in two strange capriccios Hodges produced in later years. The first shows the woman at the centre of a group clustered beneath a banana tree and at the feet of a shrouded and mysterious monk-like figure (plate 2.4). The landscape is recognisably similar to that which Hodges probably sketched in the Tuauru valley, though some of the sense of occlusion which characterised the earlier paintings of the landscape, perhaps executed in 1775 (plate 2.5),[27] has been lightened by the widening of the river valley into an expanse more reminiscent of the paintings of Vaitepiha and *Tahiti Revisited*. The second, tentatively identified as the painting Hodges exhibited at the Royal Academy in 1790 with the title *Landscape, Ruins, and Figures*, shows a similar but reorganised group of figures clustered around a herm (plate 2.6).[28] The composition of this landscape is similar to that of the two views of women bathing in the Tuauru valley in reverse, the ruins in the centre echoing those familiar from the work of Richard Wilson and Piranesi and also mimicking the outline of the rocks and trees at the centre of the *Waterfall in Tuauru*, but here there are no feathery shapes of palm trees, no bananas trees, no unmistakable allusions to Tahitian culture. The landscape here is classical European, and many Academy visitors in 1790 would I imagine not have recollected that the figure of the seated woman had first appeared in Hodges's work displaying elaborate and markedly exotic tattoos.

Both the *Landscape, Ruins, and Figures* and the *Waterfall in Tuauru* are painted on expensive large single boards, and both reveal *pentimenti*, which may suggest that Hodges worked on them extensively and over time. It would probably be a mistake to attempt to create a chronological narrative linking the two images, but the *Waterfall at Tuauru* seems within itself almost overburdened with narrative or allegorical potential. The women in the foreground on the left are adorned with unambiguous Tahitian signs of exotic specificity, in the tattooed buttocks of the two brown-skinned women, and in the idiosyncratic eyeshade of the third woman, whose pose is reminiscent of that of the similarly pale-skinned woman in the foreground of Hodges's painting of the *Resolution* and *Adventure* in Matavai Bay (plate 2.1), and alludes if anything more directly to that of Titian's *Venus*. The long leaves at the forefront of the image on the left, the spectacular cascade behind, and the palm trees high above are all clear indications of place. The women on the right could belong to a completely different landscape – as their transposition to the classical landscape of 1790 might be taken to confirm. Only the banana tree clearly marks an exotic, non-European location. The robed woman gesturing towards the water – whose feet, incidentally, position her beside the seated woman who would tower above her if she were to stand – has something of the biblical air apparent in the figures in the foreground of Hodges's Academy painting of *The War Boats of the Island of Otaheite* (plate 0.4). But the collective effect of the way each woman in the group seems posed in an effort to shield her modesty suggests a self-consciousness not usually evident in Hodges's representations of island women. It is again reminiscent of European and classical or biblical scenes of voyeuristic encounters, or bathing women surprised – Diana and Actaeon, Bathsheba or Susannah, Musidora from Thomson's *Seasons*. The bank against which the group is positioned recalls that of the valley of Tuauru, but it is also reminiscent of the sandbank in the British landscape of Hodges's painting for the Boydell Shakespeare Gallery of *Jaques and the Wounded Stag in the Forest of Arden* (1789; fig. 2.1) – a possibility that may also be marked in the oak-like configuration of the leaves of the tree above.

The women on the left seem untroubled by the presence of the monk, looming like an apparition above the right–hand group whom he seems to admonish and perhaps to shame. Possibly the contrast between the two groups suggests the distance separating the self-conscious virtue of European women from the unashamed innocence some accounts saw in the behaviour of the island women. Perhaps the arrangement of the women across the bottom of the picture space suggests the continuity linking tattooed island women to their European counterparts. Or possibly the contrast is not as great as it may initially appear. The woman with the eyeshade on the far left holds cloth across her midriff, perhaps in a gesture of modesty linking her with the women on the right, all of whom clutch some sort of material,

Figure 2.1 William Hodges, George Romney, and Sawrey Gilpin, *Jaques and the Wounded Stag in the Forest of Arden*, 1789, oil on canvas, 92.1 × 1,232 mm

while the vaguely defined form of the woman in the water might belong to either group. The seated woman central to the group on the right might have been recognisable to at least some viewers as the bather of Vaitepiha, made less exotic and perhaps more European by the absence of buttock tattoos. In keeping with this reading, the monk on the right might be seen as a sort of *momento mori*, a *vanitas* motif indicating the futility of worldly distinctions of culture and race.

In Hodges's work, of course, the monk most immediately echoes the robed figure in Richard Wilson's *The White Monk* (painted in the early 1760s), or the hermit of Wilson's *Solitude* (1762; fig. 2.2). As David Solkin pointed out, the robed figures in Wilson's emblematic landscapes of the early 1760s are opposed to contrasting images – of lovers, in the *White Monk*, and of the warlike lion in *Solitude* – and Hodges's landscape alludes to that structure in the contrast between the heavily shrouded figure of the monk and the naked-ness of the women.[29] But in Hodges's painting the contrast is addressed

Figure 2.2 Richard Wilson, *Solitude*, 1762, oil on canvas, 1,003 × 1,251 mm

not so much to the issues of domestic politics that concerned Wilson as to debates over the purposes and morality of imperial expansion – issues given a renewed urgency by the American war. Hodges's *Waterfall in Tuauru* suggests the complexity of the responses of the European spectator and arm-chair traveller as they admire and perhaps desire the apparent freedom and unselfconscious simplicity of the island women. For the image raises the question of the relation between what might be seen as the natural modesty of the women on the left, and the minatory figure of the monk on the right, apparently instilling notions of shame and turpitude into the women before him. Possibly the relation between the two groups reads from left to right in a trajectory of progressive civilisation, but the Gothic monk is hardly a figure of enlightened modernity. Perhaps the chastened and unmarked, tattoo-less women on the right suggest the increasing difficulties and loss of natural modesty that progress in civilisation and commerce involves.

Forster's reflections on island women are, I suggest, illuminated by the context Hodges's images provide, for the discrepancies between and within Forster's journals and his published *Observations* could be seen to play out aspects of the tensions in Hodges's work. The inconsistencies in Forster's writing which I have discussed in this chapter are at least in part a matter of genre. The journals detail Forster's personal experiences, and frequently emphasise the physical discomforts and inconveniences he endured, or the ailments he suffered. Passages are reflective, or evidently notes intended for revision and publication, but overall the journals are made up of private, provisional, tentative remarks, and shot through with Forster's personal grievances and hostilities. But the differences in the representation of women on which this chapter has focused also point up the way the journals, far more frequently and insistently than the *Observations*, are marked by Forster's uneasiness about the interactions of Europeans and islanders.

Forster did consider the potential influence of European manners on the islanders in his *Observations*. He noted for example that

the facility of procuring the necessaries of life, and even those articles which are here reckoned to be luxuries; together with the humane and benevolent temper of these nations have hitherto happily prevented the oppression of the Toutous; and if the morals of these people are not influenced and corrupted by the commerce and intercourse with European profligates, and by the introduction of new luxuries, which can be procured only by hard labour and drudgery, the happiness of the lowest class of people, will, probably be of long continuance.

But what he deplores here is the possible intervention in the future of 'wicked' men who might 'form a wish or plan to entail misery and wretchedness' – a contingency which he believes the vigilance of 'humanity and benevolence' can prevent (230). He represents the Tahitian way of life in sharp contrast to modern European culture because it is protected by the 'great fertility and mildness of the climate' which 'reduce the number of their wants'. He explains that the

pampered epicure in Europe hardly knows the multifarious ingredients of his disguised ragouts, and his palled appetite remains indifferent to the almost infinite variety carried to his table from every quarter of the globe; nor has he the satisfaction to know how or where these things are produced, or manufactured, while the more happy inhabitant of Taheitee plants his own breadfruit tree, and plucks the fruit for his own use; . . . there is not a single article of his food, which owes not its existence to his or his fathers industry or care. (345)[30]

In his *Observations* he imagines Tahitian society as content in the absence of the insatiable appetites of 'lust, avarice & ambition' that characterise modern commercial culture, and secure in its integrity from the complexities of a ramified social organisation and division of labour, whereas the journals detail the conflicting ambitions and desires played out in encounters between islanders and Europeans. In the *Observations* Forster's uneasiness about the nature of European civilisation, and the benefits it might extend to the South Pacific, is largely implicit, but in his journals the ambivalence of his sense of the advantages conferred by civilisation and its attendant curiosity is clear.

I mentioned in Chapter 1 that Johann Forster sometimes felt an almost 'paternal affection' for Tahitian people, with whom he believed he shared a valuable domestic intimacy. At these moments, he believed, 'All those distinctions which ambition, wealth, and luxury, have introduced, are levelled, and the inhabitant of the polar region, finds a warm and generous friend in the torrid zone or in the opposite hemisphere.' But it was these moments which also reminded him that

> our own civilized countries, notwithstanding the numberless improvements they have received from the establishment of excellent laws, and the cultivation of arts and sciences; notwithstanding the frequent occasions of still greater improvement, and the glorious encouragement to virtue and morality, were far outdone in real goodness and benevolence by a set of innocent people, so much our inferiors in many other respects.[31]

The movement here between a sense of intimacy with Tahitian culture, a belief in universal benevolence, and a sense that this very benevolence underscores the distance between Tahiti and Europe, between the innocent people of the islands and the corruptions of advanced civilisation, is, I suggest, characteristic of Forster's reflections.

The comparison between island women and 'Britannia's fair Daughters' in Forster's journals, which I discussed earlier in this chapter, is characterised by a similar movement. Forster registers the comparability of the two groups and then hastily retreats, insisting that the idea of island women must be 'effaced' as British women 'force . . . due hommage'.[32] Hodges's images of Tahitian women bathing, however, sustain the complexity of the moment in which, for the European spectator, the islanders are both similar and different. They represent them as the objects of a curiosity that desires and appropriates even as it exoticises, as people whose freedom from the desires and divisions of modern commercial societies in Europe is at once contemptible and enviable or even admirable.

3 | Curiously marked

On 14 July, 1774, Mai (or Omai) arrived in London, having travelled from Raiatea to England on board the *Adventure*. He stayed in England for two years, returning to the South Pacific with Cook on his third voyage. His story is extensively documented in E. H. McCormick's invaluable study, *Omai: Pacific Envoy* (1977). During his stay in London, he sat for Sir Joshua Reynolds, who exhibited his full-length portrait of *Mai* at the Royal Academy in 1776 (plate 3.1). Reynolds kept the portrait in his own gallery and it was sold only after his death. The portrait probably piqued the interest of Reynolds's visitors, in the wake of the 'great curiosity' that had been aroused by accounts of the Pacific islanders following Cook's first voyage to the southern hemisphere.[1]

More recently, the campaign to keep the portrait in Britain prompted debate about its importance to British history and national life – to national identity, because it was on the claim to this that the temporary bar imposed on its export depended. There was some discussion in the press of the validity of any unified notion of national identity, but, with the exception of a provocative article in the *Telegraph* which asserted that the image was 'deeply and centrally internationalist' and could therefore be appropriately housed in any country, commentators broadly agreed with Sir David Attenborough's claim that the painting is important to the nation because it 'is a vivid reminder of the way in which art can bridge cultural divides'.[2] There was, however, surprisingly little discussion of what the painting might indicate about English or British national identity in the 1770s, beyond the suggestion that this was a sympathetic portrayal of a man welcomed by courtly society in a rare moment of cultural rapprochement.

This chapter focuses on the representation of tattoos in Reynolds's portrait and in other images of Pacific islanders from the Cook voyages in order to consider the some of the ways in which aspects of national identity, or more specifically British or English masculine identity, were subject to redefinition during the 1770s. I explore the implications of the representation of Mai's tattoos in Reynolds's portrait, and their absence from William Parry's conversation piece, *Omai, Joseph Banks and Dr. Solander* (1775–6), in juxtaposition with images of tattoos from the voyages, and in the context established by my discussion of the tattoos of Tahitian women in Chapters 1 and 2. The paintings themselves may be marked by Mai's views. If he was allowed any say in how he was represented, it is possible he chose to be depicted swathed in lengths of white cloth, which was an indication of status in Tahiti and Raiatea. But unfortunately we do not know that Mai did have any choice in this matter, and there is no record of what he thought of the paintings, though many writers commented on his stay in London, and I discuss some of their assessments in Chapter 6.[3] Here I read Reynolds's and Parry's images against Reynolds's theories on costume and ornament in an attempt to imagine what their European audience in London in the 1770s might have made of them, or how they might have projected that audience. I move on to discuss representations of tattoos from the voyages in order to explore the significances Europeans attributed to their own and the islanders' tattoos. These, I suggest, indicate the instability of the voyagers' sense of their own difference from the islanders they encountered, and the fragility of European claims to a more civilised and enlightened form of masculine identity.

I

It is difficult to compare Reynolds's *Omai* to contemporary portraits of European subjects because Mai's exoticism inflects the otherwise familiar terms of his representation. This is not a private or intimately sociable image, comparable to some of Reynolds's portraits of fashionable women, or men in repose. But nor is it a portrait which indicates social or public command in its subject. Though, as Bernard Smith has pointed out, the islander assumes the pose of the 'self-confident patrician',[4] that pose here indicates the incongruity between domestic conventions of representation and exotic subjects, for Mai demonstrates patrician authority only in his ambiguous command of the spectator's gaze. His gesture does not seem to invoke the respectful attention of the spectator, but rather to spread out for display some of the tattoos on which so much European curiosity focused. The dignity of the figure is that of an orientalised 'noble savage', cleansed of characteristics that might mark his origin or history, and effaced by being endowed with what a recent biographer considers to be the 'somewhat negroid features' of 'an African princeling'.[5] The generalisation of the image makes of Mai a blank figure, available to that diversity of inscription that George Forster commented on in European assessments of his character. He wrote that: 'O-Mai has been considered either as remarkably stupid, or very intelligent, according to the different allowances which were made by those who judged of his abilities.'[6]

The blankness which made it so difficult to assess or judge Mai may however be exceeded or punctured in Reynolds's portrait by the implications of those tattoos. They mark his figure with the signs of an imperialist curiosity that perceives in the islander a specificity that resists generalisation, and that exoticises his image. Exoticism, I suggest, inscribes its object with an acultural illegibility, isolated from any coherence of origin. Exoticised subjects are characterised as sports, marked as singular tokens lacking any significance beyond that of a fragmentary and unrepresentative (perhaps unrepresentable) insularity. If Reynolds's portrait effaces those features of Mai that might distinguish him as an individual, or as a representative of his people, replacing them with the more generalised image of 'a youthful Oriental sage', then the tattoos act as a counterpoint to that generalisation, and mark his specificity removed from any context that might make it intelligible.[7] They signal an exoticism that may help to unpack the peculiar mixture of fascination and indifference that characterises British representations of the people of the South Pacific in this period.

Joseph Banks had wished to bring an islander – he had in mind Tupaia – back with him as a souvenir of his trip to the South Pacific on Cook's first voyage. He noted in his journal that government could not be expected to take an interest in this project, but, he added; 'Thank heaven I have a sufficiency and I do not know why I may not keep him as a curiosity, as well as some of my neighbours do lions and tygers at a larger expense than he will probably ever put me to.' His notorious remarks on 'the amusement I shall have'[8] from this scheme indicate the private status of ethnological curiosity, and, in the allusion to private zoos, emphasise that curiosity thrives on the isolation of its exotic object, on the colonialising displacement or dislocation of its object from any signs of the personal estate or cultural context that might produce legible or potent significance. Banks's curiosity demands the unmediated access that John Rickman alluded to in his account of Cook's last voyage, where he lamented the inadequacy of 'the feeble pencil of a fribbling artist' to represent the islanders. A more gratifying object of study might have been provided, he suggested, by 'the importation of a native from every climate', to stock an academy with 'living pictures'.[9] The generalisation of landscape, clothing, and physiognomy that makes an orientalised figure of Mai in Reynolds's portrait is given specificity by the colonialist curiosity animating Pacific expansion, which demands that its objects be presented stripped of context, and feeds on the wondrous exoticism which that nakedness enforces.[10]

The project of Pacific exploration was exceptional, and perhaps unrepresentative in the history of European expansion, because it was perceived to depend on curiosity. A voyager commented, in an account of the South Pacific published in 1793, that the islanders' 'remote situation from European powers has deprived them of the culture of civilized life, as they neither serve to swell the ambitious views of conquest, nor the avarice of commerce. Here the sacred finger of Omnipotence has interposed, and rendered our vices the instruments of virtue.'[11] The writer alludes to what he sees as the criminal vices of Fletcher Christian and the *Bounty* mutineers, which he argues might inadvertently work to civilise or enlighten the islanders. He imagines that the mutineers, isolated as a result of their rebellion, might establish proto European communities in the Pacific. He suggests that European powers more usually fulfil what is understood as their imperial destiny as a result of avarice or ambition, which find their moralised expression through the incidental imposition of the 'culture of civilized life'. In the South Pacific, where the desires that animate conquest or commerce find inadequate gratification, the hand of Providence has to resort to more explicitly immoral means. But what is I think significant, in this reflection on late eighteenth-century European expansion, is the suggestion that the underdetermined nature of European interest in the South Pacific makes the moral conflicts and inversions involved in spreading the 'culture of civilized life' much more apparent, much more explicit. The British repeatedly claimed, as we have seen, that their interest in the South Pacific was motivated by the underdetermined and ambiguously transactive notion of curiosity – what Boswell identified as 'the enthusiasm of curiosity and adventure', experienced when 'one is carried away with the general grand and indistinct notion of A VOYAGE ROUND THE WORLD'.[12] The sense that this project is somehow set apart from the ambitious views of conquest, trade, and settlement by the whimsicality, licentiousness, or enlightened and scientific purity of curiosity points to an internal and domestic ambivalence about the demarcation of vice from virtue, and perhaps even of domestic from exotic, and provides an important context for Reynolds's portrait of Mai.

Mai was perceived by Cook to be 'dark, ugly', and therefore 'not a proper sample of the inhabitants of these happy isles, not having any advantage of birth, or acquired rank; nor being eminent in shape, figure, or complexion'.[13] Mai was not a proper sample or specimen because he was physically 'ugly', dark and obscure rather than patrician. He was the appropriate object of a feminised 'curiosity, levity and lewdness' – from aristocratic women, according to Johann Forster[14] – rather than of public or political recognition. That exclusion from representative status may be figured in Reynolds's image in

[margin note: Curiosity & expansion]

the prominent marking of his tattoos. The tattoos inscribe the generalised figure that Reynolds portrays with an apparently incongruous ethnographic specificity, an authenticating 'air of truth',[15] inviting to the curious investigations of the natural philosopher, or collector of exotica. The dignity or 'benign authority' which recent critics have attributed to the figure's stance is marked by those tattoos as the gesture of self-display appropriate to the private zoo or fairground exhibit, the exotic spectacle, rather than to the public position of the patrician. The reinscribed tattoos mark the notion of Mai as 'a simple barbarian' whose transportation to 'a christian and civilized country' would 'debase him into a spectacle and a maccaroni, and . . . invigorate the seeds of corrupted nature by a course of improved debauchery'.[16] They stigmatise Mai as the authentic object of a curiosity that finds its gratification in the singularities of nature and culture. They indicate that the islander's gesture is appropriate to his exotic and unrepresentative status, for his tattoos are incompatible with any patrician authority his posture might seem to imply. It is as though they indelibly blacken and stain the transparent legibility of that classical stance.

In writing on the South Pacific in the early nineteenth century, and in the late 1790s, tattoos were frequently represented as analogous to clothing, as a sort of textured surface that is integral to the body, but that also veils and conceals it, and lends it, perhaps, a kind of parodic social propriety. In the earlier accounts from the 1770s and 1780s which I will be considering here tattoos are perceived to have an ambiguously physical texture. One of the most frequently cited accounts of Mai's buttock tattoos, for example, compared them to veneer inlaid in mahogany, as though they were a part of the body's surface, but confirmed its exotic difference.[17] Tattoos in these earlier accounts, I suggest, mark the intersections of discourses of the exotic and domestic, and of gender difference – of discourses which also move ambiguously between physical differences, and differences of culture or of manners. In order to explore these implications of tattooing, I will look briefly at Joshua Reynolds's mention of the subject in one of his influential Discourses on the theory of art.

II

In the Discourse which Joshua Reynolds delivered to the Royal Academy in December 1776 he discusses all those contingent or 'ornamental' aspects of painting that do not contribute directly to the high moral purposes of art. He begins by dismissing 'ornament' as transitory, superficial, and accidental – as a debased and sensual pleasure. He writes, for example, that colouring in painting 'can never be considered as of equal importance with the art of unfolding truths that are useful to mankind, and which make us better or wiser'. He implies that colouring is important only to 'those works which remind us of the poverty and meanness of our nature', rather than to work which 'excites ideas of grandeur, or raises and dignifies humanity'. It diminishes the spectator because, Reynolds explained, 'the help of meretricious ornaments, however elegant and graceful, captivates the sensuality . . . of our taste'. Attention to the changing nature of fashionable dress is also, he claims, a reminder of meanness. He suggests that fashionable dress points up how far the individual falls short of the unchanging and universal ideal form. Reynolds's characterisation of ornament here is reminiscent of his Discourse of 1771, where he argued that the 'seducing qualities' of the ornamental style worked to 'debauch the young and inexperienced'.[18]

Later in his seventh Discourse, however, Reynolds argued that ornament could justifiably be represented in high art because its local interest and appeal 'procures lovers and admirers to the more valuable excellencies of the art'. He claimed that

Though we by no means ought to rank these [ornaments] with positive and substantial beauties, yet it must be allowed that a knowledge of both is essentially requisite towards forming a complete, whole, and perfect taste . . . in them we find the characteristical mark of a national taste; as by throwing up a feather in the air, we know which way the wind blows, better than by a more heavy matter.

Ornament in painting becomes acceptable here because it is a sign of 'national taste' developed through custom. Reynolds begins to advocate a sort of cultural relativism, where the judicious spectator knows that ornament or fashion are merely arbitrary or accidental distractions from universal truth with its 'substantial beauties', but he can nevertheless value and appreciate them as expressions of national character. So he argues that in the encounter between a fashionable European and a Cherokee man, 'whoever of these two despises the other for his attention to the fashion of his country, which ever first feels himself provoked to laugh, is the barbarian'. He suggests that each man will show his civility, his civilised urbanity, in the respect he shows for the other's national character.[19]

At this stage of his argument, however, Reynolds introduces some exceptions to this new tolerance for accidental detail. He writes that all 'fashions are very innocent . . . The only circumstances against which indignation may reasonably be moved, is where the operation is painful or destructive of health, such as some of the practices at Otaheite, and the strait lacing of the English ladies.'[20] The Tahitian custom which was repeatedly associated with pain and the risk of infection was, of course, tattooing. This custom, along with the restrictive stays worn by English ladies, licenses the spectator to depart from his civilised respect for ornament or fashion as the sign of national character, and allows him to give vent to the sort of prejudices which, in the encounter between the fashionable man and the Cherokee, had indicated barbarism. These ornamental customs perhaps bite too deeply into the smooth surface of the body to be tolerated as expressions of custom. Instead Reynolds suggests that they reveal an unhealthy physicality which is more properly the subject of the lectures of 'the professor of Anatomy'.[21] Reynolds's seventh Discourse charts a descent from the substantial beauties of universal truth, to the more meretricious charms of local or national custom, which are then contrasted with apparently pathological adornments of tattoos and stays; and that descent also signals changes in the identity of the masculine spectator, who is dignified by the first, seduced by the second, and it would seem physically repulsed and perhaps barbarised by the third.

III

Although portraiture is not the art form that Reynolds has in mind in this seventh Discourse, his argument may illuminate the intriguing omission of Mai's tattoos from the conversation piece that William Parry produced for Joseph Banks (plate 3.2).[22] Here Banks is shown gesturing towards the unmarked – untattooed – hand of Mai, as if to point up that the figure is here identified, not by the ambiguous ornaments of ethnographic particularity or national character, but through his presentation in the isolation appropriate to an exotic spectacle. The black background, which throws the figure of the Tahitian into relief, contrasts with the richly elaborate colours of the right-hand third of the canvas, where Daniel Solander sits. Solander, a Swede who had studied botany with Linnaeus at Uppsala, had travelled with Banks on Cook's first voyage, and it is presumably in his role as a natural philosopher that he is represented here, apparently poised to record and classify the curiosity that his patron Banks discovers to him.

Mai is here posed, again with ambiguously orientalised dignity, or as though he had been caught in transition, the turn of his body suggesting that his attention has been diverted from the other men, and redirected downwards, towards the artist and spectator. His face is open to the spectator's curious gaze, and isolated in contrast to the apparently unselfconscious absorption of Banks and Solander, engaged in the mutually interesting tasks of observation and display. The warmth and detail of what looks like an oriental rug on the table at Solander's elbow, and the depth of the rural scene behind him, emphasise the displacement from the Tahitian, fixed against that flat blackness, of the ornaments that indicate national or ethnic identity. For the physical definition of the draped Tahitian figure is thrown into relief both by the empty space he occupies and by the absence of the detail of his tattoos – a detail that might have interested many of those who viewed the painting at least as much as his carefully depicted features.[23]

The distinctive sense in which Mai is stripped of cultural or ethnographic detail is clearest in the contrast between his prominence and luminosity in the image, and the relatively self-effacing and modest position of Banks. Banks's proprietorial gesture, and the tidiness and restraint of his dark suit, claim for him a masculinity that stands aloof from the colourful display of his protégées, and that distinguishes his patrician authority from their peripheral and dependent positions. Reading the painting in the context of Reynolds's seventh Discourse, it is as though the more luminous and colourful figures of the two protégées cast the sober-suited Banks in the position of the civilised spectator, free from any attachment to personal material ornament, except for those minimal details that indicate his acceptance of the customs of his country. In particular, it is as though Banks's patronage of the Tahitian indicated his capacity for worldly tolerance, for the urbane politeness Reynolds had wanted to see in the encounter between the fashionable European and the Cherokee. Mai is the ornament Banks tolerates, does not ridicule, but in relation to which he establishes his own superior difference. The clarity of the contrast between patron and islander may depend on the erasure of Mai's tattoos, for that blankness brings into focus, into relief, the inscription of the whole figure of the Tahitian as exoticised spectacle. He is the object of a philosophical curiosity that does not need to call attention to the marks of exoticisation because it so clearly isolates him and indicates his deferential dependence on the two Europeans.

Parry's conversation piece and Reynolds's portrait each present Mai as a curious spectacle, but they do so in very different ways. In Reynolds's portrait, the tattoos indicate the curious and exotic status of the islander, and undercut the apparent authority of his solitary pose. In Parry's conversation piece, in contrast, the relations between the three men cast Mai as an exotic spectacle. I have suggested that these images of Mai are illuminated by Reynolds's changing attitudes to ornament and fashion. In particular I think they are marked by the changing nature of civilised masculinity in Reynolds's discussion. For in Reynolds's seventh Discourse the severe ideal of masculinity which had disdained the sensual appeal of ornament is softened, and perhaps feminised, when the seductive charms of ornament become acceptable as signs of national character. Mai in his flowing white robes is presented in these images as an ornamental spectacle, as a figure whose potential masculine authority is compromised and attenuated by display. In this he bears an uneasy resemblance to the masculine spectator, seduced by his respect for national taste and custom into a compromising interest in ornament and fashionable dress. But in Reynolds's image the tattoos which mark Mai's exoticism deny that resemblance, as does the isolation of the islander in Parry's conversation piece. Reynolds's argument suggests that those tattoos indicate an unhealthy or painful physicality which the spectator is able to regard with indignation and distaste, despite his own compromised position. Representations of Joseph Banks in the 1770s provide an interesting indication of the instability of masculine identity in the decade, and I will now look at two examples which, I think, offer a useful comparison with the images of Mai that I have been discussing.

The first of these two paintings is one of a pair of representations of the *Members of the Society of Dilettanti* (fig. 3.1), which Reynolds completed in 1779, and which shows Banks seated on the extreme right; and the second is Benjamin West's portrait of 1771–3 (plate 3.3), painted soon after Banks's return from the South Pacific. In both, Banks is portrayed as a collector and connoisseur of curiosities. In Reynolds's painting the gentlemen are admiring a collection of antique gems while enjoying their claret. They demonstrate both the sensuality and the correctness of their taste here, as they do perhaps yet more obviously in the companion piece, where other members of the society admire antique vases and a lady's garter. But what this painting images most clearly is their conviviality, the bonds of social affection and affiliation evidenced in the co-ordinated gesticulations of their hands, and the common interest in curiosities that they point to. The gentlemen are the knowledgeable and judicious spectators of the tiny ornaments they hold between finger and thumb, and their shared fascination, as well as the complex sociality of their compositional relations one to another, seems to close them in an esoteric grouping that shields them from the intrusions of curiosity. The elaborate network of relations between the men portrayed suggests their sociable masculine equality within the limited social sphere of the club.[24]

West's portrait of Banks the world tourist is more immediately comparable to Reynolds's *Omai*, but here Banks's direct gaze asserts his ownership of

Figure 3.1 Joshua Reynolds, *Members of the Society of Dilettanti*, 1779, oil on canvas, 1,968 × 1,422 mm

the diverse artefacts that surround him, whereas Mai seemed open to the spectator's curiosity because he looks diffidently away. The figure of Banks dominates the litter of curiosities, which indicate the comprehensive scope of his civilised survey, and contrast in their apparent disorder with his central and single illuminated form. But in the absence of those clear markers of common sociality – of fraternity that Reynolds's image of the dilettanti celebrates, there is some peripheral ambiguity in West's image of Banks. In the pantomime, *Omai, Or, A Trip round the World*, which was presented on the London stage in the mid-1780s, the character based on the islander 'most whimsically and pantomimicaly dressed himself in a piece of the habit of each country he had met with', perhaps as Banks does in this image. It is as though Banks at once celebrates and stares down the more frivolous aspects of his dilettantism, and of his reputation as a macaroni, 'a kind of animal, neither male nor female, a thing of the neuter gender', as the *Oxford Magazine* had defined that term in 1770.[25] For the distinction between Banks and the spectacular array of curiosities arranged around him seems porous and uncertain, perhaps as a result of the isolation in which he is portrayed.

In the group portrait of the Society of Dilettanti it is companionship, the mutual reciprocity of looks and gestures, that confirms the manliness of their common interest in antique ornaments. In Parry's conversation piece, the relation between the three figures emphasises the masculine integrity of Banks, but represents the figure of Mai as open to speculation. The ambiguity of gender in West's portrait of Banks, which seems to represent the great collector as a curious spectacle comparable to Reynolds's *Omai*, may be produced by the absence of a visible and defining network of social relations. National affiliation, Reynolds's Discourse suggests, is manifested in social encounters between men, in their recognition of the ornaments and fashions that constitute relative customary identities, and in their shared disapprobation of tattooed islanders and corseted women. He argues that modes of dress deserve approbation when they are sanctioned by custom or the example of those 'who have the high and powerful advantages of rank, birth, or fortune'.[26] Banks's exotic dress, in West's portrait, is not authorised by local custom, or by anyone possessing 'powerful advantages' except himself, and it may therefore cast doubt on his masculinity, or even his national identity. Banks's cosmopolitan assimilation of the ornaments of different cultures may not establish his civilised detachment. It may confuse or erode the distinction between his attraction to ornament and display and that attributed to Mai.[27]

In his 'Thoughts on the manners of Otaheite' of 1773, Banks noted that civilisation modified gender differences. He argued that

The regard and attention paid by us Europeans to the fair sex is certainly one of the chief reasons why our women so far exceed those of Climates more favourable to the produce of the human species in beauty as well as those Elegant qualifications of the mind which blending themselves in our manners make the Commerce between the Sexes so much more deligh[t]full to us than to the inhabitants of Africa or america in whose breasts I do not find the refinements of Love to hold the least place.

This thought alludes to the commonplace belief that the company of women civilises men because it polishes their manners and blends them with feminine elegance of mind. Banks goes on to imply that the practice of tattooing inflects the gender of Tahitian men. He writes that both the men and the women of Tahiti 'have a singular custom of inlaying under the skin certain figures in black'; a custom 'attended with considerable pain yet . . . Essential . . . to beauty.' He observes that 'I am inclind to think that as whiteness of skin is esteemed an Essential beauty these marks were originaly intended to make that whiteness appear to greater advantage by the Contrast Evidently in the same manner as the patches usd by our European beauties.'[28] The comparison between European beauties and the men and women of Tahiti elides the distinctions between what Banks recognised was an ancient custom and transitory fashion, and links the tattoos of Tahitian men with signs of feminine vanity. Banks's argument sets up a distinction between the civilising feminisation of the manners of 'us Europeans', and the barbarous femininity of Tahitian custom. If Banks's account of tattooing seems more tolerant than Reynolds's, this may be because he is more comfortable with the notion of an absolute distinction between civilisation and barbarity, which allows him to assimilate feminised qualities of mind to the manners of European men, but to suggest that the bodies rather than minds of Tahitian men are feminised by their traditional customs. In Reynolds's Discourse, in contrast, the sensually appealing ornaments which characterise national taste are much more difficult to distinguish from the rejected practices of tattooing or strait lacing. These aspects of what it means to be a modern and civilised man are, I want now to suggest, important to the way tattooed bodies are perceived in the Pacific by European voyagers, as well as to the images I have discussed.

IV

In 1773, ten men from the crew of the *Adventure* died at Grass Cove in the South Island of New Zealand. James Burney led the party which discovered their remains, and took these to be 'most horrid & undeniable proofs' that they had been cooked and eaten.[29] Perhaps the most lurid narrative of this incident was provided in one of the accounts published without the sanction of the Admiralty. Burney's party, according to this journalist,

found several of their people's baskets, and saw one of their dogs eating a piece of broiled flesh, which upon examining they suspected to be human, and having found in one of the baskets a hand, which they knew to be the left hand of Thomas Hill, by the letters T. H. being marked on it, they were no longer in suspence about the event.[30]

Burney wrote that what he had seen could 'never be mentioned or thought of, but with horror',[31] and his father observed that after his return to London he 'always spoke of it in a whisper, as if it was treason'.[32]

The indignation that marks Burney's response, and that is promoted by the melodramatic fascination of the journalist's account, is perhaps reminiscent of Reynolds's response to tattooing. It distinguishes between islanders and Europeans in terms of custom and morality. But the indignant disapproval or horror that distanced the Europeans from the islanders was not present in all of the voyagers' accounts, nor was it, perhaps, the only response available to Burney. Probably the most influential of the various reflections on the practice of anthropophagy that resulted from this voyage were those of Cook's published account, where there is a clear sense of moral distance, but where the practice also invokes a political discourse, almost 'as if it were treason'. Cook wrote that the people of the South Island of New Zealand lived 'dispersed in small parties, knowing no head but the chief of the family or tribe, whose authority may be very little'. He thought that their social isolation and dislocation resulted in continual personal danger and warfare, and argued that 'were they more united under a settled form of government, they would have fewer enemies, consequently this custom would be less in use, and might in time be . . . forgotten'.[33] The custom of cannibalism is represented as a violation of the ideal unity of the social and private body, as though it replicated social dispersal and dismemberment on the bodies of those killed in battle. It seems to indicate an almost anarchic state of social and private disarticulation and incoherence, which Europeans can speak of only in whispers, as though it were a treasonable secret.

Cook's expressions of disapproval for the practice are measured rather than indignant, but they are marked by a strong sense of cultural difference; they represent it as the object of that moral disapprobation that is a constituent of the community of national custom in Reynolds's Discourse. Cook writes that the New Zealanders 'At present . . . have but little idea of treating others as themselves would to be treated, but treat them as they *expect* to be treated.' Cannibalism, he suggests, results from a failure to perceive others as like ourselves, a failure of sympathy, which he believes can best be remedied by 'connexion or commerce with strangers'. He explains that 'An intercourse with foreigners would reform their manners, and polish their savage minds.' The contrast here is between savage isolation and civilised sympathy and sociability; between an asocial and therefore amoral condition which permits 'inhuman and savage' practices and the social and national communities which enforce European moral values.[34] Cook's account suggests that cannibalism might either be seen as one of the 'ancient customs' which have been 'handed down . . . from the earliest times',[35] and which, because it is a social and historical custom, points to the possibility of a more coherent political organisation among the islanders, or as the sign of an inhuman isolation that can only be mitigated or moralised by colonial intervention.

Perceptions of the islanders as either lacking government, or lacking civilised humanity and sympathy, provide the context for accounts of tattooing, incision, or scarification as signs of 'ancient customs'. Representations of the islanders' tattoos in the sketchbooks of the artists on Cook's voyages most usually show elaborate designs loosely framed by outlines that suggest isolated parts of the anatomy, disarticulated knees, thighs, and buttocks – or the profiles of lightly sketched faces, as in drawings by Sydney Parkinson and Herman Spöring (figs. 3.2 and 3.3). These two men were both employed to depict specimens of flora and fauna on the first voyage, and there seems to be little variation from the technique appropriate to botanical and zoological draughtsmanship in these representations of tattoos as curiosities fixed for the perusal of the natural philosopher. Parkinson's more fully worked-up drawings of the New Zealanders are similarly disarticulated. The images that were engraved for the posthumous publication of his journal, showing the faces of Maori men 'curiously tataowed, or mark'd, according to their manner', are precise maps of elaborate facial incisions which seem dislocated from the features they adorn, or fixed in transient and impassioned expressions that are represented as mask-like (fig. 3.4).[36] There is an incoherence in these drawings that is reminiscent of the dislocation and discontinuity Cook attributed to the social formations of the New Zealanders, and that is, I think, apparent in voyagers' written reflections on Maori tattoos. The surgeon on the first voyage, for example, wrote of incisions he found 'extreamly curious' on a man's forehead, looking 'as if a plate for example had been graved with numberless little flourishes confined within two arched lines, and empressed upon the part; and each little curve thus mark'd out, not by a simple line or superficial black mark but really indented in the Skin'.[37] The perception of elaborate facial incisions as analogous to engravings is not unique to this account, and it may have been implicit in Rickman's comments on the islanders as 'living pictures'. It may suggest that the islanders are beyond representation in their exotic isolation, that

Figure 3.2 Sydney Parkinson, *Black Stains in the Skin called Tattoo*, 1769, pen and ink, top left 273 × 184 mm, top right 273 × 184 mm, bottom left 286 × 229 mm, bottom right 149 × 120 mm

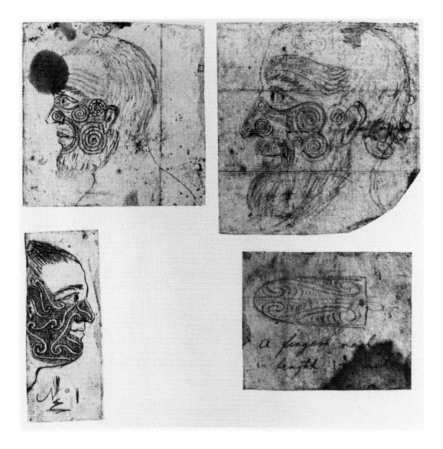

Figure 3.3 Herman Spöring, *Black Stains on the Skin called Tattoo*, 1769, pencil, top left 102 × 104 mm, top right 118 × 121 mm, bottom left 102 × 45 mm, bottom right 76 × 99 mm

they are, as it were, already the only possible image of themselves, already ethnologically specified to a degree that makes representation and cultural assimilation redundant.

The representation of tattoos in some degree of isolation from the body they mark, in European texts, seems peculiarly interchangeable with the perception of them as 'really indented in the Skin'. The dislocation and incoherence of these indentations and inscriptions is linked, I have suggested, with what was seen as an excessively masculine or savage absence of convivial sympathy – in contrast to, for example, the initials on the hand of Thomas Hill, which confirm the former coherence of his bodily identity and legible social place as a sailor proudly adorned with a Tahitian tattoo. The engraving of the discovery of the European's tattooed hand

Portrait of a New Zoland Man

Figure 3.4 Sydney Parkinson, *Portrait of a New Zeland Man* 1769, pen and ink wash, 394 × 298 mm

(fig. 3.5), published in the unauthorised journal of John Marra, gunner's mate of the *Resolution*, represents the dissevered member as the focus for cohesive relations of what might be described as convivial horror among the European party. Those drawings which represent incisions as integral to the expression of the face they adorn – for example, William Hodges's

Figure 3.5 Artist unknown, plate from [John Marra], *Journal of the Resolution's Voyage* (London: F. Newbury, 1775), 31 × 63 mm

image of an *Old Maori man with a Grey Beard* (plate 3.4) – suggest in contrast a sentimental appropriation which perceives in tattoos the marks of private and individual character. The old man is portrayed with an expression of dignified resignation comparable to that of members of the English rural poor in, for example, images by Gainsborough.[38] He has little of the spectacular exoticism or ambiguously patrician authority that characterises Reynolds's more formal and public representation of Mai. In Hodges's drawing, the inscription of the man's brow, in juxtaposition with his earring, suggests the kind of customary ornamentation which the spectator must view with dispassionate tolerance if he is to show himself a civilised man of the world.

Nicholas Thomas writes, in his invaluable account of the Cook voyages, that 'It is odd that [Hodges] made no greater effort' to represent the extraordinary variety of the tattooing he must have seen in New Zealand, Tonga, the Marquesas and Tahiti, except in the images of Vaitepiha which I discussed in Chapters 1 and 2. He suggests perceptively that Hodges's 'failure' may have been because 'he had been taught always to respond to form, and had no pictorial language for "punctures"'.[39] Hodges's representations of Maori *moko* are certainly much less dramatic than the detailed maps of facial incisions that Sydney Parkinson produced (fig. 3.6). Hodges's drawings seem to attempt to incorporate tattoos as though they were extensions of the features or expressive lines of the faces he draws, as if to emphasise the analogy between his work of portraiture, and that of the tattooist (plates 3.5, 3.6). Possibly Hodges felt encouraged to adapt facial ornament in this way by the positive responses of his Maori sitters. George Forster described the voyagers' encounter with a small group of Maori at Dusky Bay in the South Island of New Zealand, and added that

A short conversation ensued, of which very little was understood on both sides, for want of a competent knowledge of the language. Mr. Hodges immediately took sketches of their countenances, and their gestures shewed that they clearly understood what he was doing; on which they called him *t'oä-t'oä*, that term being probably applicable to the imitative arts.

Anne Salmond points out that the Maori's fascination may have been increased by Hodges's use of 'red pastel, the tapu colour'. When the group visited the ship, one of the women approached Hodges, and 'having a tuft of feathers, dipt in oil, on a string round her neck, insisted upon dressing him out with it, and he was forced to wear the odiferous present, in pure civility'. Salmond explains that the gift was 'a sign of mana (prestige and power)'. Hodges's drawings of Maori, both at Dusky Bay and in the

Figure 3.6 T. Chambers after Sydney Parkinson, *The Head of a Chief of New Zealand, the Face Curiously Tataow'd, or Marked according to their Manner*, from Sydney Parkinson, *A Journal of a Voyage to the South Seas* (London, 1784), pl. 16, opposite p. 90, 251 × 184 mm

North Island, overcame the obstacles of 'unintelligible conversation' and mutual apprehension, and provided the occasion for a shared, sympathetic enjoyment and interest experienced all too rarely during the voyagers' stay in New Zealand.[40] His depictions of tattoos and facial incisions are sometimes almost indistinguishable from delicate shading, or marks of expression (plate 3.7), and sometimes boldly marked (plate 3.8). They work both as signs of the exotic and marks which European spectators might view with sympathetic recognition, as signs of sentiment, and that dual inscription may indicate the value attached to those few occasions of cross-cultural sympathy.

In Hodges's drawings, the representation of tattoos works both to confirm the exoticism of the New Zealanders, and to soften their remoteness, to make possible a kind of sympathy that written accounts of them usually denied. The doubled significance of ornament, as confirmation of both similarity and difference, is also apparent in the reflections on women, ornament, and civilisation of John Ledyard, who served as a corporal on Cook's last voyage. He wrote that

I observe that among all nations the Women ornament themselves more than the men: I observe too that Woman wherever found is the same kind, civil, obliging, humane, tender being ... I do not think the Character of Woman so well ascertained in that Society which is highly civilized & polished as in the obscure and plain walks of life ... Climate & Education makes a greater difference in the Character of Men than Women.[41]

His remarks suggest a complicated interplay between discourses on gender difference and civilisation. On one hand, women are undifferentiated, 'wherever found ... the same', whereas men seem capable of a much greater individual variety – a differentiation which, as we shall see in the next chapter, is usually understood to be the effect of the division of labour, as Ledyard may imply in alluding to the effects of education, or what we would call culture. And the universality of women's predilection for ornament confirms their uniform character. But on the other hand, in the context of Reynolds's association of ornament with national character, Ledyard's remarks imply that women restricted to 'the obscure and plain walks of life' remain close to national character in a customary, almost natural state to which ornament is appropriate, whereas man in 'highly civilized & polished' societies rise above customary differences, and the seductive appeal of ornament.

Joseph Banks, like John Ledyard, Sydney Parkinson, and many of the other voyagers, was tattooed during his stay in Tahiti, marking what has often been described as the inauguration of a nautical tradition.[42] They seem to have understood the islanders' tattoos to possess customary or ritual significance, and to mark status, membership in a social group, or a particular attainment, such as puberty. But they usually suggest that the designs that make up the tattoo are arbitrary and whimsical, dependent on the vagaries of individual character and personal choice. They conceived of tattoos as the markers of an esoteric diversity which could be imitated and appropriated. John Elliott, who travelled as midshipman on the second circumnavigation, recollected in his memoirs of Tahiti that he and his companions particularly admired the warriors of Bora Bora – men whom Cook thought troublesome and anarchic. Elliott writes that these men had 'particular marks tattooed on the Legs etc. We therefore called them the Knights of Bora Bora, and all our mess conceived the idea of having some mark put on ourselves, as connecting us together, as well as to commemorate our having been at Otaheite.' Elliott's messmates had a star tattooed on the left breast, and called themselves the 'Knights of Otaheite'. He notes that they intended to keep their badge secret, but 'we no sooner began to bathe, than it spread halfway through the ship'.[43]

The tattoos Elliott describes mark the appropriation of what are conceived of as signs of ethnic or national identity to a secret and exotic definition. The notion of a brotherhood of knights alludes to that sentimental fondness for Gothic institutions which was to be important to, for example, Edmund Burke's conception of custom. But here those chivalric orders are identified with the esoteric orders of the men of Bora Bora, and they seem to stain the Europeans with a kind of exotic perversion of domestic and national identity. Several of the *Bounty* mutineers were distinguished by the badge Elliott describes, and one of them combined this star with the tattooed mark of 'a Garter around his Left Leg with the Motto Honi Soit Qui Mal Y Pense',[44] in parody of the insignia of the Order of the Garter, of a custom endorsed (as Reynolds had argued customs should be) by 'the high and powerful advantages of rank'.[45] The star and occasional garter that the men favoured are both the insignia of their national identity and the sign of their exoticisation.

If Reynolds's *Portrait of Omai* does contribute to national history by reminding us of the way art can bridge cultural divides, as David Attenborough has claimed, it does so by reminding us of the complexity of that process. The British elite may have thought of Mai as an exotic ornament to their civilised connoisseurship, their capacity to survey mankind with dispassionate authority. Mai might have thought he could use them to enhance his status and endow him with arms. But as we shall see in later chapters, Mai's association with fashionable metropolitan society did not improve his status at home, and lent him at best an ambiguous dignity in London. Proximity to the exotic could also blur distinctions of gender and physical definition important to European masculinity, and implicitly modify what it meant to be a connoisseur and collector of curiosities. The tattoos of the islanders of New Zealand and Tahiti were perceived as signs of a potentially asocial diversity and specificity, or the cryptic insignia of esoteric achievements and orders. When John Elliott and his messmates chose to distinguish themselves as 'Knights of Otaheite', they parodied the insignia of elites that were both exotic and a part of their domestic national identity in a gesture which indicated the fragility and permeability of distinctions between different national characters, between the domestic and the exotic, and between civilisation and those it excluded, and which acknowledged the unstable and shifting nature of cultural differences.

4 | Terms of trade in Tonga and Vanuatu

I

Tongan culture presented a peculiarly intractable puzzle for the expeditions commanded by James Cook; a problem of representation and of knowledge. Cook's ships visited the islands of Tonga on both his second and third voyages. During the second circumnavigation of 1772–5, Cook's ships anchored at the southern islands of Tonga for a few days in October of 1773, returning to the northern islands for another brief stay the following July. In 1777, unable to reach his intended anchorage in Tahiti, Cook landed at Nomuka on 1 May, and stayed among the Tongan islands until mid-July (see fig. 4.1). The two voyages produced a very considerable body of writing about the Tongan islands, in the range of unpublished journals kept by officers and men, and in the accounts published with or without official sanction by Cook, by officers and sea men, and by Johann and George Forster. The eleven weeks spent among the islands in 1777 produced, in particular, lengthy and quite detailed accounts of the manners and customs of the islanders from James Cook himself, and from William Anderson, the surgeon on the sloop *Resolution*. But somehow all this documentation, rich with anecdote and theorisation, quotidian observation and general reflection, seems to assert and imply continually the sense that Tongan culture remains enigmatic, a curious object of investigation that eludes the researches of the Europeans.

There is of course a sense in which all the island cultures of the South Pacific remain strange, exotic, to their European visitors, and Tongan society presented – perhaps more than most – particular historical problems. The Pacific historian O. H. K. Spate notes that by the time Cook arrived at Tonga, different chiefly people there functioned severally as religious, nominal, and executive authorities, and relations between them were complex. He concludes that: 'the system of ranking was most intricate. Cook . . . confessed himself baffled, and no wonder.'[1] Though both Johann Forster on the second voyage and William Anderson on the third seem to have found the Tongan language relatively unproblematic, because of its closeness to that of Tahiti and the Society Islands, Cook experienced considerable difficulties.

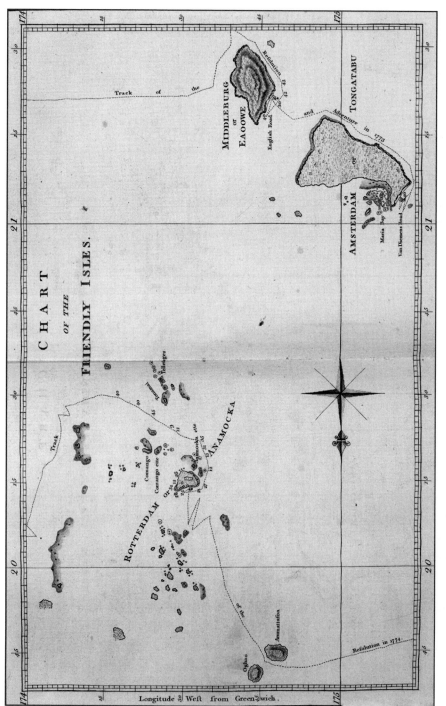

Figure 4.1 James Cook, *Chart of the Friendly Isles*, in Cook, *Voyage* (1777), I, pl. XIV

On the third voyage he resorted to the interpreting skills of Mai, but he noted despondently that Mai frequently misunderstood the islanders.[2] He concluded at the end of his stay that

It may indeed be expected that after spending between two and three Months among these islands, I should be enable[d] to give a good account of the customs, opinions, and arts of the inhabitants, especially as we had a person on board who understood their language and he ours. But unless the object or thing we wanted to enquire after was before us, we found it difficult to gain a tolerable knowledge of it from information only without falling into a hundred mistakes.[3]

Cook excuses or explains what he clearly regards as an embarrassing failure of knowledge on a number of grounds. He blames Mai, whom, he writes, 'never gave himself the trouble to gain knowledge for himself, so that when he was disposed to explain things to us his account was often very confused'. And he blames the islanders themselves, complaining that

It was . . . very rare we found a person both able and willing to giving us the information we wanted, for the most of them hate to be troubled with what they probably think idle questions. Our situation at *Tongatabu* where we remained the longest, was likewise unfavourable; it was in a part of the country where there were few inhabitants except fishers; it was always holiday with our visitors as well as with those we visited, so that we had but few oppertunities of seeing into their domistick way of living.[4]

There is a strong suggestion that the islanders resist investigation; that they are indifferent or even hostile to a properly intellectual curiosity. They deny the European the opportunities his quest for knowledge demands, opportunities of observing them as though he were not present. Here Cook seems to diffuse his irritation with the islanders' recalcitrance by implying that it is a problem of class difference. He had not been happy with the choice of Mai, a low-ranking islander, as a 'proper sample' to take back to London, and here he is clearly suggesting that Mai suffers from a vulgar lack of curiosity, and inability to organise his ideas. Most of the Tongans he encounters, he may also suggest, are too busy, too relaxed, too rustic to supply appropriate information, for they are fishermen or working people who 'hate to be troubled with what they probably think idle questions'.[5] Cook's lack of confidence in the knowledge he did gain and record in his journal, I suggest, is intensified by the nature of the interaction between islanders and voyagers at Tonga, and the sorts of problems of representation or knowledge that it poses.

My discussion focuses on representations of the southern islands of Tongatapu and Eua, which had been named Amsterdam and Middleburg by

Figure 4.2 J. K. Sherwin after William Hodges, *The Landing at Middleburgh one of the Friendly Islands*, in Cook, *Voyage* (1777), II, pl. LIV (fp. 192), 275 × 515 mm

Abel Tasman in 1643. William Hodges produced only a handful of drawings of these islands, and no portraits of Tongan women, but he did produce an image which provided the basis for J. K. Sherwin's engraving of *The Landing at Middleburgh* [Eua] *One of the Friendly Isles*, published in Cook's account of his second voyage (fig. 4.2). It seems likely that this was an oil painting, which has since been lost. The engraving is one of four landing scenes, the other three showing landings in Vanuatu (Cook's 'New Hebrides'), visited later on the voyage, and for those three, the oil sketches on which the engravings were based have survived.[6] The group constitutes a sort of subgenre of first-contact paintings, and it is partly in the context of this subgenre that I want to consider this engraving.

II

The *Landing at Middleburgh* was a controversial image. Hodges prided himself on the 'accuracy' of his work, and though it is not at all clear (as we saw in the Introduction) that what he meant by that was some kind of trans-parent realism, it was in terms which suggested transparency that his work was often praised. Johann Forster, for example, admired his 'most accu-rate representations' of Tongan canoes, and Cook wrote that these sketches made his own written description unnecessary;[7] but in the landing scene Hodges was perceived to have gone widely astray (fig. 4.3). George Forster, in his published account of the voyage, acknowledged that Hodges's work was usually and admirably 'characteristic of the objects which he meant to represent', but felt obliged to explain that this image 'does not convey any adequate idea of the natives'. He adds that it is

greatly to be feared, that Mr. Hodges has lost the sketches and drawings which he made from NATURE in the course of the voyage, and supplied the deficiency in this case, from his own elegant ideas. The connoisseur will find Greek contours and features in this picture, which have never existed in the South Sea.[8]

Specifically he pointed out that the islanders rarely covered the top halves of their bodies, and that the men shaved off their beards with shells. It might be added that the islanders seem to be offering fruits, though initially and to Cook's dismay they offered everything but food. Almost the only details here that are borne out by the journals seem to be the presence of the palisade in the top right-hand corner, and the number of shortened little fingers visible, as a result of a custom over which the Europeans puzzled endlessly.

Figure 4.3 William Hodges, *Tonga Tabu or Amsterdam*, [June 1774–], pen and indian ink wash, 619 × 1,172 mm

It may, however, be more fruitful to attempt to read the image in the context of Hodges's work elsewhere in the South Pacific. Hodges quite frequently represents the people of the South Pacific as reminiscent of representations of oriental or biblical figures rather than 'Greek contours and features'. It has been pointed out, for example, that the man in the foreground of the earlier *View of Cape Stephens in Cook's Straits with Waterspout* looks 'like Moses pacifying the Red Sea' (plate 4.1),[9] and the figures in the bottom left corner of his image of the *War Boats of Otaheite* are reminiscent of representations of the flight from Egypt (plate 0.4).[10] Neither of those images attracted the Forsters' displeasure. In the *Landing at Middleburgh*, George Forster picks out for criticism 'an elegant flowing robe which involves the whole head and body, in an island where the women very rarely cover the shoulders and breast', and 'the figure of a divine old man, with a long white beard, though all the people of Ea-oowhe shave themselves with muscle-shells'.[11] The figures clearly are ethnographically inaccurate, but they might be read as biblical rather than classical. The bearded old man suggests representations of prophets and patriarchs, and the woman with children clustered around her is reminiscent of allegorical images of Charity. Biblical or oriental allusions of this kind are a recurrent motif of Hodges's images of islanders to the east of Tonga, but not of his representations of more western islanders, which may be an indication of the division of the islanders into two groups, differentiated in terms most fully theorised and explored in the work of Johann Forster.

Nicholas Thomas has argued that it is misleading to assimilate discussions of the similarities and differences between islanders that arose from Cook's voyages to the nineteenth-century model of a racial division between Melanesians and Polynesians. Thomas points out that though Forster did write of 'two "great varieties" or "races" among the Oceanic peoples', his account of the differences between island groups depended on the analysis of a range of factors, such as climate, education, political system, migration, and population size, that could not simply be reduced to the terms of an emerging discourse on racial difference. So, for example, Thomas argues that Forster thought, on the evidence of linguistic cognates and shared customs, that the Society and Friendly islanders shared a common ancestry, but he also points out that the difference between the degree of feudal stratification structuring the two societies was important to Forster's account.[12] Forster thought that in Tonga 'government has still much oriental despotism and slavish subjection to chiefs', whereas the people of Tahiti had 'arrived at that happy mean which assigns the just bounds of prerogative to each rank of people'.[13]

Figure 4.4 J. K. Sherwin after William Hodges, *The Landing at Tanna, One of the New Hebrides*, in Cook, *Voyage* (1777), II, pl. LIX (fp. 54), 235 × 473 mm

The visual vocabulary of Hodges's paintings may indicate the sort of uneven and tentative processes of classification that Thomas describes. The biblical allusions in the *Landing at Middleburgh* may signal the oriental character of Tongan society, and thus indicate a degree of continuity between the cultural polity of Tonga, and of the islands to the west, which were perceived to be marked by the more or less faint vestiges of oriental manners. For the way that the cluster of Tongan men is, as it were, almost entirely enclosed by the outlines of women certainly works to distinguish this landing scene from those Hodges produced of Vanuatu. These paintings all dramatise the notion of first contact as an occasion which emphasises difference, the contrast between the dressed Europeans in their boats and the bodies of the islanders. In the engravings produced for Cook's published account of the voyage, the contrast between the islanders, represented as taller and more muscular than the accompanying text would suggest, and the Europeans, often seated, with flowing locks, and outlines softened by their clothing, points towards the difference between the graceful femininity of the civilised and the excessive masculinity attributed to those thought to be savage or barbarian (figs. 4.4, 4.5) These are not all scenes of potential conflict. In *The Landing at Mallicolo* [Malakula] (fig. 4.6), the islanders appear to welcome the Europeans; but the one who extends his hand also brandishes his weapon, and the Europeans too seem apprehensive and well-armed, their group dominated by the height of the armed marine on the right. Many of the Europeans are seated, unlike the islanders, but the vertical lines of muskets and masts and of the officers' bodies more than counterbalance in height the upright figures of the islanders. The tension between the two wary groups perhaps indicates the sorts of mixed feelings Cook voiced in his unpleasant concession that 'had we made a longer stay, we might soon have been upon good terms with this ape-like nation'.[14]

The contrast that in the later landings is emphasised by the imaginary viewing position of the artist, from which the two groups are clearly separated by the shoreline, is attenuated in the *Landing at Middleburgh* by the presence of the islander in the boat, the line of the leaf or branch he holds to signify welcome paralleled in the upended musket of the standing officer. The way the subgenre of first-contact images seems to privilege confrontation is softened by the kneeling, almost supplicant position of the man in the centre, surrounded by women and children. Here it may be the Tongans who appear feminised, softened, submissive. But the painting is still a landing scene; it is, with whatever qualifications, a representation of difference, of the contrast between the mobility of the Europeans, whose ship looms large in the distance, and the islanders they visit – a contrast less obviously

Figure 4.5 J. K. Sherwin after William Hodges, *The Landing at Erramanga, One of the New Hebrides*, in Cook, *Voyage* (1777), II, pl. LXII (fp. 46)

Figure 4.6 J. Basire after William Hodges, *The Landing at Mallicolo, One of the New Hebrides*, in Cook, *Voyage* (1777), II, pl. LX (fp. 30)

Figure 4.7 William Hodges, [*A Party of Maori in a Canoe*], [June 1773–], pen and indian ink wash, with tints of watercolour, 375 × 545 mm

important in images of encounters between Europeans and Society Islanders or New Zealanders, who approach the ship in canoes (fig. 4.7).

III

My discussion suggests, then, that the inaccuracies pointed out by George Forster in *The Landing at Middleburgh* may most fruitfully be seen as signs of a problem of representation, the puzzle of how to understand the Tongans in relation to European categorisations of either the Society Islanders or the New Hebrideans. This is a problem apparent in the gendered language or visual vocabulary seen as appropriate to the islanders. In images of landings in Vanuatu, the Europeans seem softened and feminised by civilisation, in contrast to the masculine figures of the islanders. In the Society Islands, that binary is reversed: the literature that resulted from Bougainville's voyage of 1766–9 had established the idea of the islands as a feminine and sensual paradise, and Hawkesworth's account of Cook's first voyage had given flesh and detail to that idea.[15] So that, for example, by the time of Cook's third voyage, comparisons of the Tahitians with the Tongans could more or less take for granted the notion of the feminisation of the Society Islanders. James King (then second lieutenant on the *Resolution*) wrote that

the men here [at Tahiti] fall far short in my Idea, in shape, air, sweetness & manliness, of those at Tongataboo . . . they are effeminately and loosely made to what the others are, & Sloth & Idleness affect their manners as well as shapes; We certainly saw some Chiefs whose fine smooth & fair skins made them much more beautiful than those at Tonga-taboo; On the whole as to figure if we want'd a Model for an Apollo or a Bachus we must look for it at Otaheite, & shall find it to perfection, but if for a Hercules or an Ajax at the friendly Isles.[16]

Broadly speaking, the Society Islanders are perceived to be feminised to a degree that gives the Europeans a kind of right to exploit them as though that were a natural masculine prerogative; whereas the people of Vanuatu are attributed an impoverished masculinity, which in Cook's account verges on animality, because they are perceived to be undesirable subjects, isolated from the feminine softness of civilised sociability. A form of manliness that is less impoverished, more immediately complementary to the feminised image of the Tahitians, tends to be attributed to the New Zealanders, perceived as barbarous warriors who can be respected for their bravery while their apparent lack of domestic affections is deplored.[17] But the Tongans are a good deal more difficult to assimilate to this model.

King's comparison of the Tongans and Tahitians begins to suggest the difficulty. The notion that the Tongans resemble Ajax and Hercules to the Tahitian's Bacchus and Apollo suggests that the two groups do share terms of reference, but the Tongans were known as the friendly islanders because they appeared not to be at war with anyone, which hardly suits the idea of Ajax. For Cook, the contrast placed the Tongans somewhere on the border between the two great varieties or races Johann Forster identified. Cook wrote of the Tongans that 'With respect to their persons and colour I neither think them ugly nor handsome, there are none so fair, so tall or so well made as some of the natives of Otaheite and the neighbouring isles: on the other hand they are not so dark, so little or ill shaped as some we see at these isles'.[18] For Cook the Tongans occupy a median position – neither ugly nor handsome, dark nor fair – almost as though they shared the normative qualities attributed to Europeans, though this is a negative account, a list of what they are not.

Perhaps the most intriguing description is Johann Forster's. He writes of the Tongans that: The people here are in general of a middling Stature or something above it. The outlines of their bodies are not so beautifull & soft, as those of the people at *Otahaitee* & its neighbouring Isles, but they are compact, proportionate & Symmetric, however more musculated & expressive than those at *Otahaitee*. They are all here more laborious & industrious, & therefore have stronger Expression in their Musculation; whereas the Natives of *Otahaitee* are more addicted to Sloth & indolence.[19]

The passage is from Forster's journal, and not from a text intended for publication, and perhaps because of that it seems unusually meditative, marked by the uncertain processes of assessment. At first, the comparison seems to work in favour of the Tahitians, whose bodies are beautiful and soft. The notion that the Tongans' bodies are 'compact, proportionate & Symmetric' seems only a small consolation for their lack of beauty. But with the introduction of the notion of expression, and its association with labour and industry, the balance begins to tip in favour of the Tongans. Labour and industry are after all privileged categories, cardinal virtues, in the commercial cultures of late eighteenth-century northern Europe. And these are linked, perhaps at first rather oddly, with admiration for the 'stronger Expression in their Musculation'; not praise for muscle in and of itself, but for that I think implicitly painterly notion of expression or character that muscle produces. As Forster goes on to think about the contrast between the Tahitians and Tongans in the context of ideas of virtuous industry and expressive muscle, the Tahitians lose their attractive beauty. Forster writes that their muscles get a gentle soft outline & all coincide in an effeminate manner. You see Men of 6 foot 3 Inches high & broad in proportion, with fine limbs, nasty legs & the softest outline imaginable. These people here [at Tonga] are none disformed by hard labour; moderate Industry has assigned each Muscle its place, without deforming the whole. The Stature is moderate, each limb proportionate, the whole harmonically Symmetric. The colour is a lively brown inclining towards the red or Copper colour; whereas the *Otahaitee* common people are as black, if not more so, & their Chiefs are rather yellow, or like the complexion of a dropsical Person in *Europe*.[20]

In the context of this Georgic valorisation of labour, the more pastoral Tahitians appear effeminate. The relatively pale complexions of high-ranking Tahitians, which had been central to European perceptions of their beauty, seem diseased, and their beautifully soft outlines give way to 'nasty legs' and poor muscle definition. The notion of expression, usually associated with the portrayal of heroic character in painting, here seems to function to indicate not just that the muscles of the Tahitians are too fluid, but that the character of the people is somehow too indistinct, that the men 'all coincide in an effeminate' rather than heroic manner.

Forster's thoughts on the Tahitians and Tongans, in this passage, find an intriguing echo in some of the arguments of the Irish painter, James Barry, professor of painting at the Royal Academy from 1782 to 1799. In his lecture on Design, first delivered at the Royal Academy in 1785, Barry argues that the 'human frame being of all others calculated for the greatest variety of ends, the beautiful is there necessarily at its highest point'. But he goes on to argue that the ideal of beauty is always inevitably distorted in men by vigorous action. These deviations constitute either deformity or sublimity (the highest form of 'particular character', in Barry's terms) in so far as they thwart or serve the 'better purpose of effecting utility and power' in active republican citizenship. Beauty alone, he concludes, must be 'tasteless and insipid', or even 'lying and contradictory', unless it is informed by 'the superior nature of moral excellence', which causes it to deviate into something more elevated and admirable. Beauty should either be 'united with those exquisite sensations of a grateful sensibility, as it ought to be in the female', or 'improved and heightened by vigorous exertion into some admirable, generous, venerable, character in the other sex'.[21] Forster's notion that the beauty of the Tahitians is not sufficiently differentiated by industrious exertion, and his suggestion that the Tongans achieve a more admirable definition because their activity distorts or deviates from beauty, draws on a similar discursive linkage of manly character and vigorous action.

IV

In general terms, then, the Tahitians had seemed to represent a kind of exotic ideal to the Europeans; an ideal that is pastoral, feminised, and admirably civilised in its social cohesion, particularly when considered in contrast to the atomised social organisation and barbarian manners of the New Zealanders. In the context of Europeans' perceptions of the Tahitians, the Tongans appeared less beautiful, less amenable to the eroticised language of masculine desire which so insistently characterised European representations of the Society Islands, and less civilised, in their 'slavish subjection' to 'oriental despotism'. But Tongan culture could also call into play a different set of references, a discourse that privileged manly expression in industry and its associated virtues of intelligence and ingenuity. Charles Clerke (commander of the *Discovery*) remarks, for example, on this triangle of islands, that the Tongans

are by no means so much the Children of the Hour as our good friends of Otaheite and the Society Islands; they have infinitely more thought and attention to the morrow than those good Fellows, which their industry in agriculture and extensive plantations sufficiently evince. On the other hand, in respect to our hungry Acquaintance, the Zeelanders, every thing among them so immediately becomes the property of force and power, that no Man knows what may be his possessions tomorrow; consequently nothing is worth keeping that can possibly be made to accrue to our use or satisfaction to day.[22]

In this context the Society Islanders and the New Zealanders are, in different ways, infantilised by an inability to defer the gratification of their desires, whereas the Tongans, thoughtful and deliberate, possess characteristics that Europeans respect, and that they appropriate to themselves, which might make it difficult to define the subject position from which the difference and superiority of the voyagers is to be established.

The capacity for labour and industry that is attributed to the Tongans situates them, as it were, on the trajectory of progressive improvement that is more usually seen as appropriate only to the manufacturing nations of northern Europe. Forster writes, for example, that

We think ourselves much superior to these Nations in regard to Arts & Trades, & what is still more than all this, in regard to our sublime Sciences, & the use of letters. I will by no means say they are as far as we in regard to all these things, or even as far as any of the least civilized Nations, but let us only give them their due.

He argues that the Tongans 'have more civilization than we might at first out-set think', comparing their progress directly with that of northern European nations. He points out that

The greatest disadvantage to this Nation is there being totally destitute of Iron & the rest of the useful Metals; & the ways of working them. This makes that their Manufactures seem to be so imperfect & all their Works so unfinished. But were a few centuries ago the greatest part of the Northern Nations in Europe not by far more backward in their Manufactures? though they had the use of Iron & Copper than these Islanders?[23]

He suggests that Tongan culture can be defined and respected in terms of European notions of progress because they possess the intellectual qualities that progress requires, which they demonstrate in 'their ingenuity, their con-trivances', and they possess the appropriate moral qualities: 'They exercise all the Social virtues to one another, which are usual among the civilized nations. Charity, the main spring of all morality & virtue, is no where more exercised than among these people.' All that seems to slow them down, in his account, is 'the Simplicity of their tools'.[24] The polity of the Tongans is perceived as less advanced than that of Tahiti, but Forster suggests that they possess a greater aptitude for progress than the Society Islanders.

Cook is less willing than Forster seems to be to measure the Tongans' condition, as it were, against a different scale to that seen as appropriate to the Society Islanders. In his published account he notes casually, but I suspect critically, that 'Some of our gentlemen were of opinion' that the Friendly Islanders 'were a much handsomer race' than the Society Islanders, concluding that 'others maintained a contrary opinion, of which number I was one'.[25] In his account of the landscape of Tongatapu, however, the pressure of that discourse on progressive industry that so marked Forster's account of the islanders emerges. Cook writes of being conducted inland along a road:

This road, which was about sixteen feet broad, and as level as a bowling-green, seemed to be a very public one; there being many other roads from different parts, leading into it, all inclosed on each side, with neat fences made of reeds, and shaded from the scorching sun by fruit trees. I thought I was transported into the most fertile plains in Europe. There was not an inch of waste ground; the roads occupied no more space than was absolutely necessary; the fences did not take up above four inches each; and even this was not wholly lost, for in many were planted some useful trees or plants. It was everywhere the same; change of place altered not the scene. Nature, assisted by a little art, no where appears in more splendor than at this isle.[26]

Cook was by no means alone in admiring the divided and cultivated landscape, and in understanding it in the terms associated with English enclosures; the various journals recording visits to Tongatapu and Eua on the second and third voyages repeatedly dwell with admiration and delight on the pleasure of seeing enclosed plantations and houses in fenced off areas of private property – a landscape apparently defined in familiar and recognisable terms that make the voyagers feel 'transported into the most fertile plains in Europe'. Hodges's watercolour of *Tongatabu or Amsterdam* shows a road similar to that described by Cook – level, broad, and neatly fenced – where the pigs in the foreground, and chickens behind them, suggest the agricultural prosperity of the island (plate 4.2).

In Cook's account indeed it may be the very notion that this is a culture amenable to improvement, cultivation, progress, that makes him so reluctant to discard the insistent sense that the Tongans are somehow inferior to the more beautiful Tahitians. For Cook was frequently and uneasily aware, even on the second voyage, of being at a disadvantage at Tonga. On the third voyage, and largely as a result of what were understood to be errors of judgement by Cook which provoked the antagonism of the islanders, the Europeans occasionally felt that their security depended only on their weapons, and later accounts confirmed that some of the Tongans intended to capture the British ships.[27] During the visit of 1773, a Tongan defeated one of Cook's men in a boxing match, and as a result, Cook 'forbad such tryals of skill in the future. For it be highly impolitic to let them suppose that they were equal to us in anything.'[28] Boxing matches were quite frequent in 1777, but apparently the Europeans 'were always worsted', unless the Tongans let them win out of courtesy or 'the fear they were in of offending us',[29] and it was noted that 'this had rais'd a freedom & contempt of our People among the lower sort, & which they shew'd by gestures & acts'.[30] But Cook's anxieties seem to focus on the notion that Tongans and Europeans were matched on equal terms in these contests. Apparently in order to reclaim the moral high ground, Cook and his officers went to some trouble to persuade the Tongans that the sight of women boxing was offensive to European notions of propriety, and urged that no women's fights should be staged during their visit, even though women's prize fighting was a popular sport in London in the 1770s.[31]

V

What seems to have concerned Cook more pressingly than the superior physical strength and skill of the islanders was their perceived aptitude for trade. He wrote that 'No Nation in the world understand Traffick or Barter . . . better than these people, neither are there perhaps any Indians that traffick with more honisty and less distrust',[32] and these comments, from his general overview of the manners and customs of the islands, stress the advantage to Europeans of this understanding. In their understanding of traffic, the Tongans display social virtues valuable to the voyagers, as well as the superior intelligence that the Forsters praised in them and in the Malakulans.[33] But more anecdotal accounts of trade, and particularly those of incidents occurring on the landings of 1773 and 1774, make it clear that the islanders' understanding of traffic sometimes seemed to Cook rather too modern for his comfort – that it could seem to be based in an understanding of the exploitability of desire, rather than of trade as, in the words of Anderson, 'the only medium which unites all nations in a sort of friendship'.[34]

Johann Forster's journal indicates that the first landing in Eua (Middleburgh) was for him a pleasurable and enormously exciting experience. He writes that

The shore & rocks were crowded with people. They hurraed when we came near, & immediately began a trading with us, & offerred us Cloth & other trifles to sell viz. Mother of Pearl Shells, which they hung on their breast; brasselets of mother of Pearl; Fishhooks; little Paddles & Stools of Clubwood; Bows & Arrows, Clubs.[35]

And the list continues. Forster's breathless attempt to assimilate all the items available into prose form, into a catalogue without order and without the kind of analysis that his son George's later, more measured and detailed account would supply, hardly dwells on the idea of the objects as keys to Tongan culture, but suggests rather the urgent desires of a collector let loose in a curiosity shop.[36] Only finally and in passing here does he recollect the needs of the ship and perhaps the basic materials of his botanical researches, commenting that 'only a few Banana strings, CocoNuts & large Yams were brought'.[37] Cook also takes pleasure in the brief stay at Eua, though there is perhaps a note of alarm in his recollection that on landing 'Men and Women . . . crowded so thick round the boats with Cloth, Matting, &c to exchange for Nails that it was some time before we could get room to land', until 'at last the Chief cleared the way'; but he quickly decides to leave the island because the people 'did not seem desirous to part with' hogs and fowls, 'nor did they . . . offer to exchange any fruit or roots worth mentioning'.[38]

The Forsters' desires for material and natural curiosities did occasionally conflict with the need to restock the ship with food and water, to the apparent irritation of Captain Cook. But here I think their different views of Tongan trade take on a further significance. The ship proceeded to Tongatapu, where Cook records that

a great number of the Islanders [came] aboard and about the sloops . . . bringing little else with them but Cloth and other curiosities, things which I did not come here for and for which the Seamen only bartered away their clothes. In order to put a stop to this and to obtain the refreshments we wanted, I gave orders that no Curiosities should be purchased by any person whatever . . . this had the desired effect for in the morning the Natives came off with bananas and Cocoa-nutts in abundance and some Fowls and Pigs which they exchanged for Nails and peices of Cloth.[39]

On his subsequent visits to Tongan islands, Cook always initially restricted the terms of trade, and appointed the ships' gunners as the official traders. He found that he could in this way restock the ships to his satisfaction unless chiefly Tongans chose to withdraw supplies. What interests me is the way that Cook's journals represent the necessity for this restriction. On this occasion, he feels able, after a couple of days, to give 'every one leave to purchass what curiosities and other things they pleased', and he comments that

after this it was astonishing to see with what eagerness every one catched at every thing they saw, it even went so far as to become the ridicule of the Natives by offering pieces of sticks stones and what not to exchange, one waggish Boy took a piece of human excrement on the end of a stick and hild it out to every one of our people he met with.[40]

Cook seems appalled by the desirousness of his men, and uneasily entertained but alarmed by the possibility that the islanders are ridiculing their willingness to buy sticks and stones.

In Cook's account of trade, only the needs of the ship seem legitimate, and it is presumably these he has in mind when he writes approvingly of the islanders' skill and honesty as traders. When he writes of 'the Passion for Curiosities',[41] and the desires that motivate the exchanges he sees as spoiling the market, he suggests that they make the Europeans ridiculous and reduce them to a kind of subjection to the islanders. It is interesting to note that no other journal that I have seen mentions the 'waggish Boy' with the excrement, and it is tempting to speculate on the anecdote as a reflection of Cook's attitude to unregulated desire. Anderson, who commented on trade as the basis for international friendship, does report that the Tongans 'would not even part with the twig of a tree to us without asking something in exchange'; but he represents this as evidence that they have 'by some means learnt the true spirit of traffic'.[42] Forster, on the other hand, saw the willingness to supply sticks and stones as evidence of the extraordinary hospitality of the islanders. He comments that 'If any one has a thing, he immediately communicates it, to every one, who applies for it . . . if any one of us plucked a plant, there were immediately 100 hands employed in bringing us Specimens.'[43] The Forsters frequently lamented that their own interest in curiosities inspired what appeared to be a similarly indiscriminate avidity among their companions, because 'every discovery we attempted to make, was supposed to contain a treasure, which became the object of envy', even to those the Forsters thought 'utterly incapable of making use of' their discoveries 'for the benefit of science'.[44] Forster seems almost as anxious as Cook to distinguish his transactions from the impassioned exchanges of the other Europeans, whose acquisitive hunger for curiosities, and of course for women, may expose them to the ridicule of the islanders even as it strips them of their clothes.[45] Both Cook and, to some extent, Forster seem concerned that Europeans' expressions of desire will spoil their market, and Cook in particular seems alarmed by the threat desire poses to the distance and authority he wishes to maintain. And this is not only an immediate, practical problem. It is central to the Europeans' conception of themselves as able to assess the cultures they observe that they should not appear impassioned, feminised, and lacking in the self-control that seems a condition of civilised knowledge. It is this anxiety, I want to suggest, that the journalists' discussions of Tongan women indicate.

VI

Many of the journalists, as we have seen in earlier chapters, employ Addison's and Montesquieu's measure of civilised progress, paraphrased by James King in his observation that the 'behaviour of men towards Women is doubtless the best criterion to judge how near Barbarous people approach in good manners to civiliz'd Nations'. King's account of Tongan women develops in much the same way as had Forster's account of the men, beginning with the implication that they are inferior to some pastoral ideal, but concluding with admiration for them as signs of progress. Initially he observes that 'The General figure of the women' is 'too masculine to pretend to beauty', but he goes on to argue that they are treated 'with regard & tenderness' and 'enjoy equal Priviledges of honour & respect with the men', and concludes, on this basis, that 'these people are far remov'd from a savage state'.[46] Anderson thought that the domestic life of the Tongans was that which 'the most sensible part of mankind always desire', and that 'a true picture of all the women of Tonga' could be found in Solomon's' beautifull character . . . of an industrious women'. He notes that women he took to be married, as well as some single women, were not willing to trade sexual favours with the Europeans, and were indeed 'not pregnable on any terms'.[47]

Anderson also, however, writes of the sexual manners of the Tongans in terms which clearly exemplify the problematic status of the discourse on progressive civilisation seen as appropriate to the assessment of Tongan culture. He explains that marriage does not appear to be 'rigidly binding' among the Tongans, but that this 'seems . . . of less consequence' because

free intercourse between the sexes among the younger sort is not at all reckoned criminal but rather encouraged . . . In short both men and women seem to have little knowledge of what we call delicacy in Amours; they rather seem to think it unnatural to suppress an appetite originally implanted in them perhaps for the same purposes as hunger or thirst, and consequently make it often a topic of public conversation, or what is more indecent in our judgement, have been seen to cool the ardours of their mutual inclinations before the eyes of many spectators.[48]

The surgeon's language here is intriguingly doubled. On the one hand, his references to natural appetite enable him to withhold moral condemnation, and he writes with apparent admiration that: 'This extensive and gentle empire which Love has planted amongst them is so far from loosening that it cements the bands of Society. The sexes seem to live in the most perfect harmony.'[49] This strain of argument works to fold the notion of the 'free intercourse of the sexes' into the embrace of the discourse on progressive civilisation, which gives priority to the role of women in cementing the 'bands of Society'. Tongan sexuality might seem to be a part of the attitude to women that makes their domestic arrangements ideal. But on the other hand, the language of delicacy and decency emphasises that this behaviour is also a violation of those notions of domesticity most central to British commercial culture in this period. An incident related by Cook provides a dramatic example of the unease generated by the incompatibility of narratives on civilised progress and sexual delicacy.

On his visit to the northern islands of Tonga in 1774, Cook relates that an old lady offered him a girl, who asks him for preliminary payment. He explains that he has nothing to give, thinking 'by that means, to come off with flying colours; but I was mistaken; for they gave me to understand I might retire with her on credit'. When Cook refuses the offer, the old woman argues and abuses him: 'sneering in my face, saying, what sort of a man are you, thus to refuse the embraces of so fine a young woman? For the girl certainly did not want beauty; which, however, I could better withstand, than

the abuses of this worthy matron, and therefore hastened into the boat.'[50]
They try to follow him, but Cook explains that 'I had come to a Resolution not to suffer a Woman to come aboard the Ship on any pretence what
ever and had given strict orders . . . to that purpose.'[51] Cook introduces
this anecdote in his published account with the surprising remark that he
was sorry not to have seen the older woman before he left the island, 'as I
wanted to make her a present, in return for the part she had taken in all
our transactions, private as well as public.'[52] On one hand, Cook implicitly
acknowledges, in his gratitude, that the woman's capacity to regulate transactions may be taken as a sign of progressive civilisation. But on the other,
his evident alarm indicates that the incident is an affront to his sense of
propriety, and that he views the incident in the context of European notions
of bourgeois politeness rather than Tongan civilised progress. He relates
the incident with some humour – the notion that he can 'better withstand'
the girl's beauty than the upbraiding of the 'worthy matron' sounds like a
joke at the expense of older women, or even of himself. But the suggestion
that he must retreat to the pure masculine space of his ship to hide from
the importunities of women indicates the extent to which desire frustrates
knowledge even when it is denied. Cook will not enter into trade here, he
refuses the possibility of exchange because he seems to believe that it would
compromise his authority to do otherwise, and yet in his anxious retreat
he may indicate why that 'tolerable understanding' he desired is denied
him. For the Tongans seem to exceed the discursive categories available for
their representation and comprehension by the Europeans, and to oblige the
Europeans either to trade on the terms they establish or to retreat to their
ships.

The voyagers' accounts of Tongan society, I have suggested, involve at
least three different discursive strands, different narratives of progress from
barbarism through the stages of relative civilisation. To the people of the
Society Islands is attributed the most advanced polity, in contrast to the
Tongans, because they are believed to be 'capable of that noble and disinterested desire to work for the common weal as much as lies in their power,
which we call *public spirit* or *true patriotism*'.[53] But Tongan society shows
a greater capacity for 'improvement'. The Europeans find it difficult to distinguish their own position as civilised observers from that which seems
appropriate to the Tongans, because the language of progress through cultivation, industry, and invention seems appropriate to both their own and the
islanders' culture. The difficulty seems most alarming in situations which
demonstrate the Tongans' aptitude for trade, because here it is the Europeans who seem enthralled and feminised by excessive and impassioned

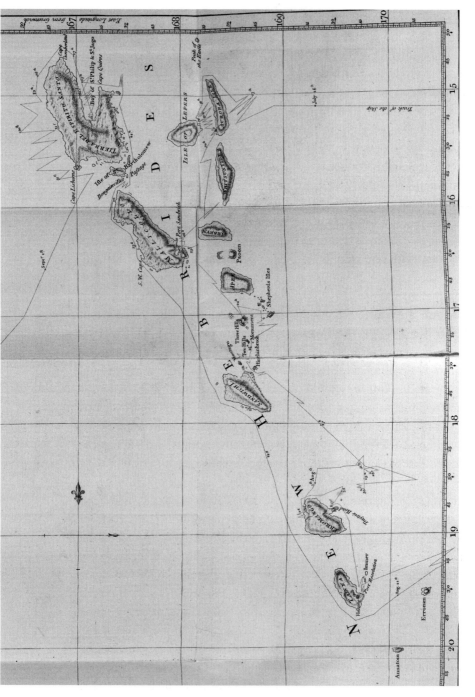

Figure 4.8 Detail from James Cook, *Chart of Discoveries Made in the South Pacific Ocean*, in Cook, *Voyage* (1777), II, pl. III

desire. The Europeans resort to the moral values of bourgeois domesticity to confirm the position of manly and knowledgeable superiority which their dependence on Tongan trading skills had threatened. But the terms of trade involved in sexual and commercial transactions are of course not so different. European responses to the sexual mores of the islanders tend to expose the voyagers' own sense of shame or embarrassment, or, in the case of Cook, to indicate again an exchange in which he feels inadequate or disadvantaged; where he feels he can only regain the upper hand by displaying some European largesse, and handing over a present. It is the continual sense of the Europeans' uncertainty, their sense of real or potential disadvantage as they attempt to assess what they encounter with the discursive tools available to them, that makes a cryptic puzzle of Tongan culture.

VII

Cook arrived in Vanuatu – the group of islands he named the New Hebrides – in mid-July 1774, and Hodges produced three paintings depicting the European voyagers landing at islands identified as Mallicollo [Malakula], Erromanga [Erromango], and Tanna (plates 4.3, 4.4, 4.5; see fig. 4.8). In the first of these, the *Landing at Mallicollo* (c. 1776), Joppien and Smith note that he 'adopted the transitional mode of history painting, the "mitigated realism" popularized by Benjamin West'.[54] The image provides a useful starting point for thinking about how the Europeans might have sought, or failed, to integrate ni-Vanuatu (the people of the islands) into their own 'schemes of historiography'. These three landing scenes, and the *Landing at Middleburgh* [Eua], which belongs to the same generic sequence, are unique among Hodges's paintings for the voyage in representing Europeans and islanders in the same image, occupying the same plane. Cook's ships, or other signs of the Europeans' presence, appear in several images where islanders are also represented, but only in these four landings are the bodies of islanders and Europeans juxtaposed. The West school of history painting to which Joppien and Smith allude is most characteristically about battles or confrontations, and in these scenes the tension on which the narrative turns focuses on the physical differences and similiarities of the two parties. In the *Landing at Mallicollo*, as in the other two landing scenes set in Vanuatu, the Europeans are clearly differentiated from the islanders by the shore line, and by the opposition between the near-nakedness of islanders and the clothing of the voyagers. But where the landings at Tanna and Erromango are marked by conflict, this painting represents a moment of uneasy reciprocity.

The open-handed gesture of the officer (perhaps Cook) in the centre of the scene, who has stepped from the boat towards the land, is repeated in the welcoming gesture of the tall islander who has also stepped forward, off the beach, and the greenery in the islander's upraised hand is mirrored as well as contrasted in the gun the officer has passed to his shipmate. The rather gracefully extended arm of the other prominent islander, to the left of the image, is echoed in the position of the officer standing in the back of the boat. In Basire's engraving for Cook's published account of the voyage perhaps more clearly than in Hodges's painting, the expressions of the islanders and mariners share both apprehension and interest.

When Hodges's second painting of this series, showing the *Landing at Erramanga*, was exhibited at the Royal Academy in 1778, the *Morning Post*'s reviewer commented critically that 'The Europeans and the savages are not discriminated in their complexion, Indians and Englishmen being described exactly of a similar colour',[55] and this observation – in the *Morning Post* it is a complaint – may be just as appropriate to the *Landing at Mallicollo*. Hodges's figures tend to be rather lumpily defined, and here the islanders and Europeans do share similarities of complexion, shape, and stature. This is remarkable because, as Joppien and Smith observe, 'Hodges's dignified presentation of the Malekulans is quite at variance with the published account',[56] where Cook notoriously wrote of this 'ape-like nation' as 'the most ugly, ill-proportioned people I ever saw . . . a very dark-coloured and rather diminutive race'.[57] Cook stressed that the amicability of the encounter on the beach was prompted by his own initiative, rather than the islanders', writing that 'seeing me advance alone, with nothing but a green branch in my hand, one of them, who seemed to be a chief, giving his bow and arrow to another, met me also in the water, bearing also a green branch'.[58] Cook was impressed by what he took to be the islanders' honesty, during the *Resolution*'s short stay, but he also implies that their lack of interest in European artifacts is a sign of their dullness, or lack of curiosity.[59] At Tanna, where Cook made a longer stay between the 6th and 20th of August 1774, he comments with I think similar implications on the indifference of the islanders to European technology. He writes that he showed 'all parts of the Ship' to a young man he 'prevailed on' to board, but 'I did not observe that any thing fixed his attention a moment or caused in him the least surprise.'[60] He observed that the old man he made his principal ally, when taken aboard the ship, 'looked on everything that was shewn him with the utmost indifference', and, noting that the man was reported to have left 'most of the articles I had given him hanging on . . . bushes' near his house, he commented that 'probably they were in his eyes of so little Value as not to be worth house room'.[61] He speculated that the reason ni-Vanuatu did not supply the ship with the stocks of food he needed 'might be our having nothing to give them in exchange, which they thought valuable'.[62] The lack of interest shown by ni-Vanuatu, which looks to later studies like confirmation of the outsider status of the voyagers, who may initially have been regarded as ghosts, perhaps of returning ancestors, is for Cook of a piece with his estimation of their 'rude state' of civilisation.[63]

Hodges's representation of the *Landing at Mallicollo* as an occasion of mixed apprehension and reciprocity is more strongly supported by the observations of George Forster, who explicitly praised Hodges's image.[64] Forster gives a detailed narrative of the wary but welcoming reception offered by the Malakulans, and emphasises their interest in European goods, noting that on their first visit to the ship 'Whatever they saw, they coveted; but they never repined at a refusal.' Like Cook, he comments on their 'ugly features, and their black colour', but though he remarks the Europeans were 'often provoked . . . to make ill-natured comparisons between them and monkies', he suggests that this has as much to do with what he regarded as the entertaining sight of them 'talking vociferously, but at the same time in such a good-humoured manner' as with their physical appearance. His most marked divergence from Cook's accounts is his assertion that 'They were the most intelligent people we had ever met with in the South Seas.'[65]

As Bronwen Douglas has argued in most detail, Forster's qualifications to the comparison between the Malakulans and monkeys were probably prompted by his desire to repudiate Lord Mondboddo's theory that orang-utans were degenerated humans who had lost the power of speech.[66] In that context it is significant that Forster's estimation of the Malakulans' intelligence is firmly linked to their language skills. He writes that

they were not only assiduous in teaching [us their language], but had curiosity enough to learn our language, which they pronounced with such accuracy, that we had reason to admire their extensive faculties and quick apprehension . . . We presently taught them our numerals, which they repeated rapidly on their fingers; in short, what they wanted in personal attraction, was amply made up in acuteness of understanding.[67]

In Tanna also, Forster remarks that the islanders' 'conversation sometimes afforded us an opportunity to admire their sagacity',[68] and though he finds their 'facility of pronunciation' less remarkable than that of the Malakulans, when he wishes to provide evidence of their 'good-humour, sprightliness, and acuteness', he uses an incident displaying linguistic 'ingenuity'.[69] Forster, like Cook, estimates that the people of Vanuatu have achieved a relatively lowly degree of civilisation, but his positive assessment of their intelligence places them on a trajectory he understands as positive and progressive. He concludes his account of Malakula with the reflection that because the islanders are 'people of quick perception; their senses acute, and their intellects very open to improvement . . . they only want the impulse of an ambitious individual to bring them into a higher state of civilization'.[70]

At Tanna, Forster emphasises the importance of music, observing that here it is 'superior to the music of all the nations in the tropical part of the South Seas, which we had hitherto heard. It ran through a much more considerable compass of notes, than is employed at Taheitee, or even at Tonga-Tabboo; and had a serious turn which distinguished it very remarkably from the softer effeminate music of those islands.'[71] Music was important to enlightenment theories of social progress. Adam Smith, for example, notes in an essay of 1777 that 'The sentiments and passions which Music can best imitate are those which unite and bind men together in society; the social, the decent, the virtuous, the interesting and affecting, the amiable and agreeable, the awful and respectable, the noble, elevating, and commanding passions.'[72] In apparent allusion to a similar theory, Forster claimed in his concluding remarks on Tanna that 'a predilection for harmonious sounds implies great sensibility, and must prepare the way for civilization'.[73]

Cook's and Forster's accounts of Vanuatu have much in common. Both read off their perceptions of ni-Vanuatu as lacking central social or political organisation against a historicised scale of progressive civilisation which identifies social dispersal into small family-based units as an early stage, and both comment on the treatment of women they observe in the islands as a definitive sign of savagery.[74] For both, the position of Vanuatu marks it as a kind of end point or limit – Forster notes that Cook named the islands the New Hebrides because they were the 'westernmost hitherto known in the South Pacific Ocean'.[75] With his survey of these islands, Cook thought he had in effect completed what Beaglehole calls his 'second sweep' of the tropical islands of the South Pacific. Where Quiros at the turn of the sixteenth century had imagined he glimpsed a continent, and where Bougainville had distinguished six islands, Cook had succeeded in dissolving the vision of any substantial landfall into an archipelago of multiple islands and intricate waterways – an achievement perhaps similar in kind to, though less dramatic than, his excursions into the ice floes south of 40 degrees, which left 'not the least room for the Possibility of their being a continent' in that region.[76] There is of course something rather disconcerting about a voyage intended to confirm an absence, about the progressive evaporation of even the fantasy of a landmass articulating and consolidating relations between the island groups glimpsed by successive European mariners. Perhaps that leaves its mark on the way the journalists of Cook's voyages articulate relations between islands, making it more difficult for them to assume, as did Henry Home, Lord Kames, that a 'great variety' of national differences in their 'original character' could be found among Oceanic 'islanders at a distance from the continent and from each other'.[77] Cook and the Forsters were clearly aware that the origins of these islanders differed from those of people they had encountered further east, and the Forsters, as Nicholas Thomas has argued, were keenly interested in theorising their difference in accordance with a range of cultural and climatic models.[78] But their discussions, as Forster's account of the music of Tanna shows, insistently compared these islanders with those they had already encountered, and reflected on the voyagers' position in relation to them.

VIII

Margaret Jolly has observed, however, that there is 'a space between the more settled adjudications of Cook and the more uncertain relativism' of George Forster's account in his *Voyage round the World*.[79] I suggest that this difference may best be understood in the context of competing historiographic narratives. The people of Vanuatu treated the European voyagers much more firmly as outsiders than did more eastern islanders. For most of their stay, for example, the Tannese were reluctant to allow them access to the island beyond the beach, and would handle things given to them by mariners only after wrapping them in leaves. Cook wrote that 'many were afraid to touch what belonged to us; and they seemed to have no notion of exchanging one thing for another', but the astronomer William Wales hesitated over whether this might 'proceed from their contempt, or rather dread of touching anything we had', and George Forster thought the practice had 'some appearance of owing its origin to a religious notion'.[80] Cook assesses this behaviour as evidence of their pre-commercial state, and perceives their apparent desire to restrict access to the island in similar terms, appropriating to himself in contrast the ability to enter into their subject position and exchange it with his own. He writes that

we found these people hospitable, civil, and good-natured, when not prompted to a contrary conduct by jealousy; a conduct I cannot tell how to blame them for, especially when I consider the light in which they must view us. It was impossible for them to know our real design; we enter their ports without their daring to oppose; we endeavour to land in their country as friends, and it is well if this succeeds; we land, nevertheless, and maintain the footing we have got, by the superiority of our fire-arms. Under such circumstances, what opinion are they to form of us? Is it not as reasonable for them to think we come to invade their country, as to pay them a friendly visit?[81]

In this tolerant or sympathetic vein, Cook can be recognised as the heroic explorer Bernard Smith has compellingly represented as the agent and ambassador of commercial culture. J. G. A. Pocock suggests that 'defined as the constant interchange of goods, words, ideas and emotions, commerce presents both the world perceived and the mind perceiving as transactional, so that the knower apprehends both the world and himself as they pass from one set of hands to another'.[82] Cook positions himself as the knowledgeable observer, capable through sympathetic transaction of projecting himself into the mind, the point of view, of the islanders with an imaginative facility that is denied to them.

Cook's comments on the indifference of the islanders are also about their reluctance to trade in the things he needs, to offer either adequate supplies to restock the ship or labour to speed its preparations. He observes on Tanna that

These people . . . are, like all the tropical race, active and nimble; and seem to excel in the use of arms, but not to be fond of labour. They never would put a hand to assist in any work we were carrying on, which the people of the other islands used to delight in. But what I judge most from, is their making the females do the most laborious work, as if they were pack-horses.[83]

His impatience here seems to be less about their progress in civilisation, though the comment on women's work alludes to that, than about the progress of work on the ship, the progress of his voyage. George Forster in contrast represents Tanna as though it were a georgic idyll of freely given labour. Strolling alone and unimpeded towards the end of his stay, he discerns a landscape of 'extensive plantations':

Here I frequently saw the natives employed in cutting down trees, or pruning them, or digging up the ground with a branch of a tree, instead of a spade, or planting yams, and other roots; and in one place, I heard a man singing at his work . . . The prospect which I beheld was so pleasing, that it did not fall much short of the beautiful scenes of Taheitee. It had this advantage besides, that all the country about me to a great distance, consisted of gentle elevations, and spacious vallies, all of which were capable of culture; whereas at Taheitee the mountains rose immediately craggy, wild and majestic from the plain, which has nowhere the breadth of two miles.[84]

The cultivated beauty of Tanna displaces the mixed beauty and sublimity of Tahiti, and this is in keeping with the scheme of relations between easterly and westerly islands apparent elsewhere in the writings of both Forsters. In summary, this scheme means that while they find the Society Islanders in the east most civilised in their polity, they also regard them as people who 'delight in an indolent life', whose 'superior degree of opulence' has produced 'many luxurious individuals . . . whose moral character appears somewhat depraved'.[85] The Tongans, further west, appear to have a polity more vitiated by 'servile submission' than that of the Tahitians, but George Forster also notes that they are much more active and industrious, which 'accounts for the regularity of their plantations, and the accurate division of property', as well as arts, such as music, cultivated by them to 'much greater perfection than [by] the Tahitians'.[86] The Tannese, inhabiting the most westerly islands, seem to possess little that Forster can recognise as political organisation, but they are more musical, and at least in this contemplative scene they reap the rewards of virtuous labour: 'The numerous smokes which ascended from every grove on the hill, revived the pleasing impressions of domestic life; nay my thoughts naturally turned upon friendship and national felicity, when I beheld large fields of plantanes all around me, which, loaded with golden clusters of fruit, seemed justly chosen emblems of peace and affluence.' The final touch to this scene, the 'cheerful voice of the labouring husbandman', confirms the sense in which the landscape is appropriated to a European or perhaps more specifically an English georgic ideal, reminiscent of the poetry of James Thomson and John Dyer.

Forster's beautiful cultivated landscape is of course precisely the scene in which fantasies of benevolent paternalism can be enacted. It is a landscape perceived to offer itself to his appropriation, where plantations 'permit the eye to take in a great extent of country'; where beauties 'deck the globe for the gratification' of the knowledgeable observer. Forster sets this up as a landscape destined for at least aesthetic colonisation, a landscape already moulded to European notions of history as progressive improvement, as is indicated when he lapses into reminiscences of how 'we sat down in their domestic circles with that harmony which befits the members of one great family' – reminiscences that confirm the Europeans' position as the 'benefactors of a numerous race' as a result of 'the pre-eminence of our civilized society'.[87]

Forster's high-point of pleasure in the Tannese landscape and satisfaction with European civilisation is succeeded immediately by his appalled account of the incident in which an islander was shot dead by a sentry, in what Forster saw as a wanton act of the 'greatest cruelty'. As Thomas and Berghof point out in their splendid edition of Forster's *Voyage*, his 'remarkable aestheticization' of the landscape 'is rhetorically amplified to prepare us for the brutal disappointment that follows'. Forster writes that this 'one dark and detestable act effaced all the hopes with which I had flattered myself', because it belies his notion that the pre-eminence of European civilisation is based in philanthropic benevolence.[88] Johann Forster commented that 'Acts of violence have been allways the beginning of settling & establishing the power of Europeans among new discovered Nations; & if we justly detest the cruelty of the Spaniards in America, we must not give a handle to other Nations to tax our conduct in the same manner.' He suggests the Spanish practised 'cruelty & inhumanity' because they inhabited a 'less refined' pre-modern age, and were Catholics, but that humanity should be expected of enlightened Protestants.[89] The Forsters understand the sentry's action, and the shore officer's support for him, as signs of a retrograde imperialism from which they emphatically distance themselves.

For the Forsters, then, the islanders are assessed in the context of a historicised narrative of progress through industry and cultivation. While they are perceived to lack the coherent social and political organisation necessary to civilisation, they can also be understood to enjoy a condition of patriarchal simplicity which encourages the arts of music and language and is amenable to improvement through paternalist and Protestant intervention. George Forster concludes his discussion of the music of Tanna with the reflection that 'If we have before observed the principle of revenge to have been active among the natives . . . we must allow at the same time, that benevolence, and a love of the fellow-creature, are not entirely banished from their hearts.' Though the islanders were initially suspicious of the Europeans, because their frequent experiences of hostility had taught them to distrust strangers, the behaviour of the voyagers, he suggests, naturally elicits benevolence towards them. He comments provocatively that 'They did not trade with us, because their affluence is not yet equal to that of the Taheitians; but hospitality does not consist in exchanging an article of which you have more than a sufficiency, for another of which you stand greatly in need.'[90] The Forster's faith in philanthropic paternalism is of course a faith in what are understood to be the beneficial effects of commercial modernity, but these do not appear to depend on engaging the islanders in commercial exchange. Cook, on the other hand, perceives the islanders in terms of a discourse which values progress achieved through affective and material exchange, a discourse which casts them as indifferent, insular, static.

The differences between Cook's commercial discourse and what might be thought of as the Forster's Christian paternalism are not of course as simple, as uniform, as this rather schematic account might suggest. The accounts of both Forsters are complicated by the transverse trajectories of their theories of migration and cultural diffusion and of geological variety. There is also a distinct sense, in the Forsters' encounters with western islanders, that they engage in a kind of sympathetic alliance with islanders because of the increasing animosity that characterises their relations with many of their fellow mariners, both officers and crew, whom they frequently stigmatise at least metaphorically as racially other. The historicising discourses that shape the voyage narratives of the ships' officers and the Forsters, and inform Hodges's work, are mixed, complex, sometimes discontinuous and fractured, and they indicate how the process of attempting to integrate the tropical Pacific through hierarchies of rank that shored up European confidence in their own pre-eminent civilisation and modernity was contested and complicated by encounters that exposed the contradictory limits of their historiography.

5 | New Zealand colonial romance

I

Writing from the North Island of New Zealand, about the Hauraki gulf and Waihou river, Joseph Banks commented in March 1770 that it 'is indeed in every respect the properest place we have yet seen for establishing a Colony' (fig. 5.1). He explained that up the river which James Cook had chosen to identify as 'The River Thames', a large ship could 'be moord [sic] to the trees as safe as alongside a wharf in London river'; and added that he deduced from local vegetation that winters were 'extreemly mild', and summers 'scarce at all hotter, tho more equably Warm' than those of England. Banks's enthusiasm is barely checked by the observation that the river banks will afford 'a safe and sure retreat in case of an attack from the natives'.[1] The perception that the Maori might not welcome colonisation is more than compensated for by the generosity with which the landscape offers refuge from them. Cook too, in these early days, thought that the fertility of the soil invited settlers, and noted that the New Zealanders were too factious to mount much effective resistance.[2]

Later journalists echo Banks's account of the physical (as opposed to cultural) hospitality of New Zealand, endorsing the notion that its climate and general appearance are familiar and welcoming to northern Europeans. John Rickman's *Journal of Captain Cook's Last Voyage* (1781), for example, commented on the arrival of Cook's ships at Queen Charlotte Sound (Totara-nui) in Cook Strait (Raukawa-Moana) that 'Not a man on board . . . did not now think himself at home, so much like Great-Britain is the Island of New Zealand.'[3] These perceptions of affinity were strongly underlined by proprietorial acts of naming, most unmistakably in that identification of the Waihou with the Thames, so frequently figured as the source and culmination of Britain's naval and imperial power. By the time of Cook's third voyage, the possibility of colonising New Zealand had become, to him at least, remote.[4] But New Zealand never the less remains a significant site of imaginative settlement – a place where fantasies about colonial power shape the actions and accounts of the European voyagers.

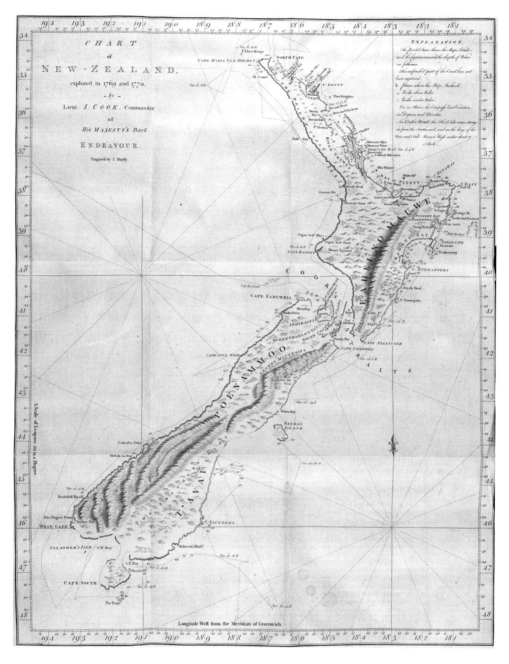

Figure 5.1 James Cook, *Chart of New Zealand, Explored in 1769 and 1770*, in Cook, *Voyage* (1773), II: 283

Those fantasies provide the theme and context for the colonial romance narrated in the journal of the last voyage attributed to John Rickman, who had served as lieutenant on both the ships that made up the expedition. Rickman's publisher, Elizabeth Newbery, must have rushed to compile the anonymous and unauthorised account, which appeared well before any official publication. The journal is, as the *Gentleman's Magazine* noted in its favourable review, 'enlivened by a love-adventure between a youth of the Discovery and a Zealander girl'; a romance that is not recounted in any other published or unpublished journal of the voyage, which lends it an uncertain status in comparison with the multiple narrations of most other episodes. We may feel able to treat parts of it more readily as fiction, drawing on fantasies about colonial power cloaked in notions of the erotic appeal of racial difference, and indebted (perhaps indirectly) to sources such as the *Aeneid*, or the tale of Inkle and Yarico. But the tale is also a valuable source of information; it relates, as the *Gentleman's Magazine* observed, 'particulars of the former massacre at Grass Cove, and also of the natural temper of the natives, and their domestic policy'.[5] Its ambiguous status does not detract from its value as a coherent and perceptive narration, but may lend greater prominence to its narrative strategies, the tricks in the telling of the tale.

In this chapter, I will compare the tale with other discussions of New Zealand, and more specifically of Queen Charlotte Sound, from Cook's second and third voyages, and juxtapose theories on civilisation and progress deriving from the Scottish enlightenment, which directly or implicitly informed the way journalists understood cultural differences, with more recent speculative accounts of Maori cultures in the period of the Cook voyages. I also look at representations of Dusky Bay (Tamatea), in the far south, from Cook's second voyage, in order to consider the different kinds of colonial vision thought appropriate to that area and to the North Island and Cook Strait. Rickman's account of the 'love-adventure' represents it (however real it may have been for the couple in history) as recognisably a version of the fantasy of equal and undivided sentimental exchange that cultures which think of themselves as more refined, more luxurious, project as their lost object of desire, and in which Mary Louise Pratt, following Peter Hulme, sees 'the mystique of reciprocity', the colonist's ideal exchange. Pratt explains that in colonial romances, 'the lovers challenge colonial hierarchies, [but] in the end they acquiesce to them . . . the European is reabsorbed by Europe, and the non-European dies an early death'.[6] Rickman's anecdote is, broadly speaking, of this kind, but along the way it speaks of the particular problems of British colonial ambition in New Zealand in ways that illuminate the potential colonists' conceptions of their imperial role.

II

Rickman writes of the young couple that

A conformity in manners and dress become significant signs between lovers. Though he appeared amiable in her eyes in the dress of a stranger, yet he wished to render himself still more so, by ornamenting his person after the fashion of her country; accordingly he submitted to be tattowed from head to foot.

In the case of the girl, 'Ghowannahe' (Ko Anahe?), the narrator claims that 'traits of her country might be traced in her locks', and in order to render this 'less offensive', Anahe is 'furnished with combs, and taught by her lover how to use them'. This is probably not about straightening her hair, which her lover would subsequently 'by the hour amuse himself with forming . . . into ringlets'(60): accounts of the New Zealanders took vehement exception to the prevalence of head lice. The youth, on the other hand, is supplemented and reinscribed, ending up 'tattowed all over', and his efforts are so thorough that 'the copy was not easily to be distinguished from the original'(70).[7] This romantic exchange is followed by the youth's attempt to desert ship. He explains that seeing the flourishing plants and livestock left by Cook's ships, and 'charmed with the beauty of the country, and the fertility of the soil', he imagines that 'he could be happy in introducing the arts of European culture into so fine a country, and in laying the foundation of civil government among its inhabitants'(74). He imagines himself as an enlightened and benevolent educationalist, whose plans will nurture, on the ground of the perceived physical resemblance between New Zealand and Britain, a growing and fruitful cultural convergence. But the narrator adds the more conventionally imperialist explanation that the youth 'was dreaming of nothing but kingdoms and diadems . . . and of being the first founder of a mighty empire' (72). Neither of these versions acknowledges the strikingly different account of relations between the voyagers and islanders which Anahe gives the sailor, as she recounts to him the circumstances in which ten men from Cook's second circumnavigation had been cooked and eaten at Grass Cove a few years earlier.

The sailor's absence is discovered as the ships are leaving, and marines are sent to recover him and his goods. Cook intends to try him as a deserter, but on hearing the boy's story, 'his resentment was converted into laughter at the wild extravagance of his romantic plan'. The sailor receives a dozen lashes. Rickman adds that Anahe's 'distress . . . is scarce to be conceived', and is demonstrated in self-bleeding, following the custom of her people (75).

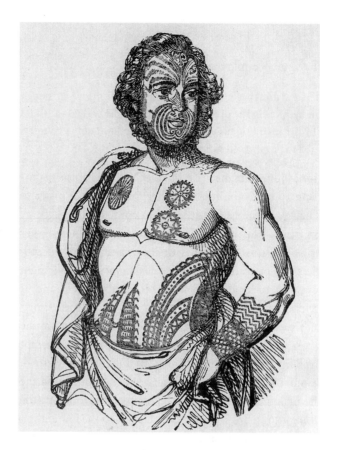

Figure 5.2 John Rutherford, from an original drawing taken in
1828, frontispiece to James Drummond, ed., *John Rutherford the
White Chief: A Story of Adventure in New Zealand* (Christchurch:
Whitcombe and Tombs Ltd, n.d.)

The 'myth of reciprocity' that structures the romance blurs the distinction
between the young European and what most of the voyagers agreed was
'the most barbarous and vindictive race of Men on the face of the Globe'.[8]
The tattooing of the sailor is central to this process, because it enables him
to conform to the desires of Anahe and pass for a Maori warrior. Some
white men were tattooed while in New Zealand during the nineteenth
century. In his study of *Moko; or Maori Tattooing* (1896), Major-General
H. G. Robley was able to devote a chapter to the various Europeans who had
been 'Mokoed', the most famous of whom was John Rutherford, whose
face was marked with the characteristic deep and convoluted incisions
during his stay among Maori people between 1816 and 1826 (fig. 5.2).
Early accounts such as Rutherford's indicate, however, that the process of

tattooing was dangerous, painful, and usually protracted. The surgeon John Savage, whose *Account of New Zealand* was first published in 1807, wrote of the operation that 'as the pain is considerable, a portion only of the intended figure can be depicted at one time; as the inflammation abates they continue their work, but it is not without a great degree of suffering that they arrive at the honour of a complete tattooing'. Samuel Marsden, the missionary, who visited New Zealand frequently between 1814 and 1837, confirmed that 'it always required several months, and sometimes several years, to tattoo a chief', whose inscriptions, he observed, would have been exceptionally extensive.[9] The men of Cook's third voyage, however, were able to go on shore only during the period of less than two weeks that the ships spent in Queen Charlotte Sound. It is, I suppose, possible that the sailor's tattoos did not include the 'deeply excavated spiral lines', carved into the face with a small chisel, that were common to most areas of New Zealand, but involved a 'relic style' patterning marked on the face with a tattooing comb, which might involve less protracted suffering.[10] But it is unlikely that the sailor could have been tattooed from head to toe during his brief stay. The tattooing is perhaps no more than a metaphor, a sign for the imaginary exoticisation of the youth, or for his transformation into a 'social personality' more acceptable to the New Zealanders than to his shipmates.[11] Even though the tattoos may lack physical and historical reality, they indicate in the narrative that the processes of cross cultural conversion involve a personal transfiguration that costs considerably more pain and effort than are suggested by the neatly complementary relation the voyagers perceived between the landscapes of Britain and its antipodean other.

For the sailors of Cook's ships, tattoos such as those I discussed in Chapter 3 were a marker of exotic experience, signs of how their voyaging had set them apart and given them a shared and exotic identity. But their tattoos seem usually to have been partial, in what Alfred Gell described as the 'disparaged' style – 'isolated motifs . . . imprinted here and there on the body in an arbitrary manner'.[12] The youth's tattoos, which are represented as clothing him from top to toe as if in a new skin, a new identity, transfigure him more thoroughly and more violently than could this nautical custom of collecting esoteric trophies on the surface of the body. Sailors' tattoos may demarcate groups who have been to particular places or shared particular experiences, or whose loyalties set them apart in some way, as we have seen, but finally their effect is to confirm that those they mark are sailors, cosmopolitan travellers, whereas the youth's tattoos expropriate him from the British ships and their companies, and localise him. Once the youth is tattooed and dressed 'in the habit of a New

Zealander' he is able to disappear into a group of Maori men and leave the ship undetected.

Peter Gathercole suggests that Maori *moko* may have been 'a symbolic representation of the ideal social personality' – a personality which was 'conventionally acceptable' within Maori culture.[13] The sailor's redefinition through tattooing indicates that he has exchanged the shared experiences of the fo'c'sle for those of a community that is yet more securely integrated, and still more remote from the centre of imperial power. His new skin signals his rejection of European attachment and of his identity as a transient voyager, and his rebirth in a form more appropriate to his new life as a 'Pakeha Maori.'[14] This new life demands more than partial loyalty, more than an isolated insignia imprinted on some part of his body, for it consumes him whole, and redefines him 'from head to foot' (60). The sailor and the narrative in which he is caught up represents a copy, a transcript of notions of Maori culture into the discourses available to the voyagers; of Maori inscriptions on to a European body of assumptions and ideas. The discrepancies between this representation of the New Zealanders and some of the other accounts produced as a result of the Cook voyages are important, I suggest, because of what they may tell a historian of Maori culture, but also because of what they indicate about British perceptions of the potential for colonial relations in New Zealand.

III

Rickman's tale juxtaposes the sailor's tattooing with an account of Anahe's self-bleeding, which Gell suggested was a parallel activity in Maori culture, and this bodily marking brings into focus what Europeans perceived as most recognisable and most disturbing in Maori culture.[15] In Rickman's story, the pain and violence of tattooing is erased, perhaps displaced into the violence with which the 'poor prisoner' is 'dragged to punishment' by the marines, who 'paid no regard to the copious tears, the cries, and lamentations of the poor deserted girl . . . who could hardly be torn from him' (72–3). But even the violence of this scene is moderated, its drama muted by bathetic practicality, as the youth and the marines have to return to collect the stores and tools, compass and fowling piece, which he had squirrelled away for his future use. The focus for the violence diffused throughout the narrative is the grief of the girl, whose sorrow is familiar – the narrator can appreciate the charge of the resonant sentimental topos of parting from the beloved person and place – and disturbingly strange, as the girl lacerates herself:

The distress of Ghowannahe is scarce to be conceived. She was left a woeful spectacle, to lament her fate. She expressed her grief, by the punctures she made in her face, arms, and wherever despair prompted her to direct the bloody instrument. It is wished, for her sake, that those savage people, whose bodies are exposed to the severities of the seasons, are not so susceptible of pain as those of a finer texture; otherwise her personal feelings must have been exquisite, independent of those of her mind. (75)

She marks her body with clear signs that she has been 'torn from' the attachment that defined her, and the signs of her suffering elicit from the narrator an unusual degree of sympathy, of imaginative projection.[16]

For the theorists of the Scottish enlightenment, and perhaps most notably for Adam Smith, the display of feeling is a sign of relative progress in civility. In his *Theory of Moral Sentiments*, Smith argued that 'natural sentiment' was common to all humans, but was modified by the situation and 'manners of different nations'. He illustrated this modification by contrasting civilised with 'rude and barbarous nations'. In the first he claimed that 'the passions of men are not commonly so furious or so desperate', but are more often 'clamorous and noisy' because they seek the spectator's sympathetic attention. In the second, passions mount 'to the highest pitch of fury', but 'are never permitted to disturb the serenity of [the] countenance or the composure of [the] conduct and behaviour'. He explained that the savage or barbarian makes no display of feeling because he 'expects no sympathy from those about him', whereas humanity is the characteristic of 'polished people, who have more sensibility to the passions of others, [and] can more readily enter into an animated and passionate behaviour'.[17]

Considered in the context of Smith's discussion of humanity, the girl's display might indicate (to European eyes) her comparatively civilised expectation of sympathy, her participation in the humanity shown by those who feel for her. Her representation as a romance heroine could also suggest a confusingly refined capacity for feeling – for forms of romantic love or sexual desire which are similar to humanity in Smith's account. John Millar, in his *The Origin of the Distinction of Ranks*, elaborated the theory that romantic love, like humanity in Smith's *Theory*, is generated by advances in civilisation. He observed that love is stimulated by obstacles to the gratification of desire – obstacles that, he argued, are not found among savages, but are produced by the inequalities of wealth that are the basis for the distinction of ranks in civilised societies. This theory led Millar to argue, in later editions of his book, that though the Tahitians enjoyed the leisure that might allow them to cultivate romantic love, they failed to do so because 'they appear to have no such differences of wealth as might restrain the free indulgence of their appetites, and by that means produce a degree of refinement in their passions'.[18] Most voyagers argued, however, that the Tahitians were considerably closer to civilisation than the New Zealanders, and in particular the Maori of Cook Strait, where the subservience of women was seen as a key indication of barbarity.[19]

When Cook's second expedition arrived at Queen Charlotte Sound in 1773, many of the voyagers were shocked by the change they saw in the treatment of the local women since their last visit with the *Endeavour*. George Forster noted, as I mentioned in Chapter 2, that the apparent collusion of some islanders and sailors in the sexual exploitation of the women was powerful evidence of the moral corruption which he believed to be only one of the detrimental effects of European imperial expansion. The incident in which some women were forcibly prostituted to mariners by their male relations seemed to him to confirm that the European presence, far from spreading civilisation, was reducing both Maori and sailors to a common level of brutality. It becomes clear, however, that Forster's moral abhorrence is strongly reinforced (at the least) by physical repugnance. He writes of the women that 'Their custom of painting their cheeks with ochre and oil, was alone sufficient to deter the more sensible from such intimate connections with them'. He refers to the smell of the oil they use, and (inevitably) to the lice, and concludes that, 'it is astonishing that persons could be found, who could gratify an animal appetite with such loathsome objects, whom a civilized education and national customs should have taught them to hold in abhorrence'.[20]

Forster's account is strongly marked by horrified fascination, which lumps together sailors and New Zealanders in an indiscriminate meld of offensive physicality and 'animal appetite'. He explicitly accepts the guilt entailed by his own part in 'our voyages of discovery', acknowledging that 'our intercourse has been wholly disadvantageous to the nations of the South Seas', and he suggests that it is only because the Europeans have 'created new wants' that the morals of the New Zealanders have been corrupted. But there is also an unmistakable implication here that had the women been less repulsive in his eyes he would have been less scrupulous, less exacting in his judgement of the behaviour of the sailors, and perhaps also of the local men. What distinguishes the display of civilised humanity and romantic love from the gratification of 'animal appetite', in Forster's account, is not only the sensibility which respects the reluctance of the women; it is also the fastidious taste which makes it impossible for him to imagine sympathetic exchange with them. In Rickman's anecdote the girl's display of passion for her loss reveals her as a tragic Dido, an exotic but sympathetic sentimental heroine. Her passion is part of an affective exchange which confirms that the narrator himself is polished and civilised in his humanity, his capacity readily to enter into the lovers' impassioned feelings. But the voyagers' experiences at Queen Charlotte Sound in 1773 suggest that affective exchanges between Maori and Europeans were no longer seen to be possible.

IV

For Adam Smith, and indeed for most enlightenment theorists, the character of the uncivilised subject is based on accounts of those they identified as 'savages in North America'.[21] Johann Forster argued, in his *Observations*, that in comparison with the North Americans the New Zealanders appeared 'one step higher in the class of rational beings' because they were more animated and passionate, which on the one hand results in 'a happy exertion of their physical and mental powers', and on the other 'breaks out into such enormities, as make the heart ache, and are humiliating to human nature'. It is significant that Forster here represents passions which advance or degrade human nature as continuous with one another rather than different in kind, for in this context, cannibalism becomes a mark of relative progress despite its humiliating implications.[22] The place in Rickman's romance narrative of the girl's exposition of the Grass Cove skirmish might be understood in the context of Forster's comments, which imply a theoretical connection between romance and anthropophagy as manifestations of a degree of passion that is incompatible with savage torpidity.

The girl is very reluctant to discuss what happened at Grass Cove; when the youth asks her if she attended the feast at which the men were eaten, 'she wept and looking wistfully at him, hung down her head' (62). But finally she tells the youth that the sailors were killed by a party of warriors from 'the hill country', led by 'a bad man' who was hostile to the voyagers because he had been punished and humiliated for taking things from the ship.[23] The bodies were subsequently divided, apparently for consumption, among the warriors and the crowd of 'women as well as men'. Once the sailor has 'by various questions in the course of several days, extorted this relation, of which, he said, he had no reason to doubt the truth, he forbore to ask her, what part her relations and herself bore in this tragedy, as there was reason to believe, they were all equally concerned' (64). The context for the girl's comments is important. She does not want to discuss the matter – it is not perhaps the most obvious use for the 'new language, consisting of words,

looks, gestures, and inarticulate tones' which the couple have developed
for 'imparting their passions'(61) – and it has to be 'extorted' from her by
'every winning way that love and curiosity suggested', and then by anger and
threats. His questions arise initially because he has been regaling her with
stories of the violence of his own people. She asks him about the women in
'the world from whence he came', and in response, perhaps in a fit of jovial
misogyny, he 'made her to understand, that the women in his world were
all *tatoo* (man-killers)' (61). Her account, in other words, is elicited from
her by a display (both in the young man's behaviour and in his anecdotes of
home) of British aggression which seems mirrored and perhaps mimicked
or parodied in what she tells him.

The narration of the cannibalistic episode is in some of the respects I
have mentioned reminiscent of what Gananath Obeyesekere identifies as 'a
British discourse about the practice of cannibalism'; a discourse initiated by
ethnological enquiry which, he suggests, reveals more about British preoc-
cupations and fantasies than about Maori practices. Obeyesekere argues that
this British discourse encouraged among the Maori 'a greater public participation, actual or vicarious, in dividing and eating the flesh of the powerful
aggressor'.[24] What interests me about Obeyesekere's argument is his emphasis on group feasting as an affirmation of collective identity for the Maori,
and as underscoring with horror and disgust the Europeans' sense of their
own difference. The girl's account of the Grass Cove incident confirms her
identification with her own family and people. Marshall Sahlins has argued
that in Maori culture of this period, time was understood as 'the recurrent
manifestation of the same experiences'. He suggests that this recurrence is
incompatible with modern Western notions of distinctions between individuals and between events, which it cuts across and collapses. He cites the
observation that 'It was a source of pure, unadulterated joy for the old time
Maori, to be able to say to an enemy, "I ate your father" or "your ancestor", although the occurrence may have occurred ten generations before his
time.'[25] The girl's reluctance to admit or deny that she participated in con-
suming the slain voyagers may indicate, as Sahlins's example suggests here,
that the idea of the feast confirms her involvement in the common cultural
identity of her people whether or not she was present.

The sailor extorts the girl's account from her by putting her in a double
bind: she does not want to tell him 'if she was at the feast' because she
worries that 'He would hate her.' But he meets her refusal with hostility:
'he turned from her, seemingly in anger, and threatened to leave her', and
then he assures her that if she will answer, he will 'love her more and more'.
He clearly suggests that silence will cost his affection, whereas speech will

increase it; and perhaps he does encourage her, with his stories of the women back home, to believe that they will after her confession share an ethos of violent consumption; that between them a new bond – like that engendered by group feasting – will be forged. He explains that her confession gives him confidence that her people will not kill and eat him – it is a confirmation of his social acceptance. The discussion of the Grass Cove feast, then, is not simply about confirming the New Zealanders' difference. Perhaps it is also about the way the youth's romantic ties, and his redefinition through tattooing, have made him a vicarious participant in the rite of the feast. In early nineteenth-century British ballads the combination of cannibalism and sexual activity is repeatedly invoked to confirm what is represented as the comically exotic character of South Pacific islanders. In journals and accounts of the Cook voyages, permeated with the discourses of Scottish enlightenment theories of civilisation, romance and anthropophagy are a more ambivalent combination, an index that oscillates between savagery and civility.[26]

George Forster was less dismayed than were his fellow voyagers by evidence of cannibal practices among the New Zealanders. He comments (with, I think, remarkable coolness in contrast to his fellow voyagers), that visual evidence

operated very strangely and differently on the beholders. Some there were who, in spite of the abhorrence which our education inspires against the eating of human flesh, did not seem greatly disinclined to feast with them … others were so unreasonably incensed against the perpetrators of this action, that they declared they could be well pleased to shoot them all; they were ready to become the most detestable butchers, in order to punish the imaginary crime of a people whom they had no right to condemn.[27]

Forster's comments on cannibalism echo his earlier remarks about the 'animal appetite' sailors show for Maori women, for in both cases he detects inclinations which education should have made abhorrent. In the case of cannibalism, Forster seems more dismayed by those who become 'unreasonably incensed', but here and in his response to sexual activity what seems to alarm Forster is precisely the evidence of common ground, of appetites shared by both Europeans and New Zealanders.

Initially the cannibal anecdote seems to dramatise the cultural differences between the lovers. It seems to indicate the redundancy of the forms of humanity, as sympathy, romantic love, or sexual desire, that had linked them. But the way the sailor extorts the narrative from the girl suggests that cannibalism, like tattooing and self-bleeding, may be a practice that both

distinguishes the Maori from the voyagers, and confirms a common humanity between them. In the context of the tale, romantic love and cannibalism
enjoy an uneasy symmetry, and though the conclusion, where the youth is
lashed and the girl slashed, seems to confirm (in Mary Louise Pratt's terms)
that this is a tale of European appropriation, the image of the completely
tattooed sailor, indistinguishable from the Maori men he copies, suggests
that this narrative is not simply about European appropriation of Maori
customs and things, about European fantasies of colonisation – but that it
may also indicate some of the anxieties and uneasiness about the fragility
of their own difference that made the British retreat from the possibility of
establishing colonial settlements in New Zealand.

V

Cook suggested that relationships between sailors and the New Zealand
women could only be appropriate in a colonial context. He noted during
the stay in Queen Charlotte Sound in 1777 that though the curiosities and
fish offered by the islanders 'always came to a good market' among the
sailors, the women who were also offered did not; and observed that

the Seaman had taken a kind of dislike to these people and were either unwilling or
affraid [sic] to associate with them; it had a good effect as I never knew a man quit
his station to go to their habitations. A connection with Women I allow because I
cannot prevent it, but never encourage tho many Men are of opinion it is one of the
greatest securities amongst Indians, and it may hold good when you intend to settle
amongst them; but with travelers and strangers, it is generally otherwise and more
men are betrayed than saved by having connection with their women, and how can
it be otherwise sence all their View are selfish without the least mixture of regard
or attatchment whatever; at least my observations which have been pretty general,
have not pointed out to me one instance to the contrary.[28]

Cook's comments rule out the possibility of the kind of relationship based
in sentimental exchange that is related in Rickman's journal. Either the
men from Cook's ships, or the Maori women, or both – Cook's grammar
is unclear – are in his judgement too deficient in sensibility to muster up
the 'least mixture of regard or attatchment'. It is interesting that for Cook
the impossibility of romance between sailors and island women is directly
linked to the absence of colonising ambition. He suggests that if colonialism
were the aim of his ships then relationships might offer security to his men,
and he implies that in those circumstances sentimental exchange might
flourish; it is because his men are 'travelers and strangers' that they are more

likely to be 'betrayed than saved'. Perhaps in Cook's terms the young sailor who hopes to be 'happy in introducing the arts of European culture into so fine a country, and in laying the foundation of civil government among its inhabitants' (74) is not a proto-colonialist at all, but a victim who, in his willingness to be 'tattowed all over' (70), acquiesces in the appropriation and consumption of European goods.

Certainly Cook's comments indicate his eagerness to disengage and distance himself and his men from the New Zealand people, in whom by 1777 he could detect no inclinations towards progress. He concludes, on this last visit to Queen Charlotte Sound, that its inhabitants are 'a people perfectly satisfied with the little knowlidge they are masters of without attempting in the least to improve it, nor are they remarkably curious either in their observations or enquires. New objects do not strike them with that surprise one expects nor do they fix their attention for a moment.'[29] His comments on the society of the New Zealanders in general resemble John Millar's account of the most primitive stages of savagery. Millar observed that 'tenderness or benevolence' resulting from sexual desire could hardly be expected from 'Nations who have so little regard to property as to live in the continual exercise of theft and rapine . . . who have the shocking barbarity to feed upon their fellow-creatures, a practice rarely to be found among the fiercest and most rapacious of the brute animals.' But even in these circumstances, Millar argued that 'human nature . . . contains the seeds of improvement'. Cook, however, explicitly denies to the New Zealanders what Millar identified as the 'disposition and capacity for improving his condition' common to man.[30] Cook's account suggests that Europeans have nothing in common with New Zealanders, and would have nothing to gain from establishing the basis of colonial relations with them.

George Forster's antipathy towards the women of Queen Charlotte Sound is also linked to his views on the potential for colonising New Zealand. Forster comments that the 'most convenient spot for an European settlement' is one where 'the country does not seem to be very populous, so that there would be little danger of quarrels with the natives'. His preference for a sparsely inhabited area for colonisation is linked explicitly to his anxiety about the inhumanity European settlers show to native people. He writes that

Perhaps in future ages, when the maritime powers of Europe lose their American colonies, they may think of making new establishments in more distant regions; and if it were ever possible for Europeans to have humanity enough to acknowledge the indigenous tribes of the South Seas as their brethren, we might have settlements which would not be defiled with the blood of innocent nations.[31]

Humanity consists in recognising and acknowledging common humanity – in perhaps the kind of sentimental response that had characterised the narrator's sympathy for the New Zealand girl in Rickman's tale – and here Forster suggests that this will be the basis for innocent colonial settlements. But Forster does not suggest that the appeal to humanity is straightforward. His reflections on the concern the New Zealanders show for news of Tupia (Tupaya), the Tahitian who had travelled with Cook to New Zealand in 1770 and later died, are illuminating. He speculates on whether

with the capacity which providence had allotted to him, and which had been cultivated no further than the simplicity of his education would permit, he was more adapted to raise the New Zeelanders to a state of civilization similar to that of his own islands, than ourselves, to whom the want of the intermediate links, which connect their narrow views to our extended sphere of knowledge, must prove an obstacle in such an undertaking.[32]

Forster's comments here suggest something like dismay at the lack of 'intermediate links', at the inability of the voyagers to 'raise the New Zeelanders'. But his reflections on European brutality, towards Maori women or in response to reports of cannibalism, indicate that what Forster perceived as common ground between New Zealanders and Europeans caused him grave concern. Forster values the enlightened extent of the European 'sphere of knowledge', and does not wish to see it punctured by the proximity of islanders whose 'narrow views' and practices resonate uncomfortably with the actions and opinions of the voyagers.

VI

Immediately before the visit to Queen Charlotte Sound in May 1773, the men of the *Resolution* had enjoyed a six-week sojourn at Dusky Bay, near the southernmost tip of the South Island (Tavai Poenamoo), recovering from an arduous voyage of four months across seas far south of Australia. John Marra, the gunner's mate, recorded that during the voyage the crew had been 'sometimes surrounded with islands of ice, out of which they could only extricate themselves by the utmost exertion of their skill in seamanship; sometimes involved in sheets of sleet and snow, and in mists so dark that a man on the forecastle could not be seen from the quarter-deck; sometimes the sea rolling mountains high'.[33] John Elliott, then a fourteen-year-old midshipman, recalled that they had endured 'frost and cold so *intense* as to cover the Rigging with Ice, like compleat christal ropes, from one End of her to the other, and even to stiffen our outer Coats on our backs, yet Capt. Cook would not allow any fire in the Gally, or anywhere else but at proper times in the day'.[34] After the hardships of the southern voyage, all the journals speak of the intense pleasure the men took in the fertile luxuriance of Dusky Bay, with its rich fishing stocks and abundance of bird life. George Forster, narrating the arrival of the *Resolution* in harbour in late March, immediately celebrated the quality of food available – 'the most delicious we had ever made in our lives' – and praised the landscape which 'conspired to complete our joy', adding more cautiously that 'so apt is mankind, after a long absence from land, to be prejudiced in favour of the wildest shore, that we looked upon the country at that time, as one of the most beautiful which nature unassisted by art could produce'.[35] Hodges's *View in Pickersgill Harbour* (plate 5.1) suggests the intense relief of the transition from Antarctic chill to comparative warmth in its luxuriant use of paint, its strong contrasts of light and warm darkness, and its use of glimmering streaks and spots of white. The figure of the sailor, with its relaxed slouch, perhaps almost bowed down by the weight of the fish he carries, is redolent of the sense of ease and plenty the Europeans experienced during their stay in Dusky Bay.

The pleasure the Europeans took in their weeks around Dusky Bay involved a very different kind of colonial enterprise and experience to that of Queen Charlotte Sound. In Hodges's painting the apparent leisure enjoyed by the sailor as he saunters back to the ship across the natural bridge provided by a fallen tree is counterbalanced by the activity suggested by the brightly illuminated geometric planes of the astronomers' tent, and the laundry hung to dry between the trees. For this was a scene of colonial industry, as George Forster explained:

The superiority of a state of civilization over that of barbarism could not be more clearly stated, than by the alterations and improvements we had made in this place. In the course of a few days, a small part of us had cleared away the woods from a surface of more than an acre, which fifty New Zealanders, with their tools of stone, could not have performed in three months. This spot, where immense numbers of plants left to themselves lived and decayed by turns, in one confused inanimate heap; this spot, we had converted into an active scene, where a hundred and twenty men pursued various branches of employment with unremitted ardour.

Forster celebrates the scene as evidence of the benevolent and enlightened nature of European expansion, which initiates through virtuous industry 'the rise of arts, and the dawn of science, in a country which had hitherto lain plunged in one long night of ignorance and barbarism!'[36]

This passage in Forster's account of the voyage is closely based on remarks in his father's journal, and both include lines from Virgil's *Aeneid*. Johann Forster frequently alludes to the *Aeneid*, which he clearly knew well, and regarded as an appropriate narrative context for his experiences. Here they cite lines in which the labour of the Tyrians in building the physical and legal framework of Carthage is compared to that of bees gathering honey for the hive. In Dryden's translation, the passage is introduced by the lines: 'The Prince, with Wonder, sees the stately Tow'rs, / Which late were Huts and Shepherd's homely Bow'rs.'[37] In the Forsters' accounts, similarly, the point is the rapidity and thoroughness of the transition. But in Dryden's translation, a part of the energetic work of the Tyrians concerns law and government: 'Some Laws ordain, and some attend the Choice / Of holy Senates, and elect by Voice.'[38] In the Forsters' vision, the place of these institutions is given to science, natural philosophy, and the 'polite arts' of painting and drawing.

Aeneas's view of the transformation of Carthage may have seemed a particularly apposite reference to the Forsters in several respects. In Virgil's epic, Aeneas, with the remnants of the Trojan fleet, seeks refuge on the Libyan coast after a dreadful storm, which has scattered and damaged the fleet. But Carthage is not where the Trojans intend to stop; it is a diversion, a temporary stay for repairs and recuperation on the destined route to Italy. The ships of Cook's second voyage, similarly, have lost track of one another at this point, and are desperately in need of temporary respite before travelling north. Perhaps the passage was also appropriate because its structure afforded no role for the Maori, but divided the action between Aeneas, whom Venus has shrouded in mists, and the industrious Tyrians – between the spectator and his fellow voyagers. George Forster, having briefly dismissed the putative labours of fifty New Zealanders, contrasts constructive European activity with plants, which 'left to themselves lived and decayed by turns, in one confused inanimate heap', as though the undisturbed confusion of the vegetation amply demonstrated the inactivity of the nomadic Maori, showing their failure to till the ground in the manner understood to be fundamental to European cultivation and civilisation.[39]

Cook thought that it was 'probable that there are Inhabitants in most of the Bays and harbours in the Southern parts of this Island', but he concluded that

they live a wandering life never remaining long in one spott, and if one can judge from appearances & circumstances few as they are they live not in perfect amity one family with another, for if they do why do they not form themselves into some society a thing not only natural to Man, but is even observed by the brute creation.[40]

Plate 0.1 William Hodges, *A View of the Monuments of Easter Island* [Rapanui], 1775, oil on panel, 775 × 1,219 mm.

Plate 0.2 William Hodges, *View of the Province of Oparee* [Pare], *Island of Otaheite, with part of the Island of Eimeo* [Moorea], [1775?], oil on panel, 762 × 1,232 mm

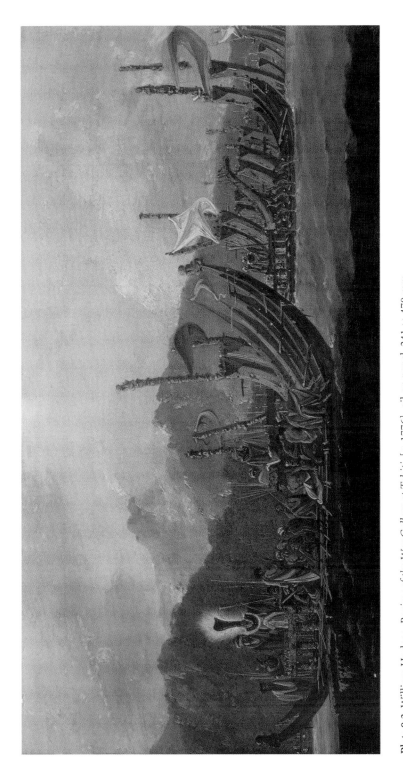

Plate 0.3 William Hodges, *Review of the War Galleys at Tahiti*, [c. 1776], oil on panel, 241 × 470 mm

Plate 0.4 William Hodges, *The War Boats of the Island of Otaheite* [Tahiti], *and the Society Isles, with a View of Part of the Harbour of Ohameneno* [Haamanino], *in the Island of Ulietea* [Raiatea], *One of the Society Islands*, 1777, oil on canvas, 1,811 × 2,743 mm

Plate 1.1 William Hodges, *A View Taken in the Bay of Otaheite Peha* [Vaitepiha], 1776, oil on canvas, 915 × 1,371 mm

Plate 1.2 William Hodges, *View of Matavai Bay in the Island of Otaheite*, 1776, oil on canvas, 915 × 1,371 mm

Plate 1.3 Detail from William Hodges, *A View Taken in the Bay of Otaheite Peha* [Vaitepiha], 1776, oil on canvas, 915 × 1,371 mm

Plate 2.1 William Hodges, [A] *View of Maitavie Bay, [in the Island of] Otaheite* [Tahiti], 1776, oil on canvas, 1,371 × 193 mm

Plate 2.2 William Hodges, *'Tahiti Revisited'* [the title 'A View taken [in] yᵉ Bay of Oaite peha OTAHEITE' is inscribed on the back of the original canvas], 1776, oil on canvas, 927 × 1,384 mm

Plate 2.3 William Hodges, [*View in Tahiti with Waterfall and Girls Bathing*], [1775], oil on panel, 301 × 457 mm

Plate 2.4 William Hodges, [*Waterfall in Tuauru*], [1775], oil on panel, 762 × 1,235 mm. Copyright 2007 The Kelton Foundation.

Plate 2.5 William Hodges, [*A Waterfall in Tahiti*], [1775], oil on panel, 489 × 616 mm

Plate 2.6 William Hodges, *Landscape, Ruins, and Figures*, 1790, oil on panel, 950 × 1,325 mm

Plate 3.1 Joshua Reynolds, *Portrait of Omai*, c. 1775–6, oil on canvas, 2,362 × 1,448 mm

Plate 3.2 William Parry, *Omai, Joseph Banks and Dr. Solander*, 1775–6, oil on canvas, 1,525 × 1,525 mm

Plate 3.3 Benjamin West, *Joseph Banks*, 1771–3, oil on canvas, 2,340 × 1,600 mm

Plate 3.4 William Hodges, *Old Maori Man with a Grey Beard*, May 1773, chalk, 542 × 379 mm

Plate 3.5 William Hodges, *Portrait of a Young Maori Man*, June 1773, red chalk, 542 × 375 mm

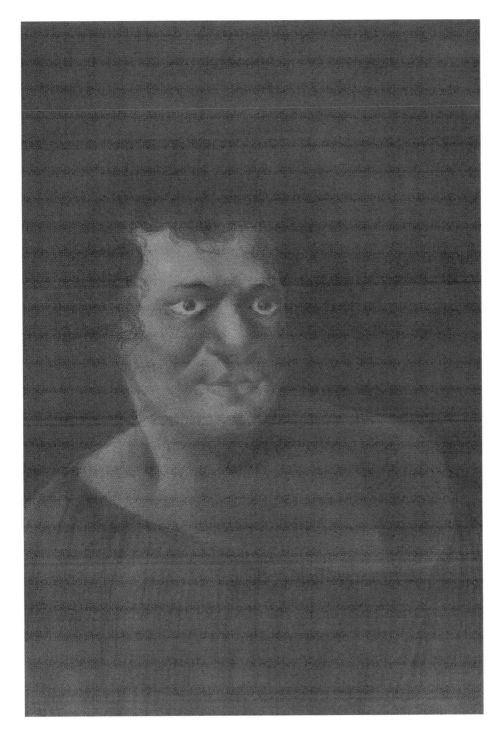

Plate 3.6 William Hodges, *Woman of* NEW ZELAND, [1773–5], red chalk,
544 × 374 mm

Plate 3.7 William Hodges, *Maori Man with Bushy Hair*, May 1773, red chalk, 544 × 375 mm

Plate 3.8 William Hodges, *Portrait of a Maori Chieftain*, October 1773, red chalk, 543 × 374 mm

Plate 4.1 William Hodges, *A View of Cape Stephens in Cook's Straits with Waterspout*, c. 1776, oil on canvas, 1,359 × 1,931 mm

Plate 4.2 William Hodges, *Tongatabu or Amsterdam*, [October 1773], watercolour, 375 × 545 mm

Plate 4.3 William Hodges, *The Landing at Mallicolo [Malakula], One of the New Hebrides*, [c. 1776], oil on panel, 241 × 457 mm

Plate 4.4 William Hodges, *The Landing at Erramanga One of the New Hebrides*, [c. 1776], oil on panel, 229 × 457 mm

Plate 4.5 William Hodges, *The Landing at Tanna One of the New Hebrides*, [c. 1775–6], oil on panel, 241 × 457 mm

Plate 5.1 William Hodges, *View in Pickersgill Harbour, Dusky Bay, New Zealand*, April 1773, oil on canvas, 654 × 731 mm

Plate 5.2 William Hodges, *Waterfall in Dusky Bay, April 1773*, 1775, oil on canvas, 1,359 × 1,930 mm

Plate 5.3 William Hodges, [*Waterfall in Dusky Bay with a Maori Canoe. II*], [c. 1776], oil on panel, 273 × 356 mm

Plate 5.4 William Hodges, [*A Maori Woman, Carrying a Child*], [April 1773], red chalk, 170 × 87 mm

Plate 5.5 William Hodges, [*A Maori Man Holding a Hatchet*], [April 1773], red chalk, 221 × 76 mm

Plate 5.6 William Hodges, *A View in Dusky Bay, New Zealand*, 1773, oil on circular wooden panel, 660 mm diam., 810 × 795 × 64 mm

Plate 6.1 Joshua Reynolds, *Head of Omai*, ?1775, 603 × 527 mm

Plate 6.2 William Hodges, *Omai*, between August 1775 and June 1776, oil on oval panel, 240 × 200 mm

Plate 6.3 John Webber, *Portrait of Captain James Cook*, 1776–80, oil on canvas, 1,095 × 695 mm

Plate 6.4 John Webber, *Portrait of Captain James Cook R. N.*, 1782, oil on canvas, 1,140 × 910 mm. National Portrait Gallery, Canberra. Purchased by the Commonwealth Government with the generous assistance of Robert Oatley and John Schaeffer 2000.

Plate 6.5 William Hodges, *Captain James Cook*, c. 1775, oil on canvas, 762 × 635 mm

Plate 6.6 Nathaniel Dance, *James Cook*, 1775–6, oil on canvas. 1,270 × 1,016 mm

Plate 6.7 John Hamilton Mortimer, [*Captain James Cook, Sir Joseph Banks, Lord Sandwich, Dr Daniel Solander and Dr John Hawkesworth*] ?1771, oil on canvas, 1,200 × 1,660 mm

Plate 7.1 Thomas Medland after William Hodges, *The Effects of Peace*, 1794, aquatint engraving, 760 × 510 mm

Plate 7.2 Thomas Medland after William Hodges, *The Consequences of War*, 1794, aquatint engraving, 760 × 510 mm

Plate 7.3 James Gillray, *Presentation of the Mahometan Credentials – or – The Final Resource of French Atheists*, London, published by H. Humphrey, 26 December 1793

Plate 7.4 [I. Cruikshank], *A Peep at the Plenipo – !!!*, London, published by S. W. Fores, 1 January 1794

Plate 7.5 Daniel Orme after Mather Brown, *The Attack on Famars*, London, 1796

Plate 7.6 Mather Brown, *Lord Howe on the Deck of the 'Queen Charlotte'*, 1794, oil on canvas, 2,591 × 3,658 mm

Plate 7.7 I. Cruikshank, *Lord Howe They Run, or the British Tars Giving the Carmignols a Dressing on Memorable 1st of June 1794*, London, published by S. W. Fores, 25 June 1794

Plate 7.8 Philippe-Jacques de Loutherbourg, *The Battle of the First of June, 1794*, 1795, oil on canvas, 2,665 × 3,735 mm

Plate 7.9 James Gillray, *The Genius of France Triumphant, or — BRITANNIA petitioning for PEACE, — Vide, The Proposals of Opposition,* London, published by H. Humphrey, 2 February 1795

Plate 7.10 I. Cruikshank, *French Happiness/English Misery*, published by S. W. Fores, January 1793

Plate 7.11 James Gillray, *Fatigues of the Campaign in Flanders*, London, published by H. Humphrey, 20 May 1793

He went to some lengths to cultivate amicable acquaintance with the few islanders he did encounter, but nevertheless it is clear that the voyagers regarded Maori with considerable apprehension, and were relieved that they were not present in large numbers. The pleasure the voyagers take in the environs of Dusky Bay is based in an aesthetic which subordinates evidence of people to picturesque natural landscape. Though Cook sees the social dispersal of the islanders as evidence of their ferocious disposition or unnatural asociality, their isolation in small groups, which the Europeans were always anxious to understand as family units, also made their presence unthreatening (plate 5.2).[41]

William Hodges was encouraged to make the most of the opportunities offered by Dusky Bay. The terse prose of Cook's journal is usually dedicated to practical matters and systematic reflections; considering the landscapes his companions found so impressive, he sees 'nothing but woods and barren cragy precipice's'. But he made a point of taking Hodges to the place he named Cascade Cove, and notes with approval that he 'took a drawing of it on Paper and afterwards painted it in oyle Colours which exhibits at one view a better description of it than I can give.'[42] George Forster, again following his father's notes closely, showed more confidence than Cook in his command of the language of picturesque description. He positions himself within the landscape in order to produce lyrical accounts of two carefully composed pictorial views, the first seen from 'the highest stone before the bason, and looking down into it', and the second framed with apparent artlessness when 'On turning round we beheld an extensive bay, strewed as it were with small islands, which are covered with lofty trees; beyond them on one side, the mountains rise majestic on the main land, capt with clouds and perpetual snow; and on the other, the immense ocean bounded our view.' But like Cook, he conceded the superiority of Hodges's efforts: 'The grandeur of this scene was such, that the powers of description fall short of the force and beauty of nature, which could only be truly imitated by the pencil of Mr. Hodges.' Forster concludes, 'We returned on board before sun-set, well pleased with our acquisitions during this excursion.' The Forsters had been gratified to find 'so beautiful' and 'so numerous' plants and birds during this expedition, and this account implies that aesthetic pleasure also figures as one of their profitable acquisitions (plate 5.3).[43]

Hodges's landscapes of Dusky Bay elicited such unqualified satisfaction, I suggest, because they thoroughly secure and confirm the voyagers' sense of the South Island as a picturesque site of extraordinary natural beauty. Recent scholarly attention has tended to focus on the representation of Maori in these paintings, and has considerably enriched our understanding of the Europeans' encounters with people in the vicinity of Dusky Bay. But it is significant that the Maori are almost always represented as diminutive figures, picturesque and exotic staffage, whose presence is subordinated to the grandeur of the landscape they inhabit. Joppien and Smith comment on the drawings of Maori which Hodges produced in preparation for more fully worked up landscapes that 'Hodges has broken through the schemata of ethnography and is now drawing the people of Dusky Bay as he might have done figures in a landscape back home in England, with a feeling for the individual posture and living presence of the person' (plates 5.4, 5.5).[44] Like the figures in English landscapes, the Maori in these paintings provide what Thomas Gainsborough called 'a little business for the Eye', a touch of exotic interest in landscapes primarily concerned to demonstrate the aesthetic sensibility of the European spectator.[45] The beauty of Hodges's landscapes appeals to what Addison had defined as a 'Polite Imagination', which gives the spectator 'a Kind of Property in everything he sees, and makes the most rude uncultivated Parts of Nature administer to his Pleasures'.[46]

The only New Zealand landscape in which the human figure occupies a prominent position is Hodges's roundel of *A View in Dusky Bay, New Zealand* (plate 5.6). The man here is dignified and impressive, but these are perhaps characteristics that can safely be attributed to him because of his absolute solitude. Like the labourers the poet William Cowper felt able to admire in his long poem *The Task* (1785), or the shepherds William Wordsworth represented as cloaked in misty nobility in *The Prelude* of 1805, this figure's dignity and stature depend on his isolation.[47] But in the majority of Hodges's views of Dusky Bay the Maori, where they are present, are so in order to supplement the natural beauty of the landscape.

Hodges produced small oil sketches of landscapes, which were often predominantly seascapes, at many of the islands he visited. But these images may have a special status, indicated by his decision to exhibit two small 'views of Dusky Bay' at the Royal Academy in 1776.[48] In their visual and written representations of this area, I suggest, Hodges and his companions celebrated picturesque landscape with exceptionally attentive fervour because, in close juxtaposition to their more challenging experiences in Queen Charlotte Sound and the North Island, they welcomed the opportunity they had created here to enjoy a relatively guiltless aesthetic colonialism. George Forster concludes his account of the clearing that is the scene of enlightened industry with the reflection that

this pleasing picture of improvement was not to last, and like a meteor, vanished as suddenly as it was formed. We re-imbarked all our instruments and utensils, and left no other vestiges of our residence, than a piece of ground, from whence we had cleared the wood. We sowed indeed a quantity of European garden seeds of the best kinds; but it is obvious that the shoots of the surrounding weeds will shortly stifle every salutary and useful plant, and that in a few years our abode no longer discernable, must return to its original chaotic state.[49]

These elegiac observations are not part of the passage from Johann Forster's journals which forms the basis for George Forster's rhapsody on improvement. The chagrin they express is mixed with relief, I suggest, because in retrospect George Forster had mixed feelings about the benefits of colonial intervention. Much as he might have liked to believe in the 'salutary and useful' consequences of temporary European residence on the South Island, he does not regard the results of their presence among the Maori of the North Island with equanimity. His vision of the original chaos to which the clearing will return is reminiscent of Cook's comments on the Maori's lack of social coherence, but here it is weeds that choke the garden of European enlightenment in a resurgence of indigenous vegetation. The consequences of interaction with the islanders are subsumed in the vision of a natural order which shows no vestigial trace of the transit of meteors or the attempted cultivation of garden seeds.

   The North Island had initially appeared to Europeans a site appropriate for colonisation because it seemed physically hospitable. Despite the presence of recalcitrant Maori, voyagers thought the landscape and climate had the potential to become a second home. Dusky Bay was not physically welcoming in the same way. George Forster observed that 'the forests had never been touched by human industry', which he suggested they actively resisted:

not only the climbing plants and shrubs obstructed our passage, but likewise numbers of rotten trees lay in our way, felled by winds and old age. A new generation of young trees, of parasitic plants, ferns, and mosses sprouted out of the rich mould to which this old timber was reduced by length of time, and a deceitful bark sometimes still covered the interior rotten substance, whereon if we attempted to step, we sunk in to the waist.[50]

What the far reaches of the South Island invited was a specular, imaginary colonisation, a picturesque appropriation which marginalised the problems of human encounter.

VII

George Forster's suggestion that the loss of the American colonies would have profound implications for the way the British thought about their presence in the South Seas was perceptive. As Bernard Smith has pointed out, Cook's posthumous reputation was shaped by the requirements of an 'ideological belief . . . in a world-wide empire dedicated to the arts of peace'; an empire in which tolerance, supported by technological progress in navigation and healthcare, would smooth the path for a Eurocentric market economy.[51] News of Cook's voyages, and later of his death, was widely reported in British papers, but the bulk of their news coverage after 1775 was inevitably dedicated to the progress of the war with the thirteen colonies. The celebration of Cook's achievements in developing what could be thought of as a new model for imperial expansion was inflected by the implications of that war, as well as by an increasingly vociferous opposition to British involvement in the slave trade, and growing unease about the British presence in India.

In 1775 a correspondent wrote to the *Morning Post* – which favoured a fairly uncompromising attitude to the thirteen colonies's demands – praising the Cook voyages for their disinterestedness: 'The voyages that have been made to the South Seas by order of his present Majesty, do incomparably more honour to his reign than any other transaction in it. The principles upon which they were planned, and the liberal manner in which they were executed, reflect infinite honour upon the monarch by whose command they were undertaken.' The correspondent went on to suggest that while it was laudable that the voyages should have been dedicated 'to the improvement of geography and oeconomy alone', those ends might be combined with something more immediately profitable. 'Why not colonize some of the new discovered islands in the South Seas?' he asks. The resources currently being used to support the army in America could then be used to 'establish a colony, which by degrees would grow into something of importance to the country, and make us amends for some of the losses we are suffering in America'.[52] George Forster was less sanguine than was the *Morning Post's* correspondent about the implications of colonisation, but his comments on the possibility of establishing settlements in New Zealand also imply the ease with which the South Pacific can be thought of as a reserve resource, a potential site for colonial expansion that might compensate for the loss of the American colonies.

A correspondent of the *Whitehall Evening-Post* writing in early 1780 expressed more direct reservations in the course of reflecting on Cook's claim to have discovered the Hawaiian Islands. The writer insisted that he did not intend his report of the discovery

to promote that bad principle which has pervaded all our European naval Powers, and has brought misery and destruction on one half of the globe, viz that a bare discovery gives a property in the land, and in the natives, as their cattle, to be killed or kept alive merely for the use, conveniency, pleasure, or pastime of the discoverers. It is to be hoped the occurrences of our own times will give the present Rulers of Europe, as well as us their Subjects, and our posterity, a surfeit of Colonization.[53]

The correspondent clearly regards dissociating the act of discovery from the processes of colonisation and annexation as a difficult but necessary feat, essential to the disentangling of Cook's voyages from the colonial policy perceived to have gone so disastrously wrong in America. The relations with islanders established by Cook's activities in the South Pacific attract careful scrutiny as models for a colonial policy that may help to salve Britain's conscience and restore British self-esteem, bruised by the American conflict.

Anna Seward's *Elegy on Captain Cook*, which was in print by the early summer of 1780,[54] distanced Cook's achievements from Britain's imperial role in east or west. She suggested that Cook was prompted to voyage to the South Pacific by his disgust for the luxurious fruits of empire corrupting London society. She asks:

Say first, what Pow'r inspir'd his dauntless breast
With scorn of danger, and inglorious rest,
To quit imperial London's gorgeous plains,
Where, rob'd in thousand tints, bright Pleasure reigns;
In cups of summer-ice her nectar pours,
And twines, mid wintry snows, her roseate bow'rs?

Seward suggests that the purgative for an imperial culture bloated with the wealth of India and America is the dedication and self-sacrifice of Cook. She concludes that his ambition is fired not by the commands of the Admiralty or the King, but by the spirit of humanity (or, in later editions, benevolence), which inspires him to reject the inglorious temptations of ill-gotten imperial gains. Seward's Cook braves 'The scorch'd Equator, and th'Antartic wave' in order to 'Unite the savage hearts and hostile hands, / In the firm compact of her gentle bands.'[55] Helen Maria Williams's elegy for Cook, *The Morai, An Ode* (1783), celebrates him as 'the Friend of human race', who has 'along the surges cast / Philanthropy's connecting zone, / And spread her loveliest blessings round.' Williams contrasts Cook's achievements with those from 'Britain's free enlighten'd land' who pursue the slave trade in Angola, and 'load with chains a brother's frame, / And plunge a dagger in the mind.' She represents Cook's virtues as a lesson to those who direct 'Ambition's lofty flame' to destructive ends.[56] For Seward and Williams, Cook is imagined to restore British self-respect because of his freedom from the vices of metropolitan corruption and imperial brutality.

In his series of conversation poems of 1781, William Cowper warned that increasing luxury and corruption would prove Britain's downfall. He represents British imperial policy in India as a particular source of concern, noting with horror that 'though suckl'd at fair freedom's breast' his countrymen 'Exported slavery to the conquer'd East.' He describes a process of reverse infection, warning the imagined nabob grown rich on the exploitation of the East that having 'Fed from the richest veins of the Mogul', he has imbibed corruption, and 'Asiatic vices stor'd thy mind.'[57] But Cowper identifies Cook as the representative of enlightened global expansion:

> Wherever he found man, to nature true,
> The rights of man were sacred in his view:
> He sooth'd with gifts and greeted with a smile
> The simple native of the new-found isle,
> He spurn'd the wretch that slighted or withstood
> The tender argument of kindred blood,
> Nor would endure that any should controul
> His free-born brethren of the southern pole.

Cook here is precisely Bernard Smith's agent of commercial expansion, who promotes 'the band of commerce . . . design'd / T'associate all the branches of mankind', and his benevolent role is contrasted with that of slave traders who pervert the nature of commerce through their 'loathsome traffic'.[58] Cowper's Cook positively resists the exploitation or control of Pacific people, defending what Kathleen Wilson has described as the 'once-glittering vision of a free and virtuous empire, founded in consent and nurtured in liberty and trade', which 'the American war tarnished'.[59]

For less distinguished poets writing in the years immediately following his death, Cook represents a vision of commercial empire that can be celebrated in its untarnished benevolence because it is associated with the spread of the benefits of science. The anonymous sea officer who composed *An Ode to the Memory of Captain James Cook* (1780) sees Cook as 'The SON of SCIENCE, free from Guile', whose achievements are motivated by the 'god-like Attribute . . . to KNOW'.[60] William Fitzgerald's *Ode* represents Cook as one of the few 'who sweep the scowling main, / Who explore deep ocean's bed, / Not impell'd by lust of gain, / But by love of science led.' The disinterestedness of Cook's mission seems to make it inevitable to Fitzgerald that, in time, '*Britannia* rules the southern isles, / And through their happy clime imparted science smiles.' In this glorious future, the 'Ills that flow from savage life' will be banished, and an era will dawn in which 'gentle sympathy' replaces sullenness, medicine treats disease, agriculture prevents food shortages and promotes population growth, Christian religion takes the place of superstition, 'freedom, giving equal laws' is bestowed in place of despotism, and, the culminating transformation, 'Blind sensual calls' are refined into love.[61] Later, *A Poem on a Voyage of Discovery* (1792) cites Cook's experience as the model for voyages which are 'the glorious works that Science loves, / That Commerce prompts, and Virtue's self approves'; voyages which 'sooth the fierceness of the savage mind', but also discover medicinal plants and advance geographical knowledge.[62]

Most of these tributes to Cook were based on their authors' knowledge of accounts of Cook's first and second circumnavigations. They were written before detailed accounts of the third voyage were available, and usually well in advance of the official narrative, published in 1784. It was the second voyage in particular, with its forays deep into the icy seas of the far south, that initiated Cook's reputation as a patriotic hero, for the first voyage had most frequently been associated with the name and achievements of Joseph Banks. The champion of humanity and commerce celebrated in these poems is most likely Cook as the narrator of the *Voyage towards the South Pole* (1777), and the science which guarantees the enlightened benevolence of his mission is primarily that of Banks and his fellow naturalists on the first voyage, and the Forsters on the second.

Cowper notes in July 1777 that he has copies of both Cook's and George Forster's accounts of the voyage of 1772–5, and observes with characteristic wryness that ''Tis well for the poor Natives of those distant Countries, that our National Expences cannot be supplied by Cargoes of Yams & Bananas. Curiosity therefore being once satisfied, they may possibly be permitted for the future to enjoy their Riches of that kind in Peace.'[63] Cowper returns to this theme with more bitterness when he writes of Mai, in *The Task* of 1785, commenting to the imagined islander that 'We found no bait / To tempt us in thy country. Doing good, / Disinterested good, is not our trade.' Commerce, and the idle 'curiosity . . . / Or else vainglory' that brought Mai to England, do not by 1785 seem to Cowper capable of disinterested or incidental benevolence.[64] But in his earlier letter he implies that the advantage of curiosity as a motive for travel is that once gratified, it is happy to move on.

To Cowper and to other poets writing in response to the news of Cook's death the narrative of Cook's second voyage seemed to offer a model for the possibility at least of colonial or commercial expansion based in the fantasy of equal and mutually beneficial exchange. The encounters between Maori and voyagers at Queen Charlotte Sound and in the North Island of New Zealand, across the three voyages, emphatically deny that possibility, and do so at the site Europeans initially regarded as most promising. These encounters seem to them to confirm their worst fears about the consequences of the spread of European commercial values. Gerald Fitzgerald summarises the most fatalistic version of these:

> whatever Advantages either the Spirit of Enterprize, or commercial and scientific Interests may derive from some Discoveries that have been made in that distant Hemisphere, it is much to be lamented, that the innocent Natives have been Sufferers by the Event: The imaginary Value annexed to European Toys and Manufactures, and the Ravages of a particular Disorder, have already injured their Morals and their Peace; even the Instruments of Iron, which so much facilitate the ordinary Operations of Industry, have been used as Weapons of Destruction, and perverted to the Purposes of Ambition and Revenge.[65]

The voyagers' experiences of Dusky Bay, however, provided some basis for the poets' praise of Cook. Here aesthetic pleasure and scientific profit seemed accessible without guilt, and only the vegetation seemed resistant – reassuring in its capacity to obliterate all sign of the European presence.

I

The arrival of Mai in London in mid-July 1774 provoked a considerable amount of interest, comment, and speculation on Cook's voyage to the Pacific. The *Westminster Magazine* for that month commented that the European voyagers:

have dived so deep into foreign parts, that they are absolutely Crusoes. But with all their penetration, I do not find that any good hath accrued to the Community. Numbers of our hardy subjects have died on the passage – many have been roasted and eaten by Cannibals – numbers have been drowned – and a great expence the nation hath been put to; and only to bring home a few seeds – some shells – stuffed fish – dried birds – voracious animals – pressed plants – and an Indian – in short, as many rare things as would set up a Necromancer or a Country Apothecary.

The journalist contrasts Cook's two circumnavigations with the expeditions of earlier 'Heroes', whose successes could be measured by the quantity of 'territories and islands . . . annexed' by their countries. Compared to the acquisitive feats of Columbus or Raleigh, he suggests, Cook's voyages have merely shopped for fashionable knick-knackery:

the present mode of exploring only appears to be an expedition to pick up shells and preserve butterflies for the Fair Sex. The Isles of Otaheite and New Zeland are not to be visited or inhabited, and therefore these jaunts to the southern latitudes are only to amuse the Court, and encrease our collections of trifles.

The trifles listed by the journalist are reminiscent of the exotic and enigmatic 'encyclopaedia of show-pieces' displayed on the walls of the quack doctor in the third engraving of Hogarth's *Marriage A-la-Mode* series (fig. 6.1), which a visitor to England in the 1770s thought were designed to afford some 'preliminary entertainment' to soften up the minds of patients in readiness for the meaningless 'jibber-jabber' of the French doctor, and which he regarded as 'a perfect general satire upon certain collectors of all the rubbish of Nature and Art'.

Figure 6.1 Bernard Baron with William Hogarth after Hogarth, *Marriage A-la-mode,*
III: *The Inspection* (London: Hogarth, April 1745), 385 × 465 mm

In the *Westminster Magazine* essay the commodity that most clearly indicates the meaninglessness and superfluous expense of British 'jaunts to the
southern latitudes' is the so-called Indian, Mai himself: 'all the world are
running to see this exotic Black. The King is to see him – the Queen is to see
him, and his velvet skin is to be touched by the Maids of Honour; and all this
is the wondrous production of a voyage of two years to the *South Seas!*' Here
the imaginary and tantalising body of the islander, whose exotic blackness
must be seen, and whose 'velvet skin' must be touched, is the measure of the
hollowness of the achievement of the voyages, the excess of an imperialism
that drains the wealth and wastes the manpower of the nation not to produce
any expansion of territory but merely in order to gratify the 'extravagant . . .
curiosity' of women and courtiers.[1] The satirist's contempt for collectors
and their curiosities focuses on the contrast between the expense of the
voyages, and the implied uselessness of Mai as an acquisition, to suggest
that the desire to see and touch the islander is a sign of the misplaced,
frivolous, or licentious ambitions of the court. Mai himself is drained of
any profit or use.

But the satirist's tirade against Mai as an unnecessary, a superfluous acquisition, may suggest, paradoxically, that he is rather more than a mere curiosity. It is intriguingly reminiscent of Adam Smith's discussion of objects of
desire in his account of 'the Effect of Utility upon the Sentiment of Approbation', in his *Theory of Moral Sentiments*. Smith explains the allure of superfluous acquisitions in an extended meditation on the appeal of gadgets:

How many people ruin themselves by laying out money on trinkets of frivolous
utility? What pleases these lovers of toys is not so much the utility, as the aptness
of the machines which are fitted to promote it. All their pockets are stuffed with
little conveniences. They contrive new pockets, unknown in the clothes of other
people, in order to carry a greater number. They walk about loaded with baubles . . .
some of which may sometimes be of some little use, but all of which might at all
times be very well spared, and of which the whole utility is certainly not worth the
fatigue of bearing the burden.

The collector admires the fitness or convenience of the object, the complexity
of its design, and accepts or even welcomes the inventiveness he has to
develop – the new pockets he has to contrive – in order to have the thing to
hand; but the possibility that the object might at some point come in handy
is at most an incidental or remote contingency. Both the function of the
gadget, and the repose it might help to secure, are endlessly deferred, but
they are also central to its present attraction, imbuing the ingenious design
of the object with an almost magical charm.

The gadgets Smith has in mind – he mentions 'the curiosity of a tooth-
pick, of an ear-picker, of a machine for cutting the nails' as well as the
perhaps more obvious hi-tech attractions of watches – do not conceal or
deny the labour that has gone into their production; indeed, the evidence of
skilled workmanship is part of their appeal. But they do veil the labour and
inconvenience entailed on their consumer behind the pleasing confirmation
of his preferential position, his relative proximity to the ideal repose that
is nature's deceptive reward. Smith writes that men 'have entirely changed
the whole face of the globe, have . . . made the trackless and barren ocean a
new fund of subsistence, and the great high road of communication to the
different nations of the earth'; and he argues that men have effected these
changes because nature deceives them into laborious pursuit of 'the idea of
a certain artificial and elegant repose which [they] may never arrive at' – a
repose that does not in itself offer any 'real satisfaction'.[2]

Mai is not an ingenious contrivance, and he no doubt understood his
sojourn in London in quite different terms – so, for example, he often spoke
of his 'desire to kill his enemy the King of Bolabola', and is reported to have

believed the trip would furnish him with 'men & guns in a Ship' to enable him to achieve this end.[3] But most of the accounts written about him show no sign of any interest in his point of view. To the satirist of the *Westminster Magazine* at least, he is the trinket of frivolous utility which indicates that the labour and contrivance invested in circumnavigating the globe have resulted only in trivial or fantastic gratifications; he is the representative of a part of the world that seems to offer no profit, no advantage to commerce or trade, and which the British do not intend to improve, colonise, or even plunder. In the issue of the *Westminster Magazine* for August 1774, only a month after the publication which had suggested that Mai was a suitable article to be included in the exotic stock of a country apothecary's 'needy shop', a fuller and more serious minded account of 'Authentic Particulars relating to O M I A H ' was published, offering what was to become a much more familiar but perhaps no more sympathetic account of him.

Omiah is so far from shewing . . . marks of simplicity and ignorance . . . that his deportment is genteel, and resembles so much that of the well-bred people here, as to make it appear very extraordinary to those who know how little a time it is since he left the South-Sea islands, where the manners, by no means savage, are yet so totally different from those of polished people in Europe.[4]

The persistence with which commentators dwell on the natural gentility of Mai is usually glossed as an allusion to the theme of the noble savage. But Smith's account of the value of objects of frivolous utility provides a means to unpack that familiar theme, for Smith, in contrast to the satirist of the *Westminster Magazine*, sees the inutility of gadgets as the indirect means to more worthwhile and complex ends; their ingenious contrivance demonstrates in synecdoche the allure of the complex economy of modern society. I want in this chapter to look again at some accounts of Mai in London and on his return to the South Pacific, to consider what they tell us about how that society thinks of itself, how it conceives of its own structuring heirarchies and differences, and their ability to accommodate the increasing demands of empire.

II

Smith argues that when we are 'charmed with the beauty of that accommodation which reigns in the palaces and oeconomy of the great', our imagination confounds the appearance with 'the system, the machine or oeconomy by means·of which it is produced'.[5] The accommodation, the fixtures and fittings of the stately edifice are in themselves 'contemptible and trifling'; but they charm because of the art and ingenuity that have produced them, and because they remind us of the aesthetically pleasing order of the economy which has made them the means of imaginary ease. Mai appears charming and indeed beautiful most immediately because he is exotic – because of the oceans that have been traversed to fetch him. Smith's argument suggests that polite London society takes pleasure in Mai because their imaginations confound him with skill and ingenuity necessary to Cook's voyages, and with the effortless increase of riches which the expansion of empire implies but does not always deliver; in praising his gentility, they displace on to Mai, who is in a sense the most immediate product of the second voyage,[6] their admiration for the extraordinary proficiency in navigation and naval healthcare that the voyage involved – they celebrate him because he is the sign of their culture's progress in technology, in manners, in civilisation, and because he seems to herald the success of imperial ambition.

One of the most familiar tropes, in accounts of meetings with Mai during his visit to England, is that which contrasts his natural civility with the barely equal or even inferior charms of a European man. Samuel Johnson, for example, claimed that he could not distinguish between the manners of Mai and Constantine Phipps, Lord Mulgrave, because 'there was so little of the savage in Omai'. Hester Thrale praised 'the savage's good breeding' at the expense of the 'impatient spirit' of Baretti (the critic and journalist), claiming that the European could be taken for the savage of the pair. Frances Burney compared Mai's manners favourably with those of Philip Stanhope, Lord Chesterfield's nephew, commenting that the islander 'appears in a *new world* like a man who had all his life studied *the Graces*, and attended with unremitting application and diligence to form his manners, and to render his appearance and behaviour *politely easy*, and thoroughly *well bred!*' Where Burney sees nature exceeding the polish of art, Johnson sees Mai's graces as the effect of the company he has kept, as a result of which 'all that [Mai] has acquired of our manners was genteel'; though Mai's gentility has a puzzling tendency to exceed that of the aristocratic examples he imitates.[7]

The sense in which these commentators perceive Mai's superabundant and perhaps superfluous social polish as evidence of their own cultural superiority and gentility may be confirmed by their reluctance to see Cook in the same terms. Neither Johnson nor Thrale met Cook, though it does not sound as if it would have been difficult to manage: Boswell dined and talked with Cook on several occasions, and visited him at Mile End, where he was staying. Burney did meet Cook when he called on her father in 1773. Her account of him is respectful, but suggests none of the pleasure she took in the society of Mai. She wrote that Cook was 'well-mannered and perfectly unpretending; but studiously wrapped up in his own purposes and pursuits; and apparently under a pressure of mental fatigue when called upon to speak, or stimulated to deliberate, upon any other'.[8] She seems more oppressed by the narrowness of Cook's conversational range than by Mai's, and more doubtful of his claim to politeness. Burney's curiosity about the South Pacific (except as the theatre for her brother's professional career) does not extend far. When she meets Mai again in 1775, a year after the encounter I have mentioned, she finds that 'He has learnt a great deal of English . . . and can with the assistance of signs and action, make himself tolerably well understood.' But despite this new fluency, she explains that: 'As we are totally unacquainted with his country, connections, and affairs, our conversation . . . consisted wholly in questions of what he had seen here.'[9] For these polite commentators, meeting Mai seems to be an experience that allows them quite thoroughly to conceal any interest they may have had in learning more about the South Pacific, or about the voyages there, or about Cook's skills as a navigator and hygienist. Where, for Burney at least, Cook himself seems too purposive, perhaps too functional, too professional and pragmatic, Mai suggests a more familiar and acceptable idea of the exotic.

The representation of Mai in these encounters seems to offer his audience no improvement or instruction, and indeed to present them with little that is unfamiliar – he seems to present them only with an improved version of aristocratic or cosmopolitan civility. The indirect and concealed implications his presence bears – the sense that he is evidence of the ambition and technical accomplishment of Cook's voyages – and the possibility that his presence may have a deferred function, in furthering British imperial expansion, are eclipsed by his more ornamental or frivolous utility; the confirmation his presence offers through comparison and contrast of the advanced state of British civilisation. Adam Ferguson, in his *Essay on the History of Civil Society* (1767), writes an account of the 'Corruption Incident to Polished Nations' which is strongly reminiscent of Smith's discussion of the charms of ingenious contrivances, and which illuminates the association of ornament and aristocracy that frequently occurs in discussions of Mai. But the displacement of ambition into trinkets of frivolous utility and fantasies of deferred ease which for Smith is the motor of civilised progress is for Ferguson the sign of incipient corruption, of distraction from the supreme ambition of serving the public good.

Ferguson argues that 'Nations are most exposed to corruption . . . when the mechanical arts, being greatly advanced, furnish numberless articles, to be applied in ornament to the person, in furniture, entertainment, or equipage; when such articles as the rich alone can procure are admired; and when consideration, precedence, and rank, are accordingly made to depend on fortune.' Ferguson claims that as nations advance in commercial civilisation, they are also progressively corrupted by the amoral instability of commercial notions of value. The worth or distinction which had been attached to moral characteristics such as 'the reputation of courage, courtly manners, and a certain elevation of mind', as well as to 'birth and titles' and 'superior fortune' becomes attached exclusively to the 'sumptuous retinue which money alone may procure'. He suggests that 'the idea of perfection' is transferred 'from the character to the equipage', to the frivolous trinkets in which the wealthy display their status. This corruption erodes all sense of relative value, and introduces a 'fatal dissolution of manners, under which men of every condition, although they are eager to acquire, or to display their wealth, have no remains of real ambition'.[10]

Ferguson's discussion of the corruptions attendant on commercial progress argues that the transfer of status on to equipage displaces moral value from people to their possessions, to the 'productions of a few mechanical arts', so that, he writes, 'excellence itself' becomes 'a mere pageant'. In Smith's argument, ornamental gadgets provide indirect evidence of the progress in complexity and sophistication of the social economy, but in Ferguson's account their pettiness indicates cultural impoverishment. Mai in London is the sign, the polished ornament of those with whom he associates, as I argued in Chapter 3. As many commentators pointed out with varying degrees of amusement or disapprobation, his associates seem to have been anxious to impress him principally with the polish and grandeur of English civilisation, rather than with any more improving information. The extent to which Mai was imagined to have been civilised by his stay in England, many commentators thought, was measured by his success in reflecting his associates' admiration for the trivial pageant of civilised excellence. The author of 'An heroic epistle from OMIAH to the QUEEN of OTAHEITE; being his REMARKS on the ENGLISH NATION', which was published in the *London Chronicle* for June 1775, has Mai respond to enquiries about 'how farther I my hours employ, / What learning gather, and what sports enjoy?' with an account of guided visits to 'plays, museums, conjurers, and shows'.[11] His English acquaintances often seem most interested, most gratified, by measuring his responses to the conjurers and shows, the spectacle of European civilisation – as Burney was. At Leicester, for example, what was claimed to be 'the greatest number of musicians hitherto assembled in England' performed Handel's *Jeptha*, with the Earl of Sandwich, first Lord of the Admiralty, on the kettle drums, all apparently in order to record Mai's 'wild amazement at what was going on'.[12] Sandwich had been at pains to impress Mai during his stay in England. He entertained Mai with a tour of the dockyard at Chatham, where Mai was taken on board *HMS Victory*, and the newspapers offered the gratifying report that 'his joy was amazing at seeing so large a ship'.[13] Mai also visited Sandwich's country house, Hinchingbrooke, in Huntingdonshire, where the islander was reported to have been 'entertained in the most magnificent manner, and where the neighbouring gentlemen vied with each other in varying his diversions, in order to raise his ideas of the splendor and gaiety of this country'.[14]

Where Mai is offered a voice, in the numerous satires spoken from his imagined subject position which reflect on similarities between British high society and a fantasy of Tahitian life, his comments are close to those of observers writing about him, and while it is unsurprising that no independent voice should emerge, it also indicates the ease with which his perceived exotic characteristics could be anglicised, could be masked or adequately expressed in the idea of his social rank – the rank attributed to him as a result of his association with high society. In Joshua Reynolds's oil sketch of the *Head of Omai* (plate 6.1) (probably painted in 1775) he has acquired at least a suggestion of the cavalier, and a sort of Van Dyck costume. Reynolds argued in his seventh Discourse, delivered at the Royal Academy in December 1776, that representations of 'fantastick dress' reminiscent of Van Dyck could make portraits appear to be 'better . . . than they really were', by which he seems to mean that their subjects appear more socially exalted. He suggests that this dress appeals to a prejudice in favour of the age of Van Dyck that is second nature to the educated viewer, and could lend the sitter something like the elevation above mundane circumstance that classical drapery effected in statuary.

Van Dyck costume does not, in Reynolds's account, have the timeless simplicity of classical drapery, however, and his account of it is a fantastic fashion, and his increasing preference for using it in portraits of children, point to the extent of its share in (what he calls) 'those whimsical capricious forms by which all other dresses are embarrassed'. In comparison with the portrait head of Mai which William Hodges painted for John Hunter, the surgeon and physiognomist, at around the same time (plate 6.2), the suggestion, in Reynolds's sketch, of Mai as a young cavalier becomes more prominent, thrown into relief by the contrast between the vigour of Hodges's painting, which suggests mobility and transient expression, and the decorative passivity of the face Reynolds portrays, with its fine features and more elegant locks. Reynolds's sketch seems to poise the islander between an ideal moment above time and change, and a curiously incongruous and anachronistic role in seventeenth-century European history.[15]

III

George Forster was disappointed by the cultural education Mai received among the English aristocracy, which he thought offered polish at the expense of improvement. He noted that from the outset of his stay, Mai was 'led to the most splendid entertainments of this great and luxurious metropolis, and presented at court amidst a brilliant circle of the first nobility'. The naturalist suggested that proximity to high life led Mai rapidly to absorb its habits: 'He naturally imitated that easy and elegant politeness which is so prevalent in all those places, and which is one of the ornaments of civilized society; he adopted the manners, the occupations, and amusements of his companions.'[16] David Samwell (surgeon on the third voyage) was also concerned. He wrote of Mai that 'he was a goodnatured sensible young fellow, of a careless Disposition, too inattentive to his own Interest', and he observed that though Mai initially seemed willing and able to learn useful lessons from his stay in England, his aristocratic guardians 'have made him more of the fine Gentlemen than anything else', and taught him 'nothing . . . but to play at cards, at which he is very expert'.[17] William Bligh (master of the *Resolution* on the third voyage) regretted that Mai had 'been led into Idleness and Dissipation as soon as he arrived in Europe',[18] and James King (then 2nd Lieutenant on the *Resolution*) commented that if, after his experiences, 'Omai remains unhappy it arises from his want of some useful Knowledge that might have made him respect'd among his Countrymen' – though he was inclined to blame Mai himself, rather than his London associates.[19] Forster was pessimistic about Mai's chances of improving his social status. He foresaw that Mai would quickly return 'to his first insignificance; whereas, had he been taught a trade, his knowledge would always have been real riches to him, and paved his road to honour and opulence among his countrymen'.[20] He lamented that Mai had gained neither useful knowledge nor skills, and concluded that the nature of his education was clearly indicated in the paraphernalia with which he was equipped when he left England in 1776, which was made up of 'an infinite variety of dresses, ornaments, and other trifles, which are daily invented in order to supply our artificial wants'.[21]

In 1789, Hester Thrale Piozzi received news of Mai's death, and heard reports of the part his possessions played in fighting between the islanders of Raiatea and Huahine. Writing to a friend, she recalled that 'poor Omai ... was no small favourite of mine', and added, more sardonically: 'Two Islands quarreling for the Possession of a German Organ and Puppet Show – Omai's best and most valuable Effects as I remember – would make an Excellent Subject for a mock Heroic Poem.'[22] Her sentimental recollection of Mai, whom she had entertained in London, rapidly hardens into disdain, as he and the islanders in general become infected with the littleness and triviality of the European toys she believes they value so highly. The possessions with which Mai returned to the South Pacific, most of which seem to have been chosen for him and not by him,[23] included the things Piozzi and Forster mention – a barrel organ, and a collection of miniature figures (of soldiers, animals, coaches, and so forth) which it was imagined he could use in his attempts to describe European life. In addition Mai was endowed with an assortment of fireworks; portraits of the King and Queen and, perhaps, of Cook; an illustrated bible; a jack-in-a-box; handkerchiefs printed with the map of England and Wales;[24] two drums, and a suit of armour. Joseph Banks presented him with an electrical machine. As if to confirm him in or at least remind him of European ways of life he was provided with cooking and eating utensils, iron tools, and a few bits of furniture, as well as with linen clothes for himself and for gifts – and he had other trading goods. He was also endowed with some livestock and poultry, and seeds for a garden. Before Cook's ships departed he also acquired a compass, globes, sea charts, and maps, as well as some guns, powder, and shot. When a site had been selected, the ships' carpenters built Mai a European-style house designed 'to contain his valuables, which would by no means have been secure in one of his own country'.[25]

The assortment of objects with which Mai was endowed on his return is freighted with the significances his English hosts had attributed to his visit. As Nigel Leask has pointed out, the collection of figures suggests that 'Mai's credit' as a narrator of European life 'is made to depend upon a miniaturized, feminized, and domesticated simulacrum of civility'.[26] My discussion suggests that Mai's dolls and trinkets may demonstrate how the progress of advanced civilisations is involved in frivolous utility and inconvenience. But Mai also acquired tools which he may have understood as more functional, such as the armaments and iron tools, as well as equipment associated with Cook's role as the emissary of imperial expansion. Anna Seward's *Elegy on Captain Cook*, for example, celebrated the navigator's attempts to encourage the cultivation of European crops and animals on the islands he visited as conclusive evidence of the disinterested humanity of his mission.[27] It was hoped that these goods would enrich the diet of the islanders, establish a resource for European ships, and, in some locations at least, provide a means of testing the feasibility of colonial settlement.

Mai's possessions, in their curious assortment of the functional or useful and the frivolous or ornamental, indicate the ambivalence with which English metropolitan society conceived of its own modernity. On one hand iron tools and ship's instruments, animals and crops look like the equipment of proto-colonial settlement. They seem to address the practical concerns of professional men such as Forster and Samwell, who understood technological advance as necessary to progressive civilisation, and perhaps they might also help to appease the ire of metropolitan critics of the luxury and inutility of the voyages. The 'editor' of the satirical poem, *Omiah's Farewell* (1776), to provide one more example of the currency of this complaint, remarked that 'OMIAH is now returning to his native isle, fraught by royal order with squibs, crackers, and a various assortment of fireworks, to show to the wild untutored Indian the great superiority of an enlightened Christian prince.'[28] The satirist points to what is clearly and repeatedly implied in accounts of Omai – the sense that the failure to return him improved with either some religious instruction or some useful knowledge both belittles him and reveals inadequacies in British culture; shortcomings that might hinder British imperial ambition. The seeds and animals to which Cook, as well as Anna Seward, attached so much importance might at least indicate an aspiration towards improvement, towards furthering the spread of European notions of cultivation. Forster, for example, emphasised the importance of the cattle and sheep, believing that their presence might 'hereafter be conducive, by many intermediate causes, to the improvement of [the islanders'] intellectual faculties'.[29]

That more practical and technological notion of progress, however, was not one that Mai's goods could do more than gesture towards. Cook's colonial gardens and Noah's ark-like collection of farm animals everywhere showed a worrying tendency to wither away and disappear. Mai himself, Cook thought, had no more than a fund of stories to his credit. In conversation with James Boswell, Cook commented wryly that he did not believe Mai's travels would improve his status, as he may have hoped: Cook 'said that for some time after Omai's return home he would be a man of great consequence, as having so many wonders to tell. That he would not foresee that when he had told all he had to tell, he would sink into his former state.' Cook concluded that he 'would take care to leave the coast before Omai had time to be dissatisfied at home'.[30] Mai's finery and toys, along with the manners which Forster saw as the 'ornaments of civilized society', perhaps took a more thorough possession of him. Forster noted, in terms reminiscent of Smith's argument, that Mai did receive a kind of aesthetic education:

He was not able to form a general comprehensive view of our whole civilized system, and to abstract from thence what appeared most strikingly useful and applicable to the improvement of his country. His senses were charmed by beauty, symmetry, harmony, and magnificence; they called aloud for gratification, and he was accustomed to obey their voice.

Mai appreciates the ornamental achievements of metropolitan civilisation, but Forster suggests that he responds to that spectacle appetitively, because 'His judgement was in its infant state' and did not equip him to form general or abstract ideas. His collection of possessions – Forster itemises 'a portable organ, an electrical machine, a coat of mail, and suit of armour' – appeal to his 'childish inclinations', his aesthetic appetite, but he is unable to deduce from them the sublime complexity of the social economy that has produced them.[31] In Smith's argument, of course, this failure of judgemental agency is all to the good; it is the beneficial imposition of nature, he argues, that leads the rich to pursue the 'gratification of their own vain and insatiable desires' for goods which, when viewed in an 'abstract and philosophical light' must 'always appear in the highest degree contemptible and trifling'.[32]

What is problematic about reading Mai's acquisitions in Smith's terms, however, may be the extent to which they do take possession of him, and make him the exemplar of anglicised civility, 'more of the fine Gentleman than anything else'; they make him, like Smith's deluded wealthy, the more or less unwitting agent of a Eurocentric conception of providential nature. On his return to the islands in the *Bounty*, Bligh heard that Mai's acquisitions had briefly increased his consequence, but that he had not 'gained any possessions or . . . higher rank than we left him in'.[33] Mai's things, however, retained their prestige longer than their owner. The missionary William Ellis reported nearly half a century later that: 'The spot where Mai's house stood is still called Beritani, or Britain, by the inhabitants of Huahine', and parts of Mai's armour were displayed on a house built on the spot. Ellis added that 'A few of the trinkets, such as a jack-in-a-box . . . were preserved with care by one of the principal chiefs, who . . . considered them great curiosities, and exhibited them, as a mark of his condescension, to particular favourites.'[34] Most accounts of Mai's return suggest that he was largely ignored or even unrecognised, until, as Cook noted, 'knowledge of his riches' had been spread, but his possessions seemed to have been imbued with lasting value as tokens of the exotic.[35] The suit of armour had been given to Mai by Sandwich, who had had it made for him by the artificers of the Tower of London.[36] Clothed in this final gesture of generosity, Mai seems briefly to be possessed by his things – to become British, like the spot where Ellis later saw the armour hanging. In 'Omiah: an ode' (published in 1784), a note explained that 'Omiah has been presented with a rich suit of armour, to enable him to conquer Otaheite. He is to hold it by charter from the Crown, and has promised to acknowledge the right of taxation, and the supremacy of the British parliament.'[37] The satirist represents Mai in his armour as the agent of British imperialism, capable of compensating Britain for the humiliations of the American war.

It is hard to see Mai, however, as the Smithian agent of commercial colonialism in the sense that Bernard Smith has argued is appropriate for Cook. Where Cook can be understood as the representative of a distinctively modern form of imperialism exercised through transaction and negotiation, Mai in his armour is a more ambiguous figure (fig. 6.2). For many British commentators, the American war offered salutary confirmation of the need for a newly modern version of imperialism, as we saw in Chapter 5. The Britishness Mai in his armour represents is as anachronistic as the Van Dyck dress that had both ennobled and infantilised him in Reynolds's sketch. In the unauthorised *Journal* of John Rickman, the only text in which Mai's return seems to make much of a splash, he is represented (in an anecdote that may well be apocryphal) in a parodic impersonation of British imperial identity. Rickman writes of the astonishment of the islanders when Cook and Mai ride out on horseback:

Omai, to excite their admiration the more, was dressed cap-a-pee in a suit of armour . . . and was mounted and caparisoned with his sword and pike, like St. George going to kill the dragon, whom he exactly represented; only that Omai had pistols in his holsters, of which the poor saint knew not the use. Omai, however, made good use of his arms, and when the crowd became clamorous, and troublesome, he every now and then pulled out a pistol and fired it among them, which never failed to send them scampering away.[38]

A central feature of Cook's characterisation as a distinctively modern hero was the notion of his humanity, manifested notably in his reputed reluctance to use firearms: 'Not a gun . . . was ever wantonly or unnecessarily fired *by his order*.'[39] If Mai was in some sense the emissary of British civilisation on his return to the South Pacific, freighted with tokens of the ingenuity and sophistication of its economy, he was not simply the agent of Smith's providential nature, which by its benevolent 'deception . . . rouses and keeps in continual motion the industry of mankind'.[40] Mai's anglicisation may confirm the global scope of British imperial ambition, but he also indicates

Figure 6.2 Royce after Dodd, *Omai's Public Entry on his First Landing at Otaheite*, print from [John Rickman], *Journal of Captain Cook's Last Voyage* (London, Newbery, 1781), opposite 136

the limitations on the cultural aspiration that desires to see admiration for the organising principles, the beauty and symmetry of the social economy, reflected from distant places. Rickman's anecdote suggests that Mai is burdened with implications of European civilisation as advanced in its taste for ornament but anachronistic in its predeliction for conquest – both forms of civilisation discordant with notions of Cook's role as the agent of commercial modernity.

Ferguson's account of the state of commercial culture in which excellence becomes 'a mere pageant' indicated the instability of the value of possessions and people in modern society. The volatility of the position of Pacific islanders taken aboard British ships is indicated in an incident reported in Prince Hoare's *Memoirs of Granville Sharpe* (1820) – an incident which must have taken place some years after Mai's return to the south seas. Hoare writes that 'a native of Otaheiti had been enticed, by the offer of presents . . . on board an English vessel, kidnapped, and brought to England. Being an expert swimmer and diver, his skill had been very profitably employed during the voyage, in the capture of seals.' When he arrived in England, the captain refused to pay him, and the merchants owning the ship told the Tahitian's representative that '"they would spend 500l. in repelling any application of the kind, rather than pay the Otaheitean a farthing"'. The use of Sharpe's name, however, obliges the merchants to accept arbitration, and in the end they have to allow the Tahitian 'the pay which had been solicited . . . which was that of an ordinary seaman'.[41] The merchants attempt to exploit the Tahitian sailor's exotic status to deny him the wages and rights of an English seaman. In a similar sense, perhaps Mai may seem emptied of value, a mere curiosity (of the kind disparaged by Ferguson) rather than a Smithian contrivance of frivolous utility, when he is considered in the context of a discourse on modernity that emphasises professional ambitions achieved through technological progress, or when accounts of Mai's gentility are juxtaposed with representations of Cook's achievements.

IV

There has of course been much discussion in the last decade or so about the extent to which Cook participates in the guilt of colonial exploitation, and I do not intend to revisit that debate here.[42] Instead I want briefly to consider the extent to which Cook, as, in Bernard Smith's words, 'a new kind of hero for a new time', is himself subject to evaluation within the terms of the commercial discourses that structured accounts of Mai in England.[43] When

James Boswell met Cook in London in 1776, he commented in the privacy of his journal that 'It was curious to see Cook, a grave steady man, and his wife, a decent plump Englishwoman, and think that he was preparing to sail round the world.' What is curious about Cook – and the mention of his wife reinforces this impression – is his domestic ordinariness, and the absence of any sign of the glamour or colour that was usually imagined to accrue to the traveller. Boswell thinks that Cook has an 'uncommon attention to veracity', and he produces an analogy for this virtue which emphasises that he sees in Cook the exactness – even the petty-mindedness – of a small shopkeeper. Boswell writes, with characteristic self-congratulation: 'My metaphor was that he [Cook] had a balance in his mind for truth as nice as the scales for weighing a guinea.' Boswell is of course enthralled by the idea of circumnavigation, and fascinated by what Cook can tell him about his experiences, but like Fanny Burney perhaps, his comments on meeting Cook suggest that he finds him disappointingly lacking in social polish or ornamental flair. Though Cook talks to him, and is, he writes, 'obliging and communicative', stimulating and feeding his interest in the voyages, he seems to lack the skills of polite conversation which were so important to the sociability of polite men and educated women in the metropolis.[44] Around the time of his death, Cook's wife was busy stitching him a waistcoat of tapa, bark-cloth from the South Pacific, to wear on his attendance at court, but the stiff white fabric would no doubt have contributed to the propriety of his dress uniform, and not lent him the exotic appeal of Mai, dressed in Manchester velvet and lace ruffles for his appearance in courtly society.[45]

After his death, Cook's very ordinariness, the notion that he is nothing more exceptional than a self-educated Yorkshireman, becomes enormously important to his eulogists. So, for example, Andrew Kippis's *Life of Cook* (1788) followed many earlier accounts in emphasising the professionalism of Cook's virtues – the sense that what he had was a double helping of the virtues every man keen to make his own way in the world should possess. In the opening paragraphs of his character of Cook, Kippis lists his genius, application, knowledge, perseverance, amiable virtues, and, finally, simplicity of manners. Cook's genius is not about the sorts of qualities of intuition or comprehensive grasp that the term usually implies in this period – it is something more practical, and, I think, less gentlemanly. Kippis begins his account of Cook's genius rather defensively:

It cannot, I think, be denied, that genius belonged to Captain Cook in an eminent degree. By genius I do not here understand imagination merely, or that power of culling the flowers of fancy which poetry delights in; but an inventive mind; a mind full of resources; and which, by its own native vigour, can suggest noble objects of pursuit, and the most effectual methods of attaining them.[46]

The opposition of Cook's skills to what seem more impractical and feminine forms of genius works to elevate practical qualities of resourcefulness and so forth which perhaps might not otherwise so readily be accepted as the hallmarks of genius.

Cook's dedication is demonstrated rather crudely in the fact that his private life largely escapes representation. He is always portrayed in his uniform. Kippis comments, in the Preface to Cook's life, that

The private incidents concerning him, though collected with the utmost diligence, can never compare, either in number or importance, with his public transactions. His public transactions are the things that mark the man, that display his mind and character; and, therefore, they are the grand objects to which the attention of his biographer must be directed.[47]

It is as though Cook hardly had a private life, hardly ever took off that uniform of office. John Webber's full-length portrait of Cook (now in the National Art Gallery in Wellington) is perhaps most reminiscent of the idea of Cook the practical and professional Yorkshireman (plate 6.3). He stands against a suitable background of waves and rocks, wearing his uniform and holding his hat and a telescope, as if to confirm his dedication to his profession; whereas in a three-quarter-length version of the portrait, now in Canberra, painted after Cook's death, his hand is unoccupied, and, with its long fingers and apparently careful manicure, rather elegant (plate 6.4). In 1826, an observer commented on Webber's portrait that Cook appeared 'raw boned . . . and capable of enduring the greatest fatigue', and the comment links together the expression of tight-lipped determination, which suggests his professional attributes of perseverance and fortitude, and his gaunt and weather-beaten complexion.[48] It is, I think, unusual for portraits of naval officers to suggest that their complexions have been marked by their profession – the two other major portraits of Cook from these years, by Nathaniel Dance and William Hodges (plate 6.5), endow him with an unlikely pallor which emphasises his raw-bonedness, perhaps because a more weathered appearance has the associations so feared and remarked on by Sir Walter Elliot, in *Persuasion*, who needs to be reassured that Admiral Croft is 'quite the gentleman in all his notions and behaviour' although he is 'a little weatherbeaten'. Sir Walter, of course, closely associates the 'deplorable looking' complexions of naval officers with his disgust for the naval profession as the 'means of bringing persons of obscure birth into undue distinction, and raising men to honours which their fathers and grandfathers never dreamt of.[49]

Bernard Smith has written of the 'realism' of William Hodges's portrait of Cook (probably painted soon after the second voyage, at around the same time as Dance's). But this is not the same kind of realism as is shown in Webber's portrait. Hodges's image removes Cook's head and gleaming linen from any informing context but that of his dimly suggested uniformed torso. This dramatic representation emphasises the alertness of Cook's expression; as though this painting, like Hodges's portrait of Mai, caught a fleeting expression. But here this animation, as Cook seems almost to strain out of the canvas, suggests that his professional dedication to his mission hardly allows him to sit still, or to be gazed at steadily. It is this image that provides the basis for one of John Flaxman's Wedgwood plaques (fig. 6.3), where the streaming hair, large eyes, and intent expression suggest the extent to which Cook's posthumous image begins more and more recognisably to bear the impress of the idea of his active, heroic genius. Nathaniel Dance's society portrait, in contrast, shows Cook sitting, bewigged, indoors (plate 6.6). He looks across and out of the frame to the right, as though interrupted in his study of the chart before him, where his finger marks his place, and he looks studious, meditative, even polite, rather than the man of action he appears in both Webber's and Hodges's portraits. His pose suggests a kind of studied informality, indicated by the undone waistcoat button and relaxed position of his legs, but this is not the confident informality of, say, Reynolds's portrait of the young Joseph Banks in his study, with the signs of his interest in global travel around him. Cook is here unambiguously professional in his dress, his attentiveness, and perhaps also in the nature of his gaze. In the Webber portrait, his look is commanding, but the context, the sea, the rocks, even the weather, make that appropriate. In Dance's portrait, he is an authoritative figure, but it is less directly an authority over the viewer – more, perhaps, that sense of a specialised professional skill, involved in the mastery of charts and ships.

Cook himself, of course, insisted that he was a 'plain man' with little formal education, and the notion of him as a self-made man is important to the idea of his heroic Britishness. His plainness is represented as though it were the antidote to the ornamental refinement and luxury of London life. So for example, the *St. James's Chronicle* commented admiringly that 'Capt. Cook's rising, from being the Son of a Day-Labourer, to the distinguished Rank he held in the British Navy, is a Proof what superiour Abilities can do, when they have a proper Field to display themselves in.'[50] The *Westminster Magazine*, in an extended essay on the 'Melancholy catastrophe of Captain

Figure 6.3 Detail from John Flaxman after William Hodges,
Wedgwood plaque bearing portrait of Cook (c. 1779–80), blue and
white jasper ware, 240 × 180 mm

Cook's death', hints that his origins were necessary to his success. The eulogist
writes that: 'no man seemed so well formed for enterprizes such as he was
engaged in. He was fond of the pursuit, and sacrificed every consideration
to them. He owed his rise entirely to his merit; and retained the modesty of
his early state after he had risen beyond the expectations of his friends, and
equal to his own.'[51] Voyages into unexplored territory through ice sheets and
across the divisions of British society seem to draw on similar reserves of
character. Sophie von La Roche recorded in her diary that during the 'general
mourning' for Cook's death 'someone expressed the view that [Cook] had
fulfilled his mission, and it was time for him to die. I would not have stirred
a finger to save him.' Frances Burney replied that this was '"a very sublime
way of considering Cook's death"' – a response La Roche found 'delicious'.[52]
For Burney and her well-educated circle, Cook is consumed, sublimed, by

his professional dedication; he is a man so heroically purposive that even his death seems a small sacrifice to provide the narrative of his mission with a fitting closure.

At moments such as this, Cook's career can seem as much an ornament to advanced civilisation as Mai's cosmopolitan gentility. John Hamilton Mortimer's *Group Portrait*, probably painted in 1771, after the first circumnavigation, shows Cook between his patrons, Lord Sandwich on the right, and Sir Joseph Banks on the left (plate 6.7). This is perhaps the 'proper Field' spoken of in the *St. James's Chronicle*. Cook gestures towards the sea, where he will again display his superior abilities. His central position makes him the focus of the attention of the other four, and the image seems ambivalently poised between the suggestion that they admire his heroic endeavours, that he commands at least their interest, and the possibility that Sandwich and Banks display him as their protégé, with the relaxed confidence, almost negligence, of the massively propertied. Cook, like Mai, may be seen as a sign of the grandeur of men more powerful than himself; the ornament of their prosperous civilisation and metropolitan polish. Cook may look like a more modern, or at least more Romantic, figure than Mai, in his professional dedication, his purposiveness, his perceived capacity for toleration and a sort of humanitarian cultural relativism. In contrast to Cook, the notions of British civilisation and imperial identity that are associated with Mai may have looked anachronistic – too dependent on ornament and display, on aristocratic inutility. The two men are marginalised, disadvantaged, exploited by metropolitan society in what are evidently very different ways – by, for example, racial or regional difference, social status, linguistic competence, and elegance of manner. But they are both also, in their differences, central to the discursive contradictions about use and ornament, technological progress and civility, in which metropolitan society conceived of its own modernity.

Epilogue: *The Effects of Peace* and *The Consequences of War* in 1794–1795

I

On 1 December 1794, an exhibition of Hodges's work opened at Orme's Gallery in Old Bond Street. The one-man show consisted of some twenty-five pictures, but the centre piece, the hero of the hour, dominating the series of newspaper advertisements for the exhibition, was the 'very large' pair of pictures showing *The Effects of Peace* and *The Consequences of War*. The sparse narrative of the exhibition that can be gleaned from Joseph Farington's *Diary* suggests that these large paintings were central to Hodges's ambitions and aspirations as an artist. He lavished 60 guineas on their frames, paid 6 guineas a week for the exhibition space, which he intended to retain for three months, and employed a man to be in attendance at 25 shillings per week.[1] The catalogue for the exhibition, apparently inviting subscriptions for prints of the two landscapes, described them at some length, and represented them as the first fruits of a new stage in Hodges's career, in which he would make the focus and explicit aim of his work the attempt to give landscape painting some of the dignity associated with more elevated genres:

It could not escape me, that other branches of the art had achieved a nobler effect – History exhibited the actions of our heroes and patriots, and the glories of past ages – and even Portrait, though more confined in its influence, strength-ened the ties of social existence. To give dignity to landscape painting is my object. Whatever may be the value of my execution, the design to amend the heart while the eye is gratified, will yield me the purest pleasure by its success. I may flatter myself even with an influence that shall never be acknowledged; and the impression of these slight productions may be felt in *juster* habits of Thought, and Conduct consequently *improved*. From slight causes, the Author of our minds has ordained that we should derive most important convictions. Perhaps the enthusiasm of the artist carries me too far; but I hope and trust that my progress in this design may be serviceable to my country, and to humanity.[2]

Hodges's avowed objective here – to freight landscape painting with some of the social and moral *gravitas* that traditionally characterised history paint-ing – is strongly reminiscent of the ambitions of the landscapes from his travels in the South Pacific. He spent his life attempting to develop the intellectual scope and energy of the genre in which he worked by introducing allusions to historical narrative, or theories of the development of civilisation. The recently rediscovered prints from the paintings central to this exhibition, with the detailed textual exegesis of Hodges's catalogue notes, provide the opportunity to explore Hodges's final and most overt attempt to create instructive and improving landscapes, and to consider the sorts of problems and difficulties which in 1794–5 debilitated the project and limited its influence.

Hodges's exhibition was not a success. After the first week Farington heard that there were no subscribers for the prints, and by the end of the second week Hodges had dismissed the paid attendant. On 26 January 1795, Farington reported that the exhibition had closed.[3] Part of the problem was the extreme cold, which froze the rivers of northern Europe and held harbours icebound, and had significant consequences for the progress of the war with revolutionary France. Farington noted on 25 January 1795 that the temperature in his painting room, with a fire lit and the window closed, stood at 19 degrees Fahrenheit, and on the staircase it was a bitter 27 degrees below freezing.[4] Attracting visitors to venture out to exhibitions in that chill must have been exceptionally difficult. The show of Loutherbourg's paintings, at the Historic Gallery in Pall Mall, for example, lured punters with the promise of 'a constant fire', but Orme's Gallery does not seem to have been able to boast this attraction.[5] The immediate event which caused Hodges' exhibition to close so prematurely, however, and on the very eve of the thaw, was the visit of the Duke of York and Prince William of Gloucester, who 'abused his pictures as being of a political tendency expressing their surprise that such pictures should be exhibited'.[6] Within a few weeks, Hodges, who was 'very low spirited' after this attack, had sold his paintings by auction and at a considerable loss and quitted London to open a bank in Dartmouth; he never painted again.[7] The *Peace* and *War* contrast made a brief reappearance at the European Museum Exhibition in 1813, but following that disappeared without trace.[8]

In the summer of 2004, just as the first major retrospective exhibition of Hodges's work at the National Maritime Museum was opening, prints of the two images by Thomas Medland, the landscape engraver and watercolourist, came to light (plates 7.1, 7.2). Though the prints are now rather discoloured, it is clear that they were designed in strong contrast. They represent what is recognisably the same landscape, but the point from which the landscape of *War* is viewed would be within the frame of the landscape of *Peace*, and what must have been warm colours in the peaceful rural scene become colder and more muted greys, blues, and browns in the stormy scene of *War*. The peaceful landscape is quite sharply divided between the sheltered view of the cottage door on the left, where an old couple sit with women and small children, and the brighter and more extensive prospect on the right, where men are busy reaping an abundant crop, while in the centre of the image the bridge and port, apparently built on a narrow tongue of land jutting into the bay, suggest the harmonious relation between country and city which peace and prosperity affords. In the image of war, the plentiful harvest scene which fills the right side of the image of peace is no longer visible, the generations of men and women have been replaced by soldiers, and the ruined cottage and desolate tree on the left are balanced by the smoke and flame pouring from the ruined port on the right. Neither image suggests activity; these are before-and-after images, not views of the process of change, or the immediate physical violence of war, and the passages from the catalogue descriptions printed beneath underline the contrast between the views, rather than suggesting a narrative of progress from one to the other. The catalogue extracts function as keys against which the images can be read, almost as though they were allegorical representations or emblems, and the close relation between image and text means that the prints need to be discussed in close conjunction with the descriptions Hodges provided.

Hodges wrote in the catalogue that 'My pictures will constantly be lessons, sometimes of what results from the impolicy of nations, or sometimes from the vices and follies of particular classes of men.'[9] It is fairly clear from his account of his intentions that the paintings were intended to impress, at the least, the need for reflection on the morality of the war with France, and to prompt debate about the justification for its continuation. He cannot have imagined, when he began work on the paintings in May 1794, that it would be either possible or desirable to represent the contrast between the blessings of peace and the devastation of war in a manner so generalised or abstracted from contemporary circumstances – from the current 'impolicy of nations' – that all controversy would be avoided. Hodges moved in Whig circles in the 1790s – the portrait of him, after Westall's, which accompanied his 'Biographical anecdotes' in the *Literary and Biographical Magazine* for May 1792, identified him as 'landscape painter to the Prince of Wales' (fig. 7.1). In 1793, he worked on commissions from Whig politicians Sir Richard Hotham and Walter Ramsden Fawkes of Farnley Hall (the latter angrily rejecting his work), and though neither Hotham nor Fawkes were actively engaged in parliamentary politics in these years, Hodges might have associated, through their connections, with others who supported the

Figure 7.1 Thornton after Richard Westall, 'William Hodges Esqr. R. A. landscape painter to the Prince of Wales', *Literary and Biographical Magazine*, June 1792

Whig opposition. The close friend who most directly influenced Hodges's painting in 1794 was the poet William Hayley, who 'had first suggested to him that Landscape painting was capable of expressing moral subjects', and whom the Tory Farington castigated in January 1795 as a 'violent Republican' – perhaps because he was about to publish a poem celebrating Erskine's conduct of the defence in the treason trials that dominated the newspapers in late 1794.[10]

Hodges's catalogue echoed Hayley's praise for the social utility of portraiture in his earlier *Essay on Painting*.[11] In correspondence, almost all of which has disappeared, the poet seems to have urged Hodges to take on an ambitious series that would change the nature of landscape as a genre, and emphasise its social and moral role. Hodges responded to Hayley, in a letter dated 19 August 1794:

I thank you most really for the Ideas in your last letter on the subject of War & peace – and I certainly think with you – that a series of pictures might tell such a tale to the World as would make hot headed and ambitious politicians blush – should there be one spark of real virtue be remaining in their minds or one atom of humanity in their hearts . . . but think for a moment what a task – for an unsupported unprotected man to undertake – and allow for a moment the pictures painted how are they to be supported – for floor Cloths I must suppose – or as stop holes in a useless garret, to prevent bad weather making depredations – can you instance a Noble, or a rich man that decorates his Walls with works of art connected with sentiment – that which should be read like a book to instruct or amend the heart. – is not the parade of fine Carriages; – racing – Gambling – or the mean vices of the Stews the occupation of the rich the Idle? – certain I am I truly think it is – but I do entertain making two large pictures from the Studies I have already made. – and they (the Studies) are not on a small scale being 6 feet by 4′3′ – and are at least I think so highly. I mean the one nearly compleated Peace – and the other may be soon finished.[12]

Hodges was well aware that a narrative series of the kind Hayley proposed would have been both controversial and uncommercial. But the letter suggests that the two friends were enthused by their shared vision of effective art, of images which demanded to be 'read like a book to instruct or amend the heart', and would deliver an unambiguous lesson designed to 'make hot headed and ambitious politicians blush'. Though Hodges rejected the plan of a series, suggesting that the venture would require the support and protection of a wealthy or aristocratic patron, the letter does indicate that he thought of the large contrast on which he was working as a contribution towards the promotion of 'art connected with sentiment'.

Hayley's explicit opposition to Pitt's government and Pitt's war, and what we can deduce about Hodges's own political sympathies, make it more likely that the images they discussed in August 1794 would have supported the liberal movement for political reform, rather than, for example, celebrating recent British naval and military triumphs. But Hodges did not openly court political controversy – his letter makes it clear that as 'an unsupported, unprotected man' he could not afford to – and neither the prints, nor Hodges's comments on them in this letter or in the exhibition catalogue, nor Farington's second-hand account of the progress of the exhibition, suggest that he intended to produce images which unmistakably 'proceeded from Democratic principles', as his outraged Royal visitors apparently believed, or which seemed to offer direct commentary on the daily events of the winter of 1794–5.[13] If in the summer of 1794, when Hodges began the two paintings, he intended to reflect in general terms on what he, like many of the Whigs of his circle, might then have seen as an unnecessary war, and to exercise a 'slight' and unacknowledged influence on the views of their audience, the events of the autumn and winter sharpened the focus of his visual 'lessons', and made them more urgently politicised, and more legible as a commentary on immediate issues and debates, than he could easily have foreseen even in mid-August. By the time the paintings were on display, British troops had been forced by a series of ignominious retreats to withdraw from northern Europe, and the failure from drought of what had been a promising harvest threatened serious food shortages.

II

In the autumn of 1794 the government succeeded in delaying the opening of parliament until 30 December, when the session opened with a firm restatement, in the King's speech, of 'the necessity of persisting in a vigorous prosecution of the just and necessary war in which we are engaged'.[14] Parliament had initially been prorogued only until 19 August and successive delays were variously attributed to the need to wait for the conclusion of the treason trials, to the progress of the war, and even, by some satirists, to Pitt's poor memory.[15] The *Morning Post* commented on 28 November that had parliament reconvened earlier, as had been expected,

Ministers foresaw the consequences, that they could be scarcely able to retain their places, while news of some mortifying disaster would arrive daily, that must urge the People not to squander more money in the hopeless projects of Ministers. By proroguing the Parliament, they conceive that both armies will go into winter quarters, and that then they may amuse the People with the brilliant prospects that offer themselves, should they approve of another Campaign.[16]

Following the king's speech, amendments urging him to 'take the earliest means of concluding a peace', put forward by the Earl of Guildford in the Lords, and William Wilberforce in the Commons, were debated with heat and urgency.[17] These debates on the soundness of the case for war must have been enormously significant in shaping the way Hodges's paintings were viewed, and it is therefore worth exploring the possible intersections of parliamentary arguments and newspaper comments with the prints and catalogue descriptions of Hodges's images.

It is significant, first of all, that Wilberforce – like the *Morning Post* in November – felt that the precise timing of the debate was important. During the debate of 28 January 1795, on Grey's motion respecting peace and the aims of the war, Wilberforce argued that had parliament met 'on the day on which had been originally summoned', allowing him to put forward his motion when Britain was in a position of relative strength, peace would have seemed a more attractive possibility.[18] He denied, of course, that there was any humiliation in suing for peace in the current situation, but the implication of his preference for an earlier opportunity to speak out against the war, the suggestion that arguments for peace had been made more controversial by the disasters of the campaigns of the autumn and winter, is unmistakable. It suggests that the anti-war lesson of Hodges's contrasting images would have been more palatable during the period when they were designed and executed than it was by the time they were on display. In July 1794, for example, The *Oracle*, which strongly supported government policy, reported favourably and in some detail on the progress of Hodges's contrast, praising him as 'the great *moral* painter of landscape'.[19] In late October 1794, the *Oracle* commented admiringly and at length on Hodges's preparatory sketches for the paintings, and noted with approval that the images were designed to 'impress upon the mind the felicity of the PEASANT in a season of PEACE, and the dreadful reverse created by WAR'.[20] Peace could seem an attractive option to the government's supporters as late in the day as 28 November 1794, when the *Times* argued, in its 'Political observations', that 'A wish for Peace is general throughout Europe', and commented hopefully that 'the sudden prorogation of Parliament, at a moment when it was least expected, has excited the attention of everyone to overtures of Peace'. But on the same day the paper's news column argued that peace could be 'a very serious misfortune to this country', because 'We then indeed could be overrun with French principles, and have more to dread from internal foes than open enemies.'[21]

The principal points of the debates on Wilberforce's and Guildford's amendments turned on the extent to which Britain could be seen as justified in continuing a war which they were understood to have provoked the French into declaring and which could no longer be understood in terms of the original *casus belli*, to support the resistance of the Netherlands – which had now entered into negotiations with France. The war now appeared to be about hostility to republican politics, and the desire to impose regime change on France in order to pre-empt the arrival of hordes of proselytising revolutionaries in Britain. The government argued that despite the fall of Robespierre, they could not enter into negotiations with French republicans, who still posed 'the greatest danger with which [Europe] has been threatened since the establishment of civilized society'.[22] Lord Mulgrave urged his fellow peers to recollect 'that not only our lives, our laws, and our liberties are at stake, but even the national character of our posterity'.[23] Windham, the secretary at war, also insisted that the war was about political principle, and that 'The advantages of war or peace were not to be estimated by the territory or the trade we might gain or lose.'[24] This high-minded attitude must have come more easily to him as a result of his belief that the costs of war 'were now so lightly to be born as hardly to be felt', a persuasion he grounded in the 'maxim, that if the rich felt no suffering, the poor also were not likely to feel any'.[25] Where the government did acknowledge that the war was costing Britain dear, they urged that French resources would be drained even faster; and concluded that the effects of peace would be far more alarming and devastating than any possible consequences of continued war.

The arguments of the Foxite opposition to the war, to which Wilberforce uneasily found himself allied, emphasised that the recent campaign had been 'unparalleled for disaster',[26] and 'calamitous beyond example'.[27] In the Lords it was pointed out that because there was nothing in the King's speech that 'in the smallest measure determined what the object of the war really was', the conflict was potentially a 'war of mutual destruction'.[28] Fox ridiculed Windham's arguments by paraphrasing them to suggest that this was a contest 'the issue of which involved, not territory or commerce, not victory or defeat in the common acceptation of the words, but our constitution, our country, our existence as a nation'.[29] These arguments, stressing the indeterminacy of the aims of the war and the consequent difficulty of bringing it to any conclusion, and emphasising its enormous cost, were repeated at meetings up and down the country, and summarised in the numerous petitions reported in the newspapers, and particularly of course in the opposition press, for January 1795. A letter from ' A DEMOCRAT ' to the *Morning Post*, for example, warned of the imminence of famine:

We should relinquish all further mad notions of prosecuting a Continental War, and keep our provisions at home to feed our own Countrymen, instead of sending it abroad to feed Foreignors . . . let Ministers look to it – for we must apprize these weak and ignorant men, that while they revel in riot and luxury, Famine *is at our doors*, and all its attendant horrors![30]

The *Courier* represented government obduracy in a colourful analogy that highlighted both its moral irresponsibility and its devastating economic cost:

Two commercial nations going to war are like two hard working men settling a Boxing match. They beat one another till they are both half dead; are three or four weeks before they can return to their usual employment; and in the mean time their families are starving, with an apothecary's bill to anticipate the earnings of future labour.[31]

Hodges's representations of peace and war directly addressed the economic consequences of conflict. Peace is characterised by abundant evidence of commercial prosperity, as the catalogue description emphasised:

The Scene represents a sea-port thronged with shipping, expressive of Commerce; the great public buildings denote its Riches; a large bay opening to the ocean, merchant ships going out, others returning, shew the extension of its trade to the most distant quarters of the globe.

From the interior of the country a river empties itself into the bay, across which is a bridge, for the convenience and communication of commerce: the loaded waggon evincing the labours of the manufacturer.

The 'vigorous executive government' which encourages commerce also nurtures agriculture: 'A rich corn field marks the industry of the peasant, and the high state of agriculture in the country.' The composition of the print suggests that the fertile productivity it images is the effect of wise and perhaps paternalistic benevolence. The family around the cottage door are grouped in a clearly demarcated shady recess. They do not look out across the landscape, the different parts of which are linked together by the spectator's eye rather than by routes or rivers within the image. In Hodges's narrative on the companion piece, the 'same scene' is shown 'under the most melancholy difference – the city on fire – ships burning in the harbour . . . Batteries of cannon now occupy the rich fields of husbandry.'[32] The viewpoint here is from within the landscape depicted in *Peace*, and where that had shown a landscape of discrete areas whose relation could best be understood from a position outside the frame, this shows a scene denuded of trees and without clear contrasts of light and shade, a landscape of uniform devastation. The Duke of York commented, according to Edwards, that

he thought no artist should employ himself on works of that kind, the effects of which might tend to impress the mind of the inferior classes of society with sentiments not suited to the public tranquillity; that the effects of war were at all times to be deplored, and therefore need not be exemplified in a way which could only serve to increase public clamour without redressing the evil.[33]

As the price of entry to Hodges's exhibition was one shilling, it seems unlikely that the paintings would have been able to impress the minds of the inferior classes with any lessons, acknowledged or not. Hodges's contrast did represent the glaringly obvious point mentioned by the Duke: war 'at all times' damages commercial and agricultural prosperity somewhere. But what makes the images a threat to 'public tranquillity', in the Duke's eyes, may be the specificity of the location for this damage, the emphasis on the effects of continental war in Britain, and on the cherished notion of the domestic content and 'happy state of the peasantry'.

In the foreground of his image of peace, Hodges paints a domestic and familial idyll which is unmistakably British, even in the Virgilian details of the vine and fig, naturalised by the conventions of patriotic georgic:

Shrouded in a rich wood is a cottage, covered with the vine and the fig-tree, and the family enjoying the breeze in a mild, soft evening. The group of figures exhibits three generations – from venerable age to infancy – with the sympathy of maternal affection, and surrounded by domestic animals, while the father and the brothers are at work in the field.

The group of figures clustered around the cottage door are strongly reminiscent of Wheatley's genre paintings and of illustrations to the *Deserted Village*. The prominently positioned fox hounds suggest specifically British rural sports, and the cattle apparently being driven home at evening allude to the opening lines of Gray's *Elegy*. The buildings of the port are a jumble of classical and gothic architectural styles, and curiously there is no visible sign of a church, but the landscape behind them suggests the smooth contours and white cliffs of the South Downs. In the contrasting image, Hodges shows 'The same scene.' But now, the 'once happy cottagers are destroyed or dispersed – the building dismantled, and the last remnant of the wood is the scathed tree . . . – soldiers of a distant region now usurp the happy retreat of the peasant – and vultures perch where domestic pigeons brooded over their young'.[34] Nathaniel Marchant, the glyptic artist, who saw Hodges's exhibition in preparation late in November 1794, commented to Farington that the pictures were 'liable to criticism, the first scene, *peace*, exhibiting an English Country and people, – the second, *War*, the same scene under circumstances of devastation'.[35] The *Oracle* also noted that the paintings showed 'the same places diversified by events'. The reporter suggested that 'to avoid all political implication', Hodges had 'drawn an imaginary scene', but implied that it was an imaginary English scene of peace in pointing out the telling detail that the 'dogs of the Lord of the Manor', in the centre of the image, 'indicate that [the family] are flourishing under a merciful landlord'.[36]

The contrast does not simply represent the catastrophic consequences of war in general; it brings them home to the British countryside and to family life in a manner that was strongly associated with opposition to the war with France, and with rejection of the foolish or cynical complacency exemplified by Windham's remarks. Sir George Beaumont told Farington that 'Wilberforce has done much mischief by his conduct in Parliament, and that it certainly appears as if the solicitation of the Dissenters had strongly operated on his mind.'[37] The arguments of Wilberforce and Fox followed those of prominent dissenters in stressing the domestic consequences of the war, and insisting that though the scenes of bloodshed and devastation might seem comfortably distant from mainland Britain, both their effects and the responsibility for them inevitably came home, and potentially violated the domestic intimacies of 'once happy cottagers', disrupting the ties of familial affection and the mutual dependence of the generations. In the print of Hodges's image of *War* the soldiers are positioned relatively close to the frame, and turned from the viewer, where the more distant cottagers of *Peace* had invited our gaze. In *War* the viewer shares the perspective of the invaders on the destruction they have wreaked.

In her influential Discourse for the Fast of 19 April 1793, *Sins of Government, Sins of the Nation*, which lucidly articulated the misgivings of many dissenters, Anna Laetitia Barbauld had argued that though in recent years 'we have known none of the calamities of war in our own country but the wasteful expence of it', and have 'calmly voted slaughter and merchandized destruction', private individuals should never the less '*translate* this word war into language more intelligible to us', and reckon the cost of their acquiescence in human terms:

so much for killing, so much for maiming, so much for making widows and orphans, so much for bringing famine upon a district, so much for corrupting citizens and subjects into spies and traitors, so much for ruining tradesmen and making bankrupts (of that species of distress at least, we *can* form an idea,) so much for letting loose the daemons of fury, rapine, and lust, within the fold of cultivated society, and giving to the brutal ferocity of the most ferocious, its full scope and range of invention.

She detailed the effects of war on family life and personal integrity in Britain as well as on the Continent, and concluded that 'Every good man owes it to his country and to his own character, to lift his voice against a ruinous war', because this opposition 'is the only way reformations can ever be brought about'.[38] Coleridge's *Religious Musings* (written in 1794–6) echoed Barbauld's Discourse in their condemnation of the war:

> Mistrust and Enmity have burst the bands
> Of social peace; and listening Treachery lurks
> With pious fraud to snare a brother's life;
> And childless widows o'er the groaning land
> Wail numberless; and orphans weep for bread![39]

Joseph Fawcet, in his *The Art of War. A Poem* (1795), similarly emphasised the responsibility of private individuals for the devastation war effected on the battlefield, and for its domestic consequences in the grief and economic distress of the bereaved and wounded, detailing how 'complicated traffic's trembling web' carries the reverberations of war to the 'domestic scene':

> The city feels the strife that's in the field.
> To the connected, sympathising scene
> The battle's blows their dire vibrations send.
> In other ruins rages there the war;
> There falling fortunes answer falling lives,
> And broken hearts to broken limbs reply.[40]

The *Morning Chronicle*, which was consistently critical of government policy in the winter of 1794, expressed enthusiastic admiration for the 'imagination and execution' of Hodges's work, and negotiated the implications of their representations of contrasting British scenes with conspicuous delicacy. Peace, they argued emphatically, showed 'the present glorious and happy internal state of Great Britain at this moment', whereas the contrasting image showed 'what would, and what must be the inevitable consequence of disunion in this great Empire', without the support of its present 'glorious Constitution'. The journalist was able to support his praise on the basis of the 'testimony . . . by that most upright and amiable Nobleman' the second Earl of Dartmouth and his family. The Earl, known for his piety and sympathy for Calvinistic dissent, probably shared the disquiet about the war common among the conservative and evangelical associates of Wilberforce.[41]

Hodges's own comments suggest that the depiction of England as the scene of invasion and pillage in *War* had been intended to shock. He wrote to Hayley that 'I declare I revolt at the picture myself.'[42] His sensitivity to the changing political climate of the autumn of 1794 may have led him to revise his design for *War*, and tone down its more repulsive features. The *Oracle* reported in July that Hodges was at work on moral landscapes of 'WAR and PEACE', and added more detailed information: 'The latter is cottage security, innocence and labour. The former, its full contrast, is the cottage burnt, and wretched Peasants lying slaughtered by the merciless progress of the Soldier!'[43] There are no slaughtered peasants in Medland's image, and none are mentioned in the various descriptions of the finished painting, including the reliable and detailed account provided by the *Oracle* in October. It seems probable that Hodges had begun work on, or at least intended to produce, an image that would have portrayed the bloody process of war more immediately than his final rather static contrast could, but that he had shrunk from the controversy such an image was likely to provoke. The *Oracle* commented on the image in October that 'the soldier usurps the peasant's habitation', indicating that the presence of the soldiers replaces and erases the corpses of the cottagers, as it does in Medland's print. The *European Museum* noted in 1813 that even the soldiers, 'inured to war, bloodshed and plunder, seem moved with the extensive scene of misery and desolation with which they are surrounded', and their emotion, and the interest of the vultures, may be the only indications of slaughtered cottagers in the finished image.[44] Marchant criticised the 'Vultures introduced as symbols', not because they exoticised the scene, but because they 'relate to the *past* and not to the *present*', pointing perhaps to the bloodshed which the image now only suggested had taken place.[45] But though the contrast between the final prints no more than hints at the violent fate of the rustic family, the devastation of the British landscape of *Peace* clearly had the power to shock its audience with the horrors of scenes from which they wished to remain distanced.

III

The soldiers in the foreground of Hodges's image are armed with curved swords and daggers, and wear conspicuously long moustaches and tall, fez-like hats. When the *Oracle* reported on the paintings in October, it noted that their 'dress is fancied . . . between that of the CROAT and the HUNGARIAN'.[46] Nathaniel Marchant noted with more confidence that

the image showed '*Turkish* soldiers only in the front.'[47] The flag to the right
of the image is recognisably based on that of the Ottoman empire. Hodges
might have chosen to represent the 'soldiers of a distant region [who] now
usurp the happy retreat of the peasant' as recognisably Turkish because while
Islamic religion and a reputation for Francophilia made the Ottoman empire
an obvious candidate for animosity, the empire was also sufficiently remote
to pose an unlikely threat of invasion to mainland Britain. But by the winter
of 1794/5, the image of the Turks had acquired a sharper definition which
might to some extent have been in conflict with the potential appropriation
of his contrast to the campaign for peace as well as with the direction of
government policy.

Yusuf Agah Efendi, the first permanent ambassador from Turkey, had
arrived in London with his suite late in 1793, and Gillray's print, *Presentation
of the Mahometan Credentials – or – The Final Resource of French Atheists*
(plate 7.3), was published on 26 December within days of his arrival.[48] It
imagined the ambassador alarming the King and Queen with the exaggerated
manliness of the credentials he wields, as well as by allusions to the Turkish
association with revolutionary France inscribed in his unmistakably phallic
scroll, and blazoned by the tricolour fluttering behind him. Fox, Sheridan,
and Priestley, wearing bonnets-rouge to emphasise their support for the
revolution, kneel in his train, while Pitt, caricatured as a chained monkey,
cowers against George's knee. The ambassador was the subject of lively public
curiosity and comment, however, and was not only cast as the emissary of
revolution. In Cruikshank's *A Peep at the Plenipo – !!!* (plate 7.4) of 1 January
1794, he is shown at court, his masculine potency arousing the admiration
of the Countess of Buckinghamshire, Mrs Fitzherbert, and other fashionable
women. The Duke and Duchess of York are prominent in the surrounding
crowd. On 29 January 1795 the ambassador made his 'long talked of Public
Entry into London', journeying in the King's state coach at the head of a
splendid cavalcade in procession from Chelsea Hospital to St James's Palace,
where he presented 'his credentials to the King on his Throne, with the
ceremonies usual on such occasions; and afterwards to the Queen on her
Throne, in her Majesty's apartment of State'. The *Morning Post* reported that
the 'concourse of People was immense', and the *Times* concurred that 'The
day being fine, the procession afforded a pleasing sight to a great number of
spectators.'[49]

The representatives of the fading Ottoman empire were welcomed so
warmly despite the empire's tradition of friendship with the French because
it was perceived to be increasingly necessary to support the Turks as a
check on the power and ambition of Russia. Suvorov, the Russian general

responsible for the brutal defeat of Ottoman forces at Ismael (Izmayil) in 1790, at which Russian troops were reported to have behaved like cannibals, succeeded in crushing the Polish rebellion in November 1794 in a 'horrible massacre' which led a correspondent to the *Courier* to remark that 'Had we the accounts complete, I am of opinion we could not bear to read the dreadful narrative.' This defeat of Poland significantly increased the possibility that 'the Turkish empire in Europe [might] be annihilated' by Russia 'before the European powers, interested in its preservation, could have time to prepare for its defence', giving Russia access to the Mediterranean and seriously destabilising the balance of power in Europe.[50] By the winter of 1794/5, the fate of Poland reinvigorated memories of the massacre at Ismael, and reinforced the perceived need to check the Russians which had brought Britain to the brink of war in 1791. The *Courier*, for example, published a poetical 'Farewell to the year 1794', on 31 December, reiterating the link between the Turkish and Polish massacres. The poem begins by lamenting that 1794 has been a 'long year of Massacre', before praising the Polish revolutionary leader, Koscuisko:

> Illustrious Chief! – *sure 'tis no treason here*
>   To pay an heartfelt tribute to thy worth;
> O'er suff'ring Liberty to drop a tear,
>   *And curse the bloody Tygress of the North.*
>
> Lo! Ismael's brutal Conqu'ror from afar
>   Leads on his myrmidons in scent of prey;
> Train'd up to all the cruelties of war,
>   To age, to sex, they no distinction pay!
>
> Ill-fated Praga yielded to their rage,
>   And, oh! the massacre that there ensued!
> In blood of blooming youth, and hoary age,
>   Their savage hands were wickedly imbrued![51]

Pitt's government found itself in the awkward position of balancing its desire to maintain the Ottoman empire as a bulwark against the expansive ambitions of Russia, at the same time as negotiating the treaty with Russia which Catherine the Great signed on 7 February 1795.[52] The opposition press in particular emphasised the link between Polish and Turkish oppression by Russia in order to increase the government's difficulties. A 'Friend to Peace and Humanity' wrote to the *Courier*, for example, expressing revulsion at the possibility of a British alliance with 'the cruel and detestable Catherine':

That scourge of mankind, the Empress of Russia, with whom we were not long since on the very point of entering into a War, *to preserve the balance of Europe,* (but whose powerful co-operation we are now so frequently told of) has been most basely employing her power in enslaving the virtuous and unfortunate Poles.

The Friend went on explicitly to compare the atrocities of Russian action at Ismael and Warsaw.[53] Hodges's depiction of 'an English Country and people' suffering under invasion by '*Turkish* soldiers only' might have seemed 'liable to criticism' by the time it was exhibited because it reawakened memories of antagonism towards Turkey that were out of tune in different ways with both opposition sympathies and government policy.

IV

The reception of Hodges's ambitious paintings was further complicated by the immediate circumstances of the exhibition. Hodges, as I have mentioned, paid for his exhibition space in Orme's Gallery, but he did not have exclusive use of the rooms. Since 2 April 1794 (and perhaps earlier), Daniel Orme had also been exhibiting Mather Brown's massive 17-foot painting of *The Attack on Famars* (Orme's print of which is reproduced as plate 7.5), and on 1 January 1795 this was joined by Brown's equally enormous companion-piece, *Lord Howe on the Deck of the 'Queen Charlotte'* (plate 7.6). It was presumably the desire to admire the heroic representation of himself leading the attack at Famars, in the hills near Valenciennes, in juxtaposition with Howe's celebrated victory of the glorious first of June, that attracted the Duke of York to make his fateful visit to Orme's Gallery. Hodges's paintings were viewed not only in contrast with each other, but in contrast with Brown's celebratory visions of all-too-scarce recent British triumphs. The styles of painting and the attitudes to war on display in the gallery could hardly have been more different.

Mather Brown's career as an artist in the 1780s and 1790s has been fully documented by Dorinda Evans in her valuable study. It followed a very different trajectory to Hodges's. Hodges seems to have sacrificed personal fortune to his lofty ambitions for his art, as Edwards reported without much sympathy, sinking such riches as he gained from his years in India in the splendid elephant folio publication of his *Select Views in India* and the costs of his final exhibition, whereas Brown, having arrived in London as an unknown American disciple of Benjamin West, rapidly secured commercial success at the expense of artistic prestige. The *Morning Post* commented in 1786 that Brown had 'devised an ingenious expedient for procuring a name', by painting well-known people without having secured a commission, and noted that 'the artist by this kind of *popular painting* contrives to derive more profit from his exertions than many of a much higher repute and long standing in the profession'.[54] By 1790, Brown was able to style himself 'Painter to their Royal Highnesses the Dukes of York and Clarence', and, having entered into a financial arrangement with Daniel Orme, the engraver, he became 'the first major history painter to have his topical subjects immediately engraved and published so as to capitalize on sustained public interest'.[55] His paintings of the 1790s displayed what Evans aptly describes as 'that strange mixture of contemporary reportage and grandiosity that characterized the genre' in that decade, and functioned as loss-leaders for Orme's prints – a role which seems to have driven, for example, the decision to display *The Attack on Famars* before it had been completed. Brown's later reputation inevitably paid the price for his commercial success. Farington commented rather acidly on Loutherbourg's topical painting of Valenciennes that 'When the novelty is over these pictures appear very deficient', and Brown's work was subject, at least in some quarters, to a similar deflation of respect. Farington noted in October 1794 that Brown's was a name 'I certainly would not vote' for election to the Royal Academy.[56] Brown's friend C. R. Leslie, who visited his studio after he had become able to retire on his profits, lamented that 'a more melancholy display of imbecility I never saw'. Among all the amassed 'world of canvasses', Leslie saw 'not one single idea, nor any one beauty of art. He seemed to possess facility but nothing else. Those of his canvasses that looked most like pictures exhibited a feeble imitation of the manner of West, but wholly destitute of any one principle of his master.'[57]

Evans notes that 'the topical print was usually advertised in the newspapers, and this publicity at times bordered on the sensational'.[58] Small uniform advertisements for Hodges's exhibition were published in a range of newspapers, stating baldly that at Orme's Gallery 'Amongst many others, will be exhibited the MAGNIFICENT PICTURES, painted by WILLIAM HODGES, R. A. Elucidating the Effects of Peace, and the Consequences of War.' The first series of advertisements, in the *Oracle*, were headed with the address of the gallery, but in later versions they carried the more provocative heading 'PEACE and WAR', echoing the headline used for the announcement of petitions.[59] Hodges's notices are modestly restrained in contrast to Brown's sensational publicity. Advertisements for Brown's celebration of Howe's victory were large, and took a number of forms, often including lengthy descriptions of the painting spread across substantial areas of the page. But in Brown's advertisements (as in those for Loutherbourg's show), the name of the artist did not figure prominently. The topicality of the subject, and the authority of those who sanctioned or approved it, were more important selling points. The largest advertisement I have seen appeared in the *Courier*, in the position of a modern banner headline, running across the top of all four columns of the front page. Its headlines announced in large capitals: 'Description of **THE MAGNIFICENT PICTURE** NOW EXHIBIT- ING AT MR. ORME'S, OLD BOND STREET, *PAINTED UNDER THE SANCTION OF HIS MAJESTY, AND THE LORDS OF THE ADMI- RALTY,* REPRESENTING THE VICTORY BY LORD HOWE, ON THE GLORIOUS FIRST OF JUNE.' adding in smaller type, 'And which met with the most gracious reception from Their Majesties when at the Queen's Palace'. Five paragraphs of detailed description followed, in which other fea- tures salient to the commercial success of the engraving were drawn to the attention of the public. The advertisement details the ships and officers and the precise stage of the battle represented, and even records events that were beyond the scope of the image, such as the death and public commemoration of Captain John Harvey of the *Brunswick*, as if to suggest it could provide a window through to the unfolding of the battle.[60] The advertisement implies that the engraving will be an attractive purchase for the patriotic public, for friends and families of the officers represented, and also for all those connected with officers present at the battle but not actually portrayed.

Hodges's paintings in his later years were not known for high finish or exact detail – it was the 'slightly painted' character of his Yorkshire land- scapes, as well as their high-handed approach to topographical fidelity, that led Fawkes to claim they were not worth the price he charged for them, as Farington reported with perhaps some degree of *schadenfreude*.[61] Hodges's work was praised instead for 'brilliancy and effect', the 'conception of grand and poetic scenery; where the minor excellencies of execution and detail are unattended to in the broad expansion of the *idea*'.[62] The landscapes of *Peace* and *War* did not attempt to represent a known landscape, and though it is difficult to deduce much about execution or detail from the prints, they may suggest that Hodges's last grand landscapes were primarily driven by the 'broad expansion of the *ideas*' his catalogue descriptions detailed. The documentary accuracy of Brown's work, in contrast, was a major selling point. The large advertisement which appeared in the *True Briton* repeated the description given in the *Courier*, with some further additions. It made much of Brown's careful research:

Mr. BROWN had the singular opportunity of *actually residing* on board the *Queen Charlotte*, at Spithead . . . and he there had the opportunity of not only painting the Portraits of the principal Officers . . . but likewise that of taking measurements of the different parts of the Ship, and obtaining the first sources of documentary information . . . The minutae of the Ship has not been neglected by the Artist, who has particularly pourtrayed the rigging, the cannon (with the locks, as now generally adopted by the Navy), and the mode of stowing the hammocks.

It claimed that 'most of the Admirals of the Fleet have given their advice and assistance', and suggested that the King and Queen had been 'particularly pleased' with the recognisable verisimilitude of the portraits.[63] Orme and Brown did not underestimate the appeal of documentary accuracy to their principle market. Vice-Admiral Dillon, who had participated in the action of the First of June as a thirteen-year-old midshipman, remembered having attended the crowded exhibition, and recalled that the planks of the deck were 'laid – I ought to say painted – in an improper direction', which lead him to remark to the assembled company that 'Most certainly . . . that blunder has spoiled the whole in the opinion of a seaman.'[64]

The advertisements claimed that Brown's picture was 'entirely novel' as a result of its 'introduction of Portraits into a Naval Picture', and as a result of this practice, which was of course already characteristic of the work of West and Copley, the *Times* concluded that 'Out of the multitude of Pictures commemorating that glorious action on the First of June, that sanctioned by the Admiralty, in Old Bond-street, is the only one deserving the Public attention.'[65] It was these portraits that most obviously supported the claim of the key to the print (fig. 7.2), which Orme issued on 1 January 1795, that though 'the most brilliant Scenes, for the Executions of the Historian and the Artist' had been afforded by earlier British naval victories, 'never was Triumph so complete, or Magananimity so conspicuous, as when upon this glorious Occasion, an Howe despensed the Vengeance, and directed the *Thunders of Britain*'.[66] The key included outline sketches of the heads of the officers portrayed, suggesting in the representation of the flowing locks and emotive expressions of the younger officers the sentimental heroism celebrated by the painting. 'Black Dick', as Lord Howe liked to be called at sea,[67] appears to have suspended his attention to the battle around him to show sympathy with the grief of the officers bearing the dead form of Captain Neville. The magnanimity of the officers Brown portrayed is displayed in their capacity to show feeling in the heat of battle for their dead and wounded fellow officers – though not it would seem for the sailor whose foreshortened body appears in the centre of the painting. William Parker, a young midshipman aboard one of the ships of Howe's fleet, recorded in his journal that when the *Vengeur* sank, after a three-hour battle with the

Figure 7.2 *Key to the Print from the Great Picture of Lord Howe's Victory Exhibiting at Orme's Gallery, Old Bond Street, London, D. Orme,*
1795

Brunswick, British seamen were moved to tears by the sight of hundreds of French seamen struggling and drowning in the water.[68] But in Brown's image the officers on the quarterdeck of the *Queen Charlotte* all turn their backs on the Frenchmen represented at the moment of explosive impact in the waves behind them.

Brown's use of portraiture represented the officers as men of sensibility, but their humanity was not expressed in compassion for the suffering inflicted on the French, or on ordinary sea men. This is a portrait of group sympathy, of fellow feeling in loss as well as in victory. The death of Neville, and the wounding of Sir Andrew Snape Douglas, do not detract from the sense in which this is a triumphant and celebratory image, but suggest that victory is an occasion for magnanimity, an occasion on which it is appropriate to temper glory with humanity. The representation of the small group of Frenchmen apparently caught by cannon fire in the centre of the image is most obviously in line with the way popular prints had represented the victory soon after news of it reached London. Cruikshank, for example, in a print of 25 June 1794, represented the victory as a bout of fisticuffs between stout British tars and emaciated half-naked Frenchmen, with the caption Lord Howe *they run, or the British Tars Giving the Carmignols a Dressing on Memorable 1st of June 1794* (plate 7.7). In an earlier print of 16 June. *The* British Neptune *Riding Triumphant, or the Carmignols Dancing to the Tune of* Rule Britannia (fig. 7.3), Cruikshank had sketched a slightly more decorous scene, in which Lord Howe is mounted on a shell drawn by dolphins while beneath his feet starved-looking Frenchmen struggle and drown in the water.[69] By the time Brown's painting went on display, in January 1795, glee at French suffering may have seemed less appropriate, certainly to more elevated genres. Loutherbourg's representation of the victory (plate 7.8), which was on display in Pall Mall from 2 March, emphasised the devastating human cost of the battle, as did the paintings by Robert Cleveley, on display from 21 February 1795 as advertisements for Anthony Poggi's prints, which Thomas Medland also worked on (fig. 7.4).[70] In Orme's print after Brown, the distressed Frenchman were no longer the centre of the composition, their presence barely suggested (fig. 7.5).

This emphasis on sensibility and even compassion does not seem to be about a new sympathy for the French. Both Loutherbourg and Brown exhibited their representations of Howe's victory as companion pieces to scenes of the Duke of York's triumph, at Valenciennes – scenes on which I have suggested the Duke might well have wished to dwell. In early December 1794, the Duke had returned to Britain with his tail between his legs, hastening back to the comforts of London and abandoning his defeated army to find its own

Figure 7.3 I. Cruikshank, *The* BRITISH NEPTUNE *Riding Triumphant, or the Carmignols Dancing to the Tune of* RULE BRITANNIA, London, published by S. W. Fores, 16 June 1794

Figure 7.4 T. Medland after Robert Cleveley, *The End of the Battle*, London, A. Poggi, 1795

Figure 7.5 D. Orme after M. Brown, *Lord Howe on the Deck of the 'Queen Charlotte'*, London, D. Orme, 1795

way in the retreat from Flanders. The *Oracle* reported on 8 December that 'The D U K E . . . to the joy of every British subject, possesses the most perfect state of health', noting, in the adjacent column, that 'A mortality pervades the B R I T I S H A R M Y'.[71] Neither the Duke nor the patriotic public wished to be reminded of the contrast between the successes enjoyed by the navy, and the disasters of the land campaign, or the miseries the retreating army were then enduring. The emphasis on death and the display of group sympathy in Brown's image may have had the effect, I suggest, of tactfully smoothing over the contrast been land and sea, triumph and catastrophe, as well as human-ising the face of the navy. Hodges's *The Consequences of War*, in contrast to Brown's vision of Howe's victory, represented the appalling effects of defeat on land, without any mitigating display of sentimental heroism, or (in the print at least) that attention to detail that served to displace viewers' atten-tion from the theatricality of Brown's work.[72] Hodges's contrast, I suggest, was dragged into an immediate topicality by the retreat of the army, and by the proximity of Brown's work. In juxtaposition with Brown's documentary realism, it acquired by the infection of comparison a potentially sensational appearance of reportage which would have made it seriously offensive to the Duke and his supporters, and set it at odds with Hodges's own ambitions to aspire to the status of academic history painting.

V

It was this infection of reportage, I think, that made Hodges's grandly ambitious paintings available for appropriation by James Gillray, in his unashamedly topical contrast of *The Blessings of* P E A C E / *The Curses of* W A R (fig. 7.6). In 1794, Gillray lived at 18 Old Bond Street, moving to 37 New Bond Street later in the year and staying there until 1797.[73] He first issued his contrast on 12 January 1795, and, as several critics have pointed out, the print seems to echo Hodges's account of his paintings, which were on display at 14 Old Bond Street, though Gillray's print follows more closely Hodges's earlier plan to represent a scene of 'cottage security' in contrast to another of 'peasants lying slaughtered'.[74] In Gillray's print, the roundel representing 'the Blessings of P E A C E, Prosperity & Domestick-Happiness' portrays a scene of rural domestic felicity; the hale and hearty father returned from his bucolic labours to the greeting of his infant children, his wife, and his well-fed dog, while an older girl places a great joint of roast beef on the table. The contrasting image of 'the Curses of W A R, Invasion, Massacre & Desola-tion' shows the same family: the three children cluster horrified around the

Figure 7.6 James Gillray, *The Blessings of PEACE / The Curses of WAR*, London, 12 January 1795

bayoneted body of the father, while the mother, dishevelled by rape, flings her arms wide in a gesture of despair. The composition of the image is strikingly similar to Hodges's *War*, with the ruined cottage and 'scathed tree' balanced by smoke and flame from the port. Across the top of the plate, the line 'Such BRITAIN was! – Such FLANDERS, SPAIN, HOLLAND, now is!', with the centrally positioned prayer 'from such a sad reverse O Gracious God, preserve Our Country!!', might be taken to suggest that Peace represents a British scene, and War a continental landscape. But the fact that the same family appears in both roundels suggests that the image of War is a prophetic vision of the 'sad reverse' threatening the rural British family.

Gillray's image was produced on commission for John Reeves's loyalist Association for the Preservation of Liberty and Property against Republicans and Levellers, also known as the Crown and Anchor Society, and its content would have been monitored by them, but as Diana Donald has persuasively argued, 'Gillray's scenes of country life make one aware of the slipperiness of the visual signs available to the ideologists of the revolutionary period.' Gillray certainly could produce unequivocal condemnations of the opposition's case for peace. He published on 2 February 1795, for example, his print of *The Genius of France triumphant, or –* BRITANNIA *petitioning for* PEACE, *– Vide, The Proposals of Opposition* (plate 7.9), which depicted the leading parliamentary proponents of peace – Fox, Sheridan, and Stanhope – cowering behind the grovelling and dishevelled figure of Britannia as she kneels in abject supplication before the monstrous seated figure representing French republicanism. The posture of Britannia is reminiscent of that of the despairing mother in *The Curses of* WAR. But Donald points out that in his image of Peace, the depiction of 'the independent cottager living well off his own livestock and produce' suggests 'a golden past' rather than the 'perceived realities' of grain shortages and 'near beggary'.[75] The proof impression bore the inscription 'of the truth of ye representation an appeal is made and submitted to the feelings of ye internal Enemies of Gt. Britain', which seems to invite the viewer to perceive the image of peace as provocatively idealised, and the scene of war not as an avoidable future prospect, but as closer to Foxite depictions of the country ravaged by famine and war-inflicted bereavement.

Hodges's landscape of peace had been designed during the summer of 1794, when fine weather, not yet become a drought, seemed to promise a bumper harvest, which might have made the depiction of rural prosperity seem cheerfully optimistic, or at least only mildly provocative. But the political implications of visual contrasts or rural scenes were extraordinarily volatile and unstable in the early nineties. Depictions of emaciated and desperate Frenchmen set in contrast to fat British farmers gorging on roast beef and plum pudding were subject to the risk that their audience – 'the poor starving, and the middle class unable to live as they were accustomed to live'[76] – might identify with the starving French rather than with the fantasy of British plenty (see, for example, plate 7.10). In Gillray's contrast of war and peace the relation between the two sides of the image, in time and in place, seems indeterminably elusive and available to different political appropriations. The savagery of war perhaps highlights the complacency of peaceful prosperity, or the scene of war may represent distanced continental misery, as opposed to the comforts politicians such as Windham wished to believe British labourers enjoyed. Or Peace may represent what many saw as the rights of British labourers to independence, beef and pudding, of which oppressive government and continued war deprived them. The contrast between the vision of prosperity and the reality of violence, poverty, and despair might suggest the need for radical constitutional change.

Gillray's relationship with Reeves and the Crown and Anchor Society was uneven, and he sometimes satirised the Society for their failure to employ him or pay him.[77] It is possible that the indeterminate meanings of his war and peace are at least partly the result of this difficult relationship. Under one version of the print there is an inscription: 'Curs'd be the Man, who owes his Greatness to his Country's Ruin!!!!!', which John Barrell has argued might have applied to Pitt or to Fox or to Reeves himself.[78] The line might also plausibly have been taken to refer to the Duke of York, who was to be promoted to the rank of field-marshal in February 1795 although he was widely blamed for the failures of the previous year's campaign.[79] Gillray had satirised the high life the Duke was reported to enjoy on active service in Flanders, while his troops sickened and starved, in his *Fatigues of the Campaign in Flanders*, of May 1793 (plate 7.11). A few months later, in September, Gillray had accompanied Loutherbourg on an expedition to Valenciennes, collecting material for Loutherbourg's grand depiction of the Duke's finest hour, and both artists spent time with the English high command and army. The Duke's forces were then in some disarray following their hasty and ignominious retreat from the siege of Dunkirk, for which the Duke had been lambasted in the British press. On their return to London Loutherbourg and Gillray were invited to show their work to the King, and Gillray was 'not overpleased' with the monarch's criticisms of the accuracy of his sketches.[80] All of this might have prompted him to a veiled jibe at the Duke's apparently unstoppable rise. Certainly, the close relation between Gillray's print and Hodges's paintings would have worked to confirm the topical reference of Hodges's work, and to enmesh his contrast inextricably in the political controversies of the day.

VI

By late January of 1795, when Hodges's exhibition closed, his grand historical landscapes had lost the power to exercise an oblique influence through subtle moral lessons. They had become a commentary on the ongoing debates and immediate circumstances that now shaped the lessons they could impart. In the context of parliamentary and newspaper discussions of war and peace in late 1794 and early 1795, they seemed to endorse the Foxite argument for peace, emphasising the economic consequences of war, and their impact on domestic and familial life in Britain. But the representation of the invaders as soldiers of the Ottoman empire complicated their alignment with the policies of the opposition. Gillray's version of the contrast, as it might have appeared to members of Reeves's Association, offered an alternative interpretation of the iconography of peace not as a past golden age of plenty, but as the present which members of the administration wished to affirm was threatened by revolutionary government in France. Hodges's image of the plenty and domestic harmony resulting from good government could be read as a rebuke to the current policy of the nation, his vision of war as the horror that bad government called down on itself; but of course peaceful prosperity could also be seen as what the government waged war to defend, rather than as the price of reckless warmongering. The theory of historical landscape painting which Hodges's paintings were designed to exemplify was undermined by juxtaposition with Mather Brown's sensational and journalistic brand of history painting. Brown's huge canvasses claimed to represent the definitive account of recent events, building that claim on detailed documentary accuracy and the approval of leading naval and military authorities and the court. Hodges's work, with its emphasis on 'the broad expansion of the *idea*' and the indirect formation of '*juster* habits of thought', appealed to notions of art and of truth that Brown's work, in which 'not one single idea, nor any one beauty of art' appeared, did not attempt to engage. The theatrical jingoism of Brown's paintings attracted large crowds who, as they debated the convenience of hammock stowage and the direction of the decking, must have been nonplussed by Hodges's grand ambitions to amend their hearts and serve humanity.[81] Hodges's images of the South Pacific and of India fulfilled an explicitly instructive role in giving the public ideas of scenes of which they knew little. That role may have licensed or even demanded their allusions to theories of the progress of civilisation and cultural difference – just as voyagers to the South Pacific, in their journals, alluded to the discursive framework of enlightenment theories of civilisation to structure their reflections on the cultures they encountered and their own relation to them. In the polarised political climate of the 1790s, however, the use of a similar visual vocabulary in European landscapes offered too explicit, too direct a commentary.

Notes

Introduction

1. James Cook, *The Journals of Captain James Cook on his Voyages of Discovery*, II: *The Voyage of the Resolution and Adventure, 1772–1775*, ed. J. C. Beaglehole Hakluyt Society Extra Series xxxv (Cambridge: Cambridge University Press for the Hakluyt Society, 1969), 322. Easter Island was known to the islanders as *Te Pito o te Whenua*.
2. James Cook, *A Voyage towards the South Pole, and round the World. Performed in His Majesty's Ships the Resolution and Adventure, in the years 1772, 1773, 1774, and 1775* (London: Strahan and Cadell, 1777), 2 vols. I: 271.
3. George Forster, *A Voyage round the World*, ed. Nicholas Thomas and Oliver Berghof, assisted by Jennifer Newell (Honolulu: Hawai'i University Press, 2000), 2 vols., continuously paginated, 300 (all references are to this edition).
4. Rüdiger Joppien and Bernard Smith, *The Art of Captain Cook's Voyages*, II: *The Voyage of the Resolution and Adventure, 1772–1775* (New Haven: Yale University Press, 1985), 76–7. They speculate that it may have been painted after the voyage had touched at the Cape, but before the return to England.
5. Bernard Smith, *European Vision and the South Pacific* (2nd edn, New Haven: Yale University Press, 1985), 71.
6. Johann Reinhold Forster, *The Resolution Journal of Johann Reinhold Forster, 1772–1775*, ed. Michael Hoare (London: Hakluyt Society, 1982), 4 vols., continuously paginated, 476.
7. Joppien and Smith, *Art*, II: 76; Cook, *Journals*, II: 354.
8. Cook, *Journals*, II: Appendix v, Journal of William Wales, 820.
9. Cook, *Journals*, II: 350.
10. Smith, *European Vision*, 80, 72–3, 1.
11. W. J. T. Mitchell, 'Imperial landscape', in W. J. T. Mitchell, ed., *Landscape and Power* (Chicago: University of Chicago Press, 1994), 19. Geoff Quilley observes that Mitchell criticises Smith 'perhaps unfairly', in his 'William Hodges, artist of empire', in Geoff Quilley and John Bonehill, eds., *William Hodges, 1744–1797: The Art of Exploration* (New Haven: Yale University Press, 2004), 6.
12. See Linda Colley, *Britons: Forging the Nation, 1707–1837* (New Haven: Yale University Press, 1992), ch. 3; Markman Ellis, *The Politics of Sensibility: Race, Gender and Commerce in the Sentimental Novel* (Cambridge: Cambridge University Press, 1996), esp. ch. 2; Kathleen Wilson, 'Citizenship, empire and modernity in

the English provinces', in Kathleen Wilson, *The Island Race: Englishness, Empire and Gender in the Eighteenth Century* (London: Routledge, 2003), 29–53.

13. Cook, *Journals*, ii: Preface, i.

14. For a succinct account of earlier voyages to the Pacific, see O. H. K. Spate, *The Pacific since Magellan*, iii: *Paradise Found and Lost* (Rushcutters Bay, NSW: ANU Press, 1988), 86–127.

15. Cook, *Journals*, ii: Appendix vii, The Ships' Companies.

16. Boswell and Cook went on to discuss the desirability of 'having some men of enquiry left for three years at each of the islands of Otaheite, New Zealand, and Nova Caledonia, so as to learn the language and . . . bring home a full account of all that can be known of people in a state so different from ours'. Charles Ryskamp and Frederick Pottle, eds., *Boswell: The Ominous Years, 1774–1776* (Melbourne: Heineman, 1963), journal entry for Thursday 18 Apr. 1776, 341.

17. See Colley, *Britons*, 101–5.

18. *Drewry's Derby Mercury*, 14–21 Jan. 1780.

19. David Samwell, *A Narrative of the Death of Captain James Cook, to Which Are Added Some Particulars concerning his Life and Character, and Observations respecting the Introduction of the Venereal Disease into the Sandwich Isles* (London: Robinson, 1786), 25.

20. See Bernard Smith, 'Cook's posthumous reputation', in Bernard Smith, *Imagining the Pacific in the Wake of the Cook Voyages* (London and New Haven: Yale University Press, 1992), esp. 233–5.

21. Wilson, 'The island race: Captain Cook and English ethnicity', in Wilson, *Island Race*, 62.

22. William Cowper, *Charity*, l. 28, in *The Poems of William Cowper*, i: *1748–1782*, ed. John D. Baird and Charles Ryskamp (Oxford: Oxford University Press, 1980); Anna Seward, *An Elegy on Captain Cook, to Which Is Added, An Ode on the Sun* (2nd edn, London: Dodsley, 1780), 14.

23. G. Forster, *Voyage*, Preface, 5.

24. Nigel Leask, *Curiosity and the Aesthetics of Travel Writing, 1770–1840: 'From an Antique Land'* (Oxford: Oxford University Press, 2002), 41.

25. The fullest account of J. R. Forster's career is Michael Hoare's *The Tactless Philosopher: Johann Reinhold Forster (1729–1798)* (Melbourne: Hawthorn Press, 1977). See also Hoare's introduction to J. Forster, *Journal*; Nicholas Thomas, 'Johann Reinhold Forster and his *Observations*', in Johann Reinhold Forster, *Observations Made during a Voyage round the World*, ed. Nicholas Thomas, Harriet Guest, and Michael Dettelbach, with a linguistic appendix by Karl H. Rensch (Honolulu: Hawai'i University Press, 1996), xv–xxii (all references are to this edition); Nicholas Thomas and Oliver Berghof, introduction to G. Forster, *Voyage*.

26. J. Forster, *Observations*, 9.

27. J. Forster, *Observations*, 239.

28. J. Forster, *Observations*, ch. vi, section 7, Heading, 239.

29. J. Forster, *Observations*, 213–14. For further discussion of this issue, see Nicholas Thomas, 'Providential cannibalism', in Jonathan Lamb, Vanessa Smith, and Nicholas Thomas, eds., *Exploration and Exchange: A South Seas Anthology, 1680–1900* (Chicago: Chicago University Press, 2000), 92–94; Marshall Sahlins, 'Heirarchy and humanity in Polynesia', in Antony Hooper and Judith Huntsman, eds., *Transformations of Polynesian Culture* (Auckland: The Polynesian Society, 1985); Gananeth Obeyesekere, '"British cannibals": contemplation of an event in the death and resurrection of James Cook, explorer', *Critical Inquiry*, 18, 4 (1992), 630–54; and Chapters 3 and 5 below.

30. G. Forster, *Voyage*, 355.

31. John Brewer observes of eighteenth-century Britain that 'With the exception of the Dutch, and the French during the American War of Independence, no other major state devoted such a high proportion of its expenditure to a floating force.' *The Sinews of Power: War, Money and the English State, 1688–1783* (London: Unwin Hyman, 1989), 31.

32. G. Forster, *Voyage*, 355, 378.

33. G. Forster, *Voyage*, 354–5.

34. Cook, *Voyage* (1777), i: 351–2.

35. See G. Forster, *Voyage*, 469 n.11.

36. Adam Ferguson, *An Essay on the History of Civil Society*, intro., Louis Schneider (1767; New Brunswick, NJ: Transaction, 1980), pt iii, sect. iv, p. 143.

37. James Thomson, *The Seasons*, ed. James Sambrook (Oxford: Oxford University Press, 1981), Autumn, ll. 124–5.

38. Joppein and Smith conclude that 'A mysterious symbol of Tahitian tribal war is thus glossed against the Christian symbol of holiness and peace'; *Art*, ii: 84. G. Forster, *Voyage*, 357, also cited in Joppien and Smith.

39. *London Packet or New Lloyd's Evening Post*, 25 Apr. 1777.

40. On the history of the Forsters' publications on the voyage, see Hoare, *Tactless*, ch. 8. On sales of George Forster's *Voyage*, see 169–70.

41. For an account of the dispute over the writing of the official account, see Hoare, *Tactless*, 152–69.

42. See Isabel Stuebe, *The Life and Works of William Hodges* (New York: Garland, 1979), 'Biographical and critical essay', 2–78, and Quilley and Bonehill, eds., *Hodges*.

43. Stuebe, *Hodges*, 11.

44. For fuller discussion of Hodges's work in India, and his relation to Warren Hastings, see Natasha Eaton, 'Hodges's visual genealogy for colonial India, 1780–1795', in Quilley and Bonehill, eds., *Hodges*.

45. [William Hodges], 'An account of Richard Wilson, Esq. landscape painter, F. R. A.', *European Magazine, and London Review*, June 1790, 404. The essay is attributed to Hodges in Stuebe, *Hodges*, 6; see also John Bonehill, '"This hapless adventurer": William Hodges and the London art world', in Quilley and Bonehill, eds., *Hodges*.

46. William Hodges to William Hayley, 27 Apr. 1793, Alexander Turnbull Library, Wellington, NZ, published in [A. A. St. C. M. Murray-Oliver], 'Oil paintings by William Hodges, R. A.', *Alexander Turnbull Library Bulletin*, 15 (1959), 6, quoted in Stuebe, *Hodges*, p. 2.

47. See David Solkin, *Richard Wilson: The Landscape of Reaction* (London: Tate Gallery, 1982), esp. 133–4.

48. *Morning Post*, Saturday, 24 May 1794.

49. For an excellent account of this see Bonehill, '"This hapless adventurer"'.

50. Solkin, *Richard Wilson*, 133–4.

51. Anne Salmond, *The Trial of the Cannibal Dog: Captain Cook in the South Seas* (London: Allen Lane, 2003), 8, 431.

52. Nicholas Thomas, *Discoveries: The Voyages of Captain Cook* (London: Allen Lane, 2003), p. 322, citing the journal of George Gilbert. Salmond comments on Gilbert's observation that 'In this respect, Cook was not unlike local leaders, for in Tonga, chiefly violence was commonplace' (344).

53. Thomas, *Discoveries*, 325, see also, for example, 305–6.

54. Jonathan Lamb, *Preserving the Self in the South Seas, 1680–1840* (Chicago: Chicago University Press, 2001), 4–5.

55. J. G. A. Pocock, 'Nature and history, self and other: European perceptions of world history in the age of encounter', in Lamb and Bridget Orr, eds., *Voyages and Beaches: Pacific Encounters, 1769–1840* (Honolulu: University of Hawai'i Press, 1999), 29, 28.

56. Paul Gilroy, *The Black Atlantic: Modernity and Double Consciousness* (London: Verso, 1993), 56, 46. Michel Foucault, 'What is enlightenment?' in Paul Rabinow, ed., *The Foucault Reader* (Harmondsworth: Penguin, 1986), 50, cited in Gilroy, *The Black Atlantic*, 56.

1   The great distinction

1. William Hodges, *Travels in India, during the Years 1780, 1781, 1782, & 1783* (London: author, 1793), preface, iv, 2–3, 2. Hodges's *Travels* are not only intended for his private friends, but are, he writes: 'submitted to a tribunal, which I have ever regarded with awful respect . . . THE PUBLIC' (preface, iv). See also *Analytical Review, or History of Literature, Domestic and Foreign*, 15 (1793), 248. This chapter is a substantially revised version of my essay first published as 'The great distinction: figures of the exotic in the work of William Hodges', *Oxford Art Journal*, 12, 2 (1989), 36–58. My research for that essay was advanced by a Visiting Fellowship awarded by the Yale Center for British Art at New Haven.

2. William Robertson, for example, remarked that before any 'warlike race was mingled' with that of India by conquest, its 'natives [were] a gentle effeminate people', in *An Historical Disquisition concerning the Knowledge which the Ancients Had of India* (London: A. Strahan and T. Cadell, 1791), 154. See also, for example,

Hugh Murray, *Historical Account of Discoveries and Travels in Asia, from the Earliest Ages to the Present Time* (Edinburgh: Archibald Constable & Co., 1820), 3 vols., II: 313; Sir William Jones, 'The third anniversary discourse, on the Hindus, delivered 2d of February, 1786', in *The Works of Sir William Jones* (London: G. G. and J. Robinson, 1799), 6 vols., I: 23–4. See also Edward W. Said, *Orientalism* (London: Routledge and Kegan Paul, 1978; Harmondsworth: Penguin, 1985), 138, 180, 182, 187, 206–8, 309, 311; and P. J. Marshall and Glyndwr Williams, *The Great Map of Mankind: British Perceptions of the World in the Age of Enlightenment* (London: Dent, 1982), 161.

3. Hodges, *Travels*, 3–4, 5. Muslim culture is implicitly constructed as masculine, in contrast to the femininity attributed to Hindu culture, in Hodges's *Travels*. Thus, for example, Hindu architecture is remarkable for its beautiful variety, whereas Muslim architecture is praised for its sublime magnificence and grandeur. See *Travels*, 60–1, 126–7, 33–5, 151–3.

4. Sir William Jones, 'An essay on the poetry of the eastern nations', in *Poems Consisting Chiefly of Translations from the Asiatick Languages. To Which Are Added Two Essays* (Oxford: Clarendon Press, 1772), 198; Robertson, *Disquisition*, 319; Hodges, *Travels*, preface, iv.

5. For an indication of the extent to which that combination was perceived as problematic, see [? Henry Mackenzie] *Mirror*, 28, 1 May 1779. See also Ramkrishna Mukherjee, *The Rise and Fall of the East India Company: A Sociological Appraisal* (rev. edn, New York: Monthly Review Press, 1974), ch. 5, and P. J. Marshall's discussion, in Marshall and Williams, *Great Map*, 158–64. On the Company in the context of developments internal to the region, see C. A. Bayly, *Imperial Meridian: The British Empire and the World, 1780–1830* (London: Longman, 1989), esp. ch. 2. On the conditions for artists working in India, see Mildred Archer, *Early Views on India: The Picturesque Journeys of Thomas and William Daniell, 1786–1794* (London: Thames & Hudson, 1980), 12; Isabel Combs Stuebe, 'William Hodges and Warren Hastings: a study in eighteenth-century patronage', *Burlington Magazine*, 115 (Oct. 1973), 659–66.

6. Hodges, *Travels*, 5. Hodges points out, in an earlier note, the connection between the dress worn in India, and the 'jam', 'well known in England, and worn by children', implying, perhaps, the childishness as well as effeminacy of the spectacle he observes (3n). Hodges writes of the Hindu temples on the banks of the Ganges: 'To a painter's mind, the fine antique figures never fail to present themselves, when he observes a beautiful female form ascending these steps from the river, with wet drapery, which perfectly displays the whole person, and with vases on their heads, carrying water to the temples' (33).

7. Hodges, *Travels*, 8, 9, 10, 5, 8. Hodges does not elaborate on the relation between this sovereignty, and the role of Madras as 'a place of no real consequence, but for its trade', perhaps because he believes that his readers will already be familiar with the issues involved (48).

8. Hodges, *Travels*, 10. I quote from Pope's 'Epistle II. To a Lady: Of the Characters of Women', *Moral Essays*, in Alexander Pope, *The Poems of Alexander Pope: A One-Volume edition of the Twickenham Text*, ed. John Butt (London: Routledge, 1968), l. 2.

9. For a discussion of this function of gender differences in colonial discourses see Chandra Talpade Mohanty, 'Under western eyes: feminist scholarship and colonial discourses', *Feminist Review*, 30 (Autumn 1988), 61–88.

10. J. Forster, *Observations*, 157. For comparisons between the South Sea islanders and the Hindu people of northern India, see Hodges, *Travels*, 26, 41–1, 66–7, 69.

11. This pair of paintings may have been exhibited in the Royal Academy of 1776. See Stuebe, *Hodges*, 146; and Joppien and Smith, *Art*, II: 59, 61. Hodges produced at least two versions of each of these paintings. The relation between the pair I have chosen to discuss and other versions is explored in Stuebe, *Hodges*, 36–9,148–9, and in Joppien and Smith, *Art*, II: 61–4, 211. See also Smith, *European Vision*, 64–5, 69, 80.

12. J. Forster, *Journal*, 237; William Blake, 'Annotations to Reynolds' *Discourses*', in Sir Joshua Reynolds, *Discourses on Art*, ed. Robert R. Wark (1959; New Haven: Yale University Press, 1975), appendix I, 307.

13. *London Packet or Lloyd's New Evening Post*, 25 Apr. 1777, quoted in Smith, *European Vision*, 75. The reviewer probably refers specifically to Hodges's *The War Boats of the Island of Otaheite* (plate 0.4). For comparable assessments, see Fuseli's entry on Hodges, in Matthew Pilkington and Henry Fuseli, *A Dictionary of Painters, from the Revival of the Art to the Present Period; by the Rev. M. Pilkington, A. M. A New Edition, with Considerable Alterations, Additions, an Appendix, and an Index, by Henry Fuseli, R. A.* (London: J. Johnson et al., 1805), 237; Edward Edwards, *Anecdotes of Painters Who Have Resided or Been Born in England: With Critical Remarks on their Productions* (London: Leigh and Sotheby, et al., 1808), 243–5; Edward Dayes, *The Works of the Late Edward Dayes: Containing an Excursion through the Principal Parts of Derbyshire and Yorkshire . . .; Essays on Painting; Instructions for Drawing and Colouring Landscapes; and Professional Sketches of Modern Artists* (London: Davies, Vernor & Hood, 1805), 332; Joseph Farington, *The Diary of Joseph Farington*, ed. Kenneth Garlick and Angus Macintyre (London: Yale University Press for the Paul Mellon Centre, 1978–98), 17 vols., I: 270, 6 Dec. 1794; William Daniell, quoted in W. G. Archer, 'Benares through the eyes of British artists', *Apollo*, 92 (Aug. 1970), 102.

14. Hodges, *Travels*, 155–6. In *A Dissertation on the Prototypes of Architecture, Hindoo, Moorish, and Gothic* (London: [s.n.], 1787), Hodges makes it clear that though his works are 'the genuine productions of truth, candour, and justice', he has, in order to achieve these aims, 'foregone the very possibility of satisfying the natural historian, architect, antiquary, and politician, who look for no

pictures of India and Indian affairs but what can be expressed in rhetorical or arithmetical figures, algebraic forms, or the shape of a cash book. These figures, and minuter particulars to which naturalists, architects, and some antiquaries attend, were totally out of my line.'

15. Sir William Jones, quoted in Nicholas Cooper, 'Indian Architecture in England, 1781–1830', *Apollo*, 92 (Aug. 1970), 127. See Mildred Archer, *Company Drawings in the India Office Library* (London: H. M. Stationery Office, 1972), 6, 74; and R. W. Lightbown, 'India discovered', in Mildred Archer and Ronald Lightbown, *India Observed: India as Viewed by British Artists, 1761–1860* (London: Victoria & Albert Museum, 1982), 30. Reynolds, *Discourses*, Discourse XIII, 242. Letter, Reynolds to the Duke of Rutland, 29 Aug. 1786, quoted in Stuebe, *Hodges*, 86.

16. Joppien and Smith, *Art*, II: 61. On the representation of the islanders' sexual practices, see Neil Rennie, *Far-Fetched Facts: The Literature of Travel and the Idea of the South Seas* (Oxford: Clarendon Press, 1995), ch. 4.

17. See, for example, William Duff, *Letters, on the Intellectual and Moral Character of Women* (Aberdeen: J. Chalmers, 1807), 65–6; Jane West, *Letters to a Young Lady, in Which the Duties and Character of Women Are Considered, Chiefly with a Reference to Prevailing Opinions* (1806; 3rd edn, London: Longman, Hurst, Rees, and Orme, 1806), 3 vols, I: 49–52, 60, and, on the specificity of this to middle-class women, 199–201; George Gregory, 'Miscellaneous observations on the history of the female sex', in *Essays Historical and Moral* (London: J. Johnson, 1785), 145–64. See, for example, Cook, *Voyage* (1777), II: 80.

18. On the cultural construction of the spectator see Louis Marin, 'Towards a theory of reading in the visual arts: Poussin's *The Arcadian Shepherds*', in Norman Bryson, ed., *Calligram: Essays in New Art History from France* (Cambridge: Cambridge University Press, 1988), 63–77; Peter de Bolla, *The Discourse of the Sublime: Readings in History, Aesthetics and the Subject* (Oxford: Oxford University Press, 1989), ch. 8. It is an aesthetic imperative in this period for landscapes to represent 'subjects . . . exactly adapted to the scene, without exercising the mind in any historical action'. My point here is that these conventional compositional structures acquire particular meanings, of the kind that I go on to discuss, in the representation of exotic subjects. In this image it might also be argued that the juxtaposition of the women may, in a sense, produce something comparable to the effect of the combination of genres, when, 'should the interest of the piece be at all equally divided, it is needless to say the eye must be distracted and unquiet'. (I quote from J. H. Pott, *An Essay on Landscape Painting. With Remarks General and Critical, in the Different Schools and Masters, Ancient and Modern* (London: J. Johnson, 1782), 26.)

19. Johann Forster argues that the *tii* is a representation of an ancestor, and believed to be possessed by the inner beings of the dead, but he insists that the 'figure is not intended to be the real figure of the invisible soul', *Journal*, 552, and see 543, 567. George Robertson, who accompanied Wallis on the first British voyage

to Tahiti, commented on the figures that the islanders 'are none of the finest carvers, but they take care to imitate nature so Exact, that no man can mistake the sex which they mean to represent'. He thought the figures were 'set-up to Commemorate some of their families after death'. *An Account of the Discovery of Tahiti: From the Journal of George Robertson, Master of H. M. S. Dolphin*, ed. Oliver Warner (London: Folio Society, 1955), 85–6. See Terence Barrow, *The Art of Tahiti and the Neighbouring Society, Austral and Cook Islands* (London: Thames & Hudson, 1979), 41–4; Marshall Sahlins, *Islands of History* (Chicago: Chicago University Press, 1985), 13–14; Dorota Czarkowska Starzecka, 'The Society Islands', in Hugh Cobbe, ed., *Cook's Voyages and the Peoples of the Pacific* (London, British Museum Publications, 1979), 48–52.

20. 'Letter the Fiftieth', in [? William Combe], *Letters of the Late Lord Lyttelton* (London: J. Bew, 1785), 2 vols., II: 161. For an example of the sense in which slavery, femininity, childishness, and emasculation become almost interchangeable attributes of those who live in the seraglio, see Murray, *Historical Account*, II: 192–3.

21. A *tupapau*, or platform bearing a shrouded corpse, is referred to in J. Forster's *Journal*, 331–2, where he describes a walk taken at Vaitepiha with his son George Forster, Sparrman, Grindall, and Hodges. He notes that the platform bore the corpse of a woman.

22. On European attitudes to Pacific curiosities, see Nicholas Thomas, *Entangled Objects: Exchange, Material Culture and Colonialism in the Pacific* (Cambridge, MA: Harvard University Press, 1991); Nicholas Thomas, 'Objects of knowledge: oceanic artifacts in European engravings', in his *In Oceania: Visions, Artifacts, Histories* (Durham NC, Duke University Press, 1997); Adrienne L. Kaeppler, *'Artificial Curiosities', Being and Exposition of Native Manufactures Collected on the Three Pacific Voyages of Captain James Cook, R. N.*, Bernice P. Bishop Museum Special Publications 65 (Honolulu: Bishop Museum Press, 1978); Adrienne L. Kaeppler, 'Pacific culture history and European voyages', in William Eisler and Bernard Smith, eds., *Terra Australis: The Furthest Shore* (Sydney: International Cultural Corporation of Australia, 1988), 141–6; P. J. P. Whitehead, 'Zoological specimens from Captain Cook's voyages', *Journal of the Society for the Bibliography of Natural History*, 5 (1969), 161–201. Johann Forster remarked on the islands of the Indian Ocean: 'what vast treasures of shell-fish their shores, massive rocks, and the bottom of their seas contain, may be gathered from hence, that for at lest a century that these seas have been frequented by *Europeans*, they have continuously been offering somewhat new to the curiosity of men whose avarice or vanity has prompted them to collect such stores from all parts' (John Reinhold Forster, 'An essay on India, its boundaries, climate, soil, and sea', trans. from the Latin by John Aikin, in Thomas Pennant, ed., *Indian Zoology* (2nd edn, London: R. Faulder, 1790), 12).

23. Reynolds, *Discourses*, Discourse VII, 137, Discourse IV, 58. I discuss Reynolds's comments in more detail in Chapter 3 below.

24. See, for example, the work of Tilly Kettle, and of Thomas and William Daniell. On the latter's use of camera obscura, see Archer and Lightbown, *India Observed*, 130.

25. Hodges, 'Wilson', 404.

26. Vicesimus Knox, 'Of the expediency of introducing Christianity into the newly discovered Islands of the South-Sea', in *Winter Evenings: Or, Lucubrations on Life and Letters* (London: C. Dilly, 1788), 3 vols., III, ch. 2, 13–4. See also Greg Denning, 'Ethnohistory in Polynesia: The value of ethnohistorical evidence', in Barrie Macdonald, comp., *Essays from the Journal of Pacific History* (Palmerston North, NZ: Journal of Pacific History, 1979), esp, 53; and Smith, *European Vision*, ch. 3. Henry Home, Lord Kames, *Sketches of the History of Man. Considerably Enlarged by the Last Additions and Corrections of the Author* (Edinburgh: A. Strahan and T. Cadell, 1788), 4 vols., II: 318–19. Robertson, *Disquisition*, 313–14. Cook, *Voyage* (1777), I: 245.

27. Andrew [Anders] Sparrman, *A Voyage to the Cape of Good Hope, towards the Antarctic Polar Circle, and round the World: But Chiefly into the Country of the Hottentots and Caffres, from the Year 1772, to 1776* (London: G. G. J. and J. Robinson, 1785), 2 vols., preface, I: iii–iv. J. Forster, *Observations*, preface, 9.

28. Reynolds, *Discourses*, Discourse XI, 199; Barry, 'Lecture I. On the history and progress of the art', in James Barry, *The Works of James Barry, Esq.* (London: T. Cadell and W. Davies, 1809), 2 vols., I: 370, and see 'Lecture IV. On composition', in *Works*, I: 480–3.

29. Entry for Friday, 17 Dec. 1773, in John Wesley, *An Extract of the Rev. John Wesley's Journal, from September 13, 1773, to January 2, 1776. No. XVII* (London: G. Whitfield, 1797), 6–7. It was more usually the peoples of New Zealand, or of Tierra del Fuego, who were perceived to be savages and to lack curiosity. Pope writes: 'Go, like the Indian, in another life / Expect thy dog, thy bottle, and thy wife', *An Essay on Man*, Epistle IV, 177–8; cf Epistle I, 99–112, in *Poems of Alexander Pope*.

30. This fictive state is attributed to the voyagers as well as the islanders in Wesley's comments. On the difficulty of defining for Wesley a specific and stable position within mid-eighteenth-century culture, see the discussion of the conditions under which his *Journals* were produced and edited in Felicity A. Nussbaum, *The Autobiographical Subject: Gender and Ideology in Eighteenth-Century England* (Baltimore: Johns Hopkins University Press, 1989), ch. 4.

31. On 'bourgeois humanism', see Stephen Copley's introduction to his anthology, *Literature and the Social Order in Eighteenth-Century England* (London: Croom Helm, 1984), 3–7; J. G. A. Pocock, *The Machiavellian Moment: Florentine Political Thought and the Atlantic Republican Tradition* (Princeton: Princeton University Press, 1975), ch. 13. For most theorists in the later decades of the eighteenth century, the 'stages' of animalism, savagery, barbarism, and civilisation are understood to be linked in a progressive process in which phylogeny recapitulates ontogeny. This process can be represented either in terms of a gradual

ripening and maturation, an organic development, or in terms of an advance achieved through cultivation, individual industry, and interactive commerce – an advance understood in terms of the economic model of progress from savage hunting and gathering. It is in terms of this second model, privileging the economic activity of the private individual, and the disposition to trade, that the state of society among the peoples encountered on Cook's circumnavigations is most commonly evaluated, and which I take to be characteristic of the cultural ideology of bourgeois humanism. For some eighteenth-century writers, the opposition between civilised cultivation and uncivilised states is marked to a degree that overrides discrimination between the states of, most usually, savagery (childhood), and barbarism (adolescence), although the model of economic progress that I have outlined may be implicit to their arguments, and specifically to the privileged value of cultivation. The distinction between the states of savagery and barbarism is, therefore, not always clear.

32. Sparrman, *Voyage*, I, preface, iii.

33. See, for example, Edmund Burke's letter to Robertson, quoted in Marshall and Williams, *Great Map*, 93. See also Paul Carter, *The Road to Botany Bay: An Essay in Spatial History* (London: Faber, 1987), ch. I.

34. Reynolds, *Discourses*, Discourse III, 50.

35. J. Forster, *Observations*, 199.

36. J. Forster, *Observations*, 223, 155.

37. J. Forster, *Observations*, 223.

38. J. Forster, *Observations*, 174. In the passage that he adapts from Milton, Forster omits the lines in which Adam praises Eve as the perfect spouse – lines which might suggest that mutual obligation as well as assent is implicit in the relation described.

39. J. Forster *Observations*, 167. See also [? G. Kearsly], *Omiah's Farewell; Inscribed to the Ladies of London* (London: G. Kearsly, 1776), Preface.

40. The incestuous implications of this impulse are central to many novels of the period, including novels of Anne Radcliffe, Horace Walpole's *The Castle of Otranto* (1764), Sara Scott's *Millenium Hall* (1762), Mary Walker [aka Hamilton]'s *Munster Village* (1778), and Samuel Richardson's *Pamela* (1740), etc., where fathers, or more usually those *in loco parentis*, threaten the heroine's virtue. For an illuminating discussion of this apparent crisis in familial relations, see Jay Fliegelman, *Prodigals and Pilgrims: The American Revolution against Patriarchal Authority, 1750–1800* (Cambridge: Cambridge University Press, 1982).

2   Curiosity and desire

1. Johann Forster, *History of the Voyages and Discoveries Made in the North. Translated from the German of John Reinhold Forster* (London: G. G. J. and J. Robinson, 1786), xiv. Parts of this chapter were first published in unrevised form in my

'Looking at women: Forster's observations in the South Pacific', in J. Forster, *Observations*.

2. G. Forster, *Voyage*, 628, 632, 630. On Sandwich's own interest in curiosities, see Peter Gathercole, 'Lord Sandwich's collection of Polynesian artefacts', in Margarette Lincoln, ed., *Science and Exploration in the Pacific: European Voyages to the Southern Oceans in the Eighteenth Century* (Woodbridge: Boydell Press and National Maritime Museum, 1998).

3. For the French ambassador's anecdote, and a fuller discussion of its implications, see Spate, *Paradise Found*, 81. See also Nigel Leask's discussion of the changing implications of curiosity in his *Curiosity*.

4. For further discussion of this issue see Chapter 4 below. See also Cook, *Journals*, ii: 531–2, and iii: 488. On Forster's motives for collecting, see Hoare, *Tactless*, 175–7. On the Forsters' sales of Pacific artefacts, see Jeremy Coote, Peter Gathercole, and Nicolette Meister, with contributions from Tim Rogers and Frieda Midgley, 'Curiosities sent to Oxford: The original documentation of the Forster collection at the Pitt Rivers Museum', *Journal of the History of Collections*, 12, 2 (2000), 177–92, esp, 181–2. See also Jennifer Newell, 'Irresistible objects: collecting in the Pacific and Australia in the reign of George III', in Kim Sloan with Andrew Burnett, ed., *Enlightenment: Discovering the World in the Eighteenth Century* (London: British Museum Press, 2003), 246–57.

5. William Wales, *Remarks on Mr. Forster's Account of Captain Cook's Last Voyage round the World, in the Years 1772, 1773, 1774, and 1775* (London: J. Nourse, 1778), 34–5, also 3. See also 54–5. The grounds of the argument between Wales and the Forsters have been extensively discussed. See, for example, Hoare, *Tactless*, 173–9. For Forster's comments on 'unofficial' collecting, see, for example, his *Journal*, xlv–xlvi.

6. Joppien and Smith, *Art*, ii: 63. On these images see also David Bindman, *Ape to Apollo: Aesthetics and the Idea of Race in the 18th Century* (London: Reaktion, 2002), 134–5.

7. I am grateful to Michael Rosenthal for alerting me to the allusion to Titian here.

8. J. Forster, *Journal*, 390. On the limited circulation of Forster's *Journal*, see Hoare, *Tactless*, 110.

9. J. Forster, *Journal*, 356–7.

10. J. Forster, *Journal*, 390. For further discussion of this comparison, see Chapter 4 below.

11. J. Forster, *Journal*, 390–1.

12. Cook, *Journals*, ii: 175.

13. G. Forster, *Voyage*, 121. See Thomas, *Discoveries*, xxiii–xxvii.

14. J. Forster, *Journal*, 302–3.

15. J. Forster, *Journal*, 308–9.

16. John Millar, *The Origin of the Distinction of Ranks: Or, an Inquiry into the Circumstances Which Give Rise to Influence and Authority, in the Different Members of Society* (3rd edn, London: J. Murray, 1779), 122, 124, 110–11.

17. Millar, *Origin*, 119. J. Forster, *Journal*, 309. Millar's argument is for a remoralisation of the principles of commerce, achieved at least in part through representing the vices associated with women as a kind of inoculation for the healthy body of society.

18. Millar sees the 'liberty of divorce' in the late days of the Roman empire as a sign of luxury and debauchery – clearly not the basis for virtuous monogamy. *Origin*, 125, and see ch. 1, sect. vi, 'The effects of great opulence, and the culture of the elegant arts, upon the relative condition of the sexes.'

19. G. Forster, *Voyage*, 277.

20. 'Hints: chiefly designed to have been incorporated in the Second Part of the Vindication of the Rights of Woman', in Mary Wollstonecraft, *The Works of Mary Wollstonecraft*, ed. Janet Todd and Marilyn Butler (London: Pickering, 1989), 7 vols., v: 271.

21. See Wollstonecraft, *Works*, v: 139.

22. Perhaps incongruously, Forster wrote of the Tahitian Arioi as though their excesses were the effect of late commercial culture, comparing them to 'our grandees' (257), although he understood Tahitian culture to be pre-commercial. He wrote of them that 'Opulence never fails to excite the appetite for sensual pleasure, and if no restraint is laid on its gratification, it grows stronger and stronger, so as at last to extinguish all the notions of propriety and decency' (254). The Arioi were an exclusive and privileged group dedicated to the worship of Oro. Europeans were impressed and alarmed by their apparent libertinage and practice of infanticide. For a lucid account of the group see Alfred Gell, *Wrapping in Images: Tattooing in Polynesia* (Oxford: Clarendon Press, 1993), 146–50.

23. See J. Forster, *Observations*, 289–90 and 243–4.

24. Charles Greig has suggested to me, in private correspondence, that plate 2.3 is in fact the earliest version of the scene.

25. G. Forster, *Voyage*, 368–9.

26. Compare, for example, Thomas Gainsborough, *Diana and Actaeon* (1784–6), Francis Wheatley, *Salmon Leap at Leixlip with Nymphs Bathing* (1783), and J. M. W. Turner, 'Drawing of the Clyde', etched J. M. W. Turner, eng. Charles Turner, printer S. Lahee, in *Liber Studiorum*, Pt 4, pl. 18 (1809). The pose of the seated woman in Wheatley's *Salmon Leap* is reminiscent of Hodges's images. See Michael Rosenthal, 'Gainsborough's *Diana and Actaeon*', in John Barrell, ed., *Painting and the Politics of Culture: New Essays on British Art, 1700–1850* (Oxford: Oxford University Press, 1992), 167–94.

27. Joppien and Smith suggest that this landscape was painted before the larger, peopled view of plate 2.3, but see n. 24 above. See *Art*, ii: 210–11, entries for 2.109 and 2.110.

28. My account is indebted to Geoff Quilley's catalogue entry for this painting in Quilley and Bonehill, eds., *Hodges*, 197–8.

29. See Solkin, *Richard Wilson*, ch. 3, 'Moral landscape art'.

30. Henry Home, Lord Kames, represents variety of food and drink as the primary form of luxurious appetite; see *Sketches*, bk 1. sketch 8, 'Progress and effects of luxury'. On breadfruit, labour, and substitution, see Vanessa Smith. 'Give us our daily breadfruit: bread substitution in the Pacific in the eighteenth-century', *Studies in Eighteenth-Century Culture*, 35 (2006), 53–75.

31. J. Forster, *Observations*, 223.

32. J. Forster, *Journal*, 390–1.

3   Curiously marked

1. The name of the islander was Mai. Most eighteenth-century British accounts call him Omai, or Omiah, mistakenly including the prefix as part of the name, as they did in referring to Tahiti as Otaheite. I quote from Frances Burney, *The Early Diary of Frances Burney, 1768–1778*, ed. Annie Raine Ellis (London: G. Bell, 1913), 2 vols., 1: 337. Parts of this chapter are a substantially revised version of parts of the essay I first published as 'Curiously marked: tattooing, masculinity, and nationality in eighteenth-century British perceptions of the South Pacific', in Barrell, ed., *Painting and the Politics of Culture*.

2. Attenborough's comments were widely reported, for example in the press release issued by the Tate Gallery on 26 Mar. 2003. Adam Nicholson, 'Reynolds wanted Omai to be a man of the world', *Telegraph*, 7 Jan. 2003.

3. 'For all Oceanic people, cloth was and is a substance of sociality, a wrapping that protects bodies spiritually as well as practically, a valuable, a sort of currency, a gift.' Thomas, *Discoveries*, 171. I discuss Mai's reception in London in greater detail in Chapter 6 below.

4. Smith, *European Vision*, 80–1.

5. E. H. McCormick, *Omai: Pacific Envoy* (Auckland, NZ: Auckland University Press, 1977), 174.

6. G. Forster, *Voyage*, Preface, 10.

7. Spate, *Paradise Found*, 256.

8. Joseph Banks, *The Endeavour Journal of Joseph Banks, 1768–1771*, ed. J. C. Beaglehole (Sydney: Trustees of the Public Library of New South Wales with Angus and Robertson, 1962, rev. edn, 1963), 2 vols., 1: 312–13. On Banks and his collections see John Gascoigne, *Joseph Banks and the English Enlightenment: Useful Knowledge and Polite Culture* (Cambridge: Cambridge University Press, 1994), chs. 3 and 4; Beth Fowkes Tobin, *Picturing Imperial Power: Colonial Subjects in Eighteenth-Century British Painting* (Durham NC.: Duke University Press, 1999), ch. 6; and, for a brief but lucid overview, Patricia Fara, *Sex, Botany and Empire: The Story of Carl Linnaeus and Joseph Banks* (Cambridge: Icon, 2003).

9. [John Rickman], *Journal of Captain Cook's Last Voyage to the Pacific Ocean, on Discovery, Performed in the Years 1776, 1777, 1778, 1779* (London: Newbery, 1781), 185.

10. See Thomas, *Entangled Objects*, ch. 4. The clothing of Reynolds's figure bears some resemblance to that represented in plate 3 of Sydney Parkinson, *A Journal of a Voyage to the South Seas* (London: Caliban Books, 1984), as well as to conceptions of oriental and classical drapery. It may be the kind of clothing Horace Walpole alluded to in his comment that the plates from Cook's published voyages showed men and women 'dressed unbecomingly as if both sexes were ladies of the highest fashion' (quoted in Michael Alexander, *Omai: Noble Savage* (London: Collins and Harvill Press, 1977), 108).

11. George Hamilton, in Capt. Edward Edwards and George Hamilton, *Voyage of the H. M. S. 'Pandora' despatched to arrest the mutineers of the 'Bounty' in the South Seas, 1790–91: Being the Narratives of Captain Edward Edwards, R. N., the Commander, and George Hamilton, the Surgeon*, with intro. and notes by Basil Thomson (London: F. Edwards, 1915), 127.

12. James Boswell, *Life of Johnson*, ed. R. W. Chapman, intro. Pat Rogers (Oxford: Oxford University Press, 1980), 722–3. On curiosity, see Spate, *Paradise Found*, 81, and Daniel A. Baugh, 'Seapower and science: the motives for Pacific exploration', in Derek Howse, ed., *Background to Discovery: Pacific Exploration from Dampier to Cook* (Berkeley: University of California Press, 1990).

13. Cook, *Journals*, ii: 428 n. 2; Cook, *Voyage* (1777), i: 169. I return to Cook's impatience with Mai in Chapter 4.

14. J. Forster, *Observations*, 167.

15. Reynolds, *Discourses*, 58.

16. Letter to the *Gentleman's Magazine*, quoted in McCormick, *Omai*, 138, and see 174. The perception of Mai as a potential 'macaroni' clearly alludes to Joseph Banks's reputation for fashionable dress and pursuits. Perhaps the most striking comparison with Mai's pose in Reynolds's portrait is the engraving of 'A merchant of Java', plate 31 in Johan Niehof, *Voyages and Travels to the East Indies 1653–1670*, intro. Anthony Reid, Oxford in Asia Hardback Reprints (Singapore: Oxford University Press, 1988). Reid points out that this was 'one of the most influential accounts of the Malay World and South India in English' in the eighteenth century (v).

17. George Colman the younger, quoted in, for example, Charles Lyte, *Sir Joseph Banks: 18th Century Explorer, Botanist and Entrepreneur* (Newton Abbot: David and Charles, 1980), 192.

18. Reynolds, *Discourses*, 130, 129, 67.

19. Reynolds, *Discourses*, 136, 135, 137. I discuss this Discourse in more detail in my earlier version of this essay, see 'Curiously marked'. For a fuller reading of Reynolds's argument see John Barrell, *The Political Theory of Painting from Reynolds to Hazlitt: The Body of the Public* (New Haven: Yale University Press, 1986), 136–58.

20. Reynolds, *Discourses*, 137. Reynolds's portrait of Mai was exhibited at the Academy with a portrait of the same size of Georgiana, Duchess of

Devonshire, in fashionable dress, almost as though in allusion to the juxta-position of unacceptable fashions in Reynolds's Discourse. See McCormick, *Omai*, 168–9, 174.

21. Reynolds, *Discourses*, 138. On morality, custom, and the constitution of com-munity in these decades see Adam Smith, *The Theory of Moral Sentiments*, ed. D. D. Raphael and A. L. Macfie (Oxford: Clarendon Press, 1976), pt I. ss. 1–2, and pt v, and John Bender, *Imagining the Penitentiary: Fiction and the Architecture of Mind in Eighteenth-Century England* (Chicago: Chicago University Press, 1987), 218–28. On anatomy and the female body in this period see Londa Schiebinger, *The Mind Has No Sex? Women and the Origins of Modern Science* (Cambridge, MA: Harvard University Press, 1989), ch. 7.

22. This painting was also subject to a temporary bar on export in 2002, because of its 'value for the study of Britain's colonial and maritime heritage, and its celebration of late 18th-century England's place as a hub of cosmopolitan society, intellectual patronage and fashionable life'. (Department for Culture, Media and Sport, press notice, 13 Feb. 2002).

23. Mai's tattoos rarely escaped detailed comment by those he met in London. Perhaps to satisfy their eager curiosity as well as his own sense of humour, Mai told several people that the nine tattoos on his right hand marked the number of his wives. See McCormick, *Omai*, 102, 139.

24. On Banks as a 'clubman', see Gascoigne, *Joseph Banks*, 70.

25. McCormick, *Omai*, 116; see also John O'Keeffe, *A Short Account of the New Pantomime Called Omai, or, A Trip round the World; Performed at the Theatre-Royal in Covent-Garden* (London: Cadell, 1785), 'Characters', where this dress is attributed to an 'Otaheitean, supposed to have accompanied Omai to England'. On the pantomime, see Greg Dening, *Mr Bligh's Bad Language: Passion, Power and Theatre on the Bounty* (Cambridge: Cambridge University Press, 1992), 269–76, and Rüdiger Joppien, *Philippe Jacques de Loutherbourg, R. A.: 1740–1812* (London: Greater London Council, 1973). *Oxford Magazine*, June 1770, cited in *OED*, macaroni, 2.

26. Reynolds, *Discourses*, 137–8.

27. Walpole joked that the artist on the *Endeavour* voyage might expect to be 'scalped by that wild man, Banks' (Alexander, *Omai*, 49). For some commentators, at least, his travels seem to have confused his national identity.

28. Banks, *Journal*, II: 330, 332–3.

29. James Burney, *With Captain James Cook in the Antarctic and Pacific*, ed. Beverley Hooper (Canberra: National Library of Australia, 1975), 96. For fuller discussion of this incident, see Chapter 5 below.

30. [John Marra] *Journal of the Resolution's Voyage* (London: F. Newbury, 1775), 94. In Burney's account, the European party initially identified what they found as dog's flesh, but in Marra's account they are credited with greater forensic per-cipience, and the dogs become accomplices in the alien savagery of the islanders.

31. Burney, *With Cook*, 97.

32. The journal of Charlotte Ann Burney, which reports Charles Burney's comments, also indicates that the discovery of the remains at Grass Cove was not universally regarded as convincing proof of cannibalism, or as an occasion for instinctive horror. David Garrick commented, on hearing of James Burney's whispers: 'Why, what, they didn't eat 'em? . . . we are not sure . . . perhaps they potted 'em!' In Burney, *Diary*, II: 283.

33. Cook, *Voyage* (1777), I: 127, 245.

34. Cook, *Voyage* (1777), I: 245–6.

35. Cook, *Voyage* (1777), I: 245.

36. Parkinson, *Journal of a Voyage*, 91. On the tattooing practices of New Zealand, see Gell, *Wrapping*; and Ko Te Riria and David Simmons, *Moko Rangatira: Maori Tattoo* (Auckland, NZ: Reed, 1989), and (for a colonial view) Major General Horatio G. Robley, *Moko; or Maori Tattooing* (London: Chapman and Hall, 1896). For further discussion of some of these issues and images see Leonard Bell, *The Maori in European Art* (Wellington: Reed, 1980); Margaret Jolly, 'Illnatured comparisons: racism and relativism in European representations of Ni-Vanuatu from Cook's second voyage', *History and Anthropology*, 5 (1990); and Bronwen Douglas, '"Cureous figures": European voyagers and *tatau*/tattoo in Polynesia, 1595–1800', in Nicholas Thomas, Anna Cole, and Bronwen Douglas, eds., *Tattoo: Bodies, Art and Exchange in the Pacific and the West* (London: Reaktion, 2005), p. 39.

37. Monkhouse's Journal, in Cook, *Journals*, I: 586.

38. I have in mind Gainsborough's *The Woodman* (see Peter Simon, after Gainsborough, *The Woodman* (London: John and Josiah Boydell, 4 June 1790), and *Shepherd Boy* (see Richard Earlom after Gainsborough, *A Shepherd* (1781)), both of which adopt the raised eyes of Murillo's *Christ Child as the Good Shepherd*.

39. Thomas, *Discoveries*, 228.

40. G. Forster, *Voyage*, 86, 98; Salmond, *Cannibal Dog*, 182, 183. Salmond also observes that the Maori called Hodges '"Tuhituhi" [painter]'. J. Forster, *Journals*, 249. See Thomas, *Discoveries*, 172.

41. *John Ledyard's Journey through Russia and Siberia, 1787–1788: The Journal and Selected Letters*, ed. Stephen D. Watrous (Madison: University of Wisconsin Press, 1966), 182–3.

42. See J. C. Beaglehole, 'The Young Banks', in Banks's *Journal*, I: 41 and n. 1. For a discussion which complicates this notion of nautical tradition see Joanna White, 'Marks of transgression: the tattooing of Europeans in the Pacific Islands', in Thomas, Cole, and Douglas, eds., *Tattoo*, 72–89.

43. John Elliott and Richard Pickersgill, *Captain Cook's Second Voyage: The Journals of Lieutenants Elliott and Pickersgill*, ed. Christine Holmes (London: Caliban Books, 1984), 20–1.

44. *The Bligh Notebook: Rough Account – 'Lieutenant Wm Bligh's Voyage in the Bounty's Launch from the Ship to Tofua & from thence to Timor', 28 April to 14 June 1789, with a Draft List of the Bounty Mutineers*, facsimile and

transciption, ed. John Bach (North Sydney: Allen & Unwin with National Library of Australia, 1987), 214. James Morrisson, who bore the star and garter tattoo, remained on Tahiti for some time after the mutiny. Writing about his stay, he argued that every line of the tattoos was significant, dismissing the distinction between public significance and private whim made by other voyagers.

45. Reynolds, *Discourses*, 137–8.

4   Terms of trade in Tonga and Vanuatu

1. Spate, *Paradise Found*, 215. The first section of this essay is a revised version of the essay I first published as 'Cook in Tonga: terms of trade', in Rod Edmond and Vanessa Smith, eds., *Islands in History and Representation* (London: Routledge, 2003).

2. James Cook, *The Journals of Captain James Cook on his Voyages of Discovery*, III: *The Voyage of the Resolution and Discovery, 1776–1780*, Parts 1 and 2, ed. J. C. Beaglehole, Hakluyt Society Extra Series XXXVI (Cambridge: Cambridge University Press, 1967), 141.

3. Cook, *Journals*, III: 166.

4. Cook, *Journals*, III: 166.

5. For discussion of Cook's perception of social rank in the Tongan islands, see Gannath Obeyesekere, *The Apotheosis of Captain Cook: European Mythmaking in the Pacific*, with an new afterword by the author (Princeton: Princeton University Press, 1997) 28–33; Marshall and Williams, *Great Map*, 286–7; on Mai's role, see McCormick, *Omai*, 211–23.

6. Joppien and Smith, *Art*, II: 70.

7. J. Forster, *Journal*, 548; Joppien and Smith, *Art*, II: 70.

8. G. Forster, *Voyage*, 232.

9. Joppien and Smith, *Art*, II: 35.

10. Joppien and Smith (*Art*, II: 84) comment on the 'Madonna-like motif of a Tahitian mother and child, of remarkably pale complexion'.

11. G. Forster, *Voyage*, 232.

12. Thomas, '"On the varieties of the human species": Forster's comparative ethnology', in J. Forster, *Observations*, xxxiii, and see xxv. See also Nicholas Thomas, 'Melanesians and Polynesians: ethnic typifications inside and outside anthropology', in his *In Oceania*.

13. J. Forster, *Observations*, 237, 229.

14. Cook, *Voyage* (1777), II: 34.

15. See Smith, *European Vision*, 41–51, and Chapter 1 above.

16. James King, 'At Tonga, May–July 1777' [Adm 55/116], in Cook, *Journals*, III: 1373.

17. On relations between Europeans and Maori, see Anne Salmond, *Two Worlds: First Meetings between Maori and Europeans, 1642–1772* (Honolulu: Hawai'i

University Press, 1991), and *Between Worlds: Early Exchanges between Maori and Europeans, 1773–1815* (Honolulu: Hawai'i University Press, 1997).

18. Cook, *Journals*, iii: 267.

19. J. Forster, *Journal*, 389–90.

20. J. Forster, *Journal*, 390.

21. James Barry, 'Lecture ii. On design', in *Works*, ii: 400–1.

22. Charles Clerke, 'Account of Tonga, 1777', in Cook, *Journals*, iii: 1306.

23. J. Forster, *Journal*, 397.

24. J. Forster, *Journal*, 395–6.

25. Cook, *Voyage* (1777), i: 217.

26. Cook, *Voyage* (1777), i: 20.

27. See William Mariner, *An Account of the Natives of the Tonga Islands, in the South Pacific Ocean. Compiled and Arranged from the Extensive Communications of Mr. William Mariner, Several Years Resident in Those Islands. By John Martin, M. D.* (1st UK edn, 1817; 1st North American edn, Boston: Charles Ewer, 1820), 304–6.

28. Elliott, in *Journals of Elliott and Pickersgill*, 21.

29. William Anderson, 'A journal of a voyage made in his Majestys Sloop Resolution', in Cook, *Journals*, iii: 901.

30. King, 'At Tonga' in Cook, *Journals*, iii, 1362; 'The natives themselves mentioned the circumstance to Mr. Mariner, stating, that they allowed the Papalangies [Europeans] to get the victory sometimes, because they did not like to beat the poor fellows so much' (Mariner, *Account*, 443).

31. See George Rudé, *The Crowd in History, 1730–1848* (New York: John Wiley, 1964), 11; Cook, *Journals*, iii: 108; Anderson, 'Journal' 963; Clerke, 'Account', 1303.

32. Cook, *Journals*, iii: 171.

33. See G. Forster, *Voyage*, 485, 495.

34. Anderson, 'Journal' in Cook, *Journals*, iii, 928.

35. J. Forster, *Journal*, 377.

36. See G. Forster, *Voyage*, 230–1.

37. J. Forster, *Journal*, 377–8.

38. Cook, *Journals*, iii: 245, 248.

39. Cook, *Journals*, iii: 249.

40. Cook, *Journals*, iii: 255.

41. Cook, *Journals*, iii: 446.

42. Anderson, 'Journal', in Cook, *Journals*, iii: 959.

43. J. Forster, *Journal*, 395.

44. G. Forster, *Voyage*, 585–6.

45. See Michael Dettelbach, '"A kind of Linnaean being": Forster in eighteenth-century natural history', in J. Forster, *Observations*, lxvi–viii.

46. King, 'At Tonga', in Cook, *Journals*, iii: 1366, 1364.

47. Anderson, 'Journal', in Cook, *Journals*, iii: 932–3, 946.

48. Anderson, 'Journal', in Cook, *Journals*, iii: 945.

49. Anderson, 'Journal', in Cook, *Journals*, III: 946.

50. Cook, *Voyage* (1777), II: 13–14.

51. Cook, *Journals*, III: 444.

52. Cook, *Voyage* (177), II:13.

53. J. Forster, *Observations*, 236.

54. Joppien and Smith, *Art*, II: 92.

55. *Morning Post*, 29 Apr. 1778, quoted in Joppien and Smith, *Art*, II: 227.

56. Joppien and Smith, *Art*, II: 93.

57. Cook, *Voyage* (1777), II: 34.

58. Cook, *Voyage* (1777), II: 30.

59. On hearing that no islander 'had been off to the ship' overnight, Cook comments that 'so soon was the curiosity of these people satisfied'. *Voyage* (1777), II: 33.

60. Cook, *Journals*, II: 488.

61. Cook, *Voyage* (1777), II: 63; Cook, *Journals*, II: 490.

62. Cook, *Voyage* (1777), II: 76.

63. Cook, *Voyage* (1777), II: 66. The Malakulans may initially have regarded the voyagers as ghosts or ancestors, and it is possible that the Tannese shared this perception, though the evidence from the encounter at Tanna is less clear. See G. Forster, *Voyage*, 813 n. 14, 818 n. 1, 819 n. 20.

64. See G. Forster, *Voyage*, 484.

65. G. Forster, *Voyage*, 481.

66. See Bronwen Douglas, 'Art as ethno-historical text: science, representations and indigenous presence in eighteenth and nineteenth century oceanic voyage literature', in Nicholas Thomas and Diane Losch, eds., and Jennifer Newell, ass. ed., *Double Vision: Art Histories and Colonial Histories in the Pacific* (Cambridge: Cambridge University Press, 1999) 95–6 n. 31.

67. G. Forster, *Voyage*, 484.

68. G. Forster, *Voyage*, 556.

69. G. Forster, *Voyage*, 520.

70. G. Forster, *Voyage*, 495.

71. G. Forster, *Voyage*, 534–5.

72. Adam Smith, 'Of the nature of that imitation which takes place in what are called the imitative arts', in W. P. D. Wightman and J. C. Bryce, and I. S. Ross, eds., *Essays on Philosophical Subjects* (Oxford: Clarendon Press, 1980), section 2, para. 13. For an account of the dating of the essay see W. P. D. Wightman's Introduction, 171–2.

73. G. Forster, *Voyage*, 555.

74. On representations of the women of Vanuatu, see Jolly, '"Ill-natured comparisons"', 341–3.

75. G. Forster, *Voyage*, 557.

76. I quote from Cook's confident pronouncements of February 1775, *Journals*, II: 643. For fuller discussion of Cook's theories about the southern continent,

see J. C. Beaglehole, *The Life of Captain James Cook* (London: Hakluyt Society, 1974), especially 286–7, 433, and ch. 16, 'The second island sweep'.

77. Henry Home, Lord Kames, *Sketches*, I: 31. Kames has in mind here 'Some islands adjacent to New Guinea . . . inhabited by Negroes, a bold, mischievous, untractable race; always ready to attack strangers when they approach the shore.' He contrasts these islanders with the New Zealanders, and later with the Tongans, Easter islanders, and Tahitians (I: 31–8).

78. See Nicholas Thomas, '"On the varieties of the human species"', in J. Forster, *Observations*, xxiii–xl.

79. Jolly, '"Ill-natured comparisons"', 331.

80. Cook, *Voyage* (1777), II: 56. William Wales, 'Journal', in Cook, *Journals*, II: 867 (Appendix v); G. Forster, *Voyage*, 555, and see 820 n. 23.

81. Cook, *Voyage* (1777), II: 65–6.

82. Pocock, 'Nature and history', 28. See Smith, 'Posthumous reputation', in *Imagining*, 236.

83. Cook, *Voyage* (1777), II: 79.

84. G. Forster, *Voyage*, 548.

85. G. Forster, *Voyage*, 419.

86. G. Forster, *Voyage*, 259–60.

87. G. Forster, *Voyage*, 548–9.

88. G. Forster, *Voyage*, 551, 822 n. 65.

89. J. Forster, *Journal*, 613.

90. G. Forster, *Voyage*, 535.

5   New Zealand colonial romance

1. Banks, *Journal*, II: 4.

2. See Salmond, *Two Worlds*, 267–8, and *Between Worlds*, 241–3; Keith Sinclair, *A History of New Zealand* (Auckland: Penguin, 1959; rev. edn, 1988), 33.

3. [Rickman], *Journal*, 47. All further references in text.

4. See Salmond, *Between Worlds*, 234–6.

5. *Gentleman's Magazine*, review of [Rickman's] *Journal*, 1781. See Peter Hulme, *Colonial Encounters: Europe and the Native Caribbean, 1492–1797* (London: Routledge, 1986), ch. 6.

6. Mary Louise Pratt, *Imperial Eyes: Travel Writing and Transculturation* (London: Routledge, 1992), 97.

7. I follow Anne Salmond's suggestion about the girl's name, in *Between Worlds*, 121. Peter Gathercole observes that the tattooing of Maori men 'was generally restricted . . . to the face and between the waist and knees'; in his 'Contexts of Maori *moko*', in Arnold Rubin, ed., *Marks of Civilization: Artistic Transformations of the Human Body* (Los Angeles: Museum of Cultural History, 1988), 171. Many European journalists from the Cook voyages comment with perhaps a suprising degree of sensitive dismay on the prevalence of headlice. By 1848, sailors of

the US navy who were 'lousy' could attract a punishment of six lashes, which leads me to imagine that the condition might also have been a punishable form of 'uncleanness' in the eighteenth-century British navy. See the 'Table of Punishments' given in J. Welles Henderson and Rodney P. Carlisle, *Jack Tar: A Sailor's Life, 1750–1910* (Woodbridge: Antique Collectors Club, 1999), 97, and N. A. M. Rodger, *The Wooden World: An Anatomy of the Georgian Navy* (London: Fontana, 1988), chs. 3, 6.

8. David Samwell, *Some Account of a Voyage to the South Sea's In 1776–1777–1778*, 13 Feb. 1777, in Cook, *Journals*, III: 1000.

9. G. L. Craik, *The New Zealanders*, The Library of Entertaining Knowledge (London: Knight, 1830), 142; John Savage, *Some Account of New Zealand; Particularly the Bay of Islands* (1807), in A. D. McKinley, ed., *Savage's Account of New Zealand in 1805, together with Schemes of 1771 and 1824 for Commerce and Colonization* (Wellington, NZ: Watkins, 1939), 53. See James Drummond, ed., *John Rutherford, The White Chief: A Story of Adventure in New Zealand* (Christchurch, NZ: Whitcombe and Tombs, 1908), 68–71, and 76–7, on Rutherford's subsequent career, 223–4 and 224n. See also Robley, *Moko*, ch. 7. On Rutherford's biography as 'romantic fantasy', see Stephan Oetterman, 'On display: tattooed entertainers in America and Germany', in Jane Caplan, ed., *Written on the Body: The Tattoo in European and American History* (London: Reaktion, 2000), 198–9. On tattooing as a sign of status, cf. Gathercole, 'Contexts of Maori *Moko*', 171–3.

10. G. Forster, *Voyage*, 125. On the different tattooing techniques, see Gell, *Wrapping*, 249–51.

11. Gathercole, 'Contexts of Maori *Moko*', 176.

12. See Gell, *Wrapping*, 286.

13. Gathercole, 'Contexts of Maori *Moko*', 176. See also Gell, *Wrapping*, 259, 311.

14. The Europeans were moved and dismayed by the grief at parting from their home displayed by the two young boys from New Zealand who joined the *Discovery* in 1777. See for example Samwell, in Cook, *Journals*, III: 1000–2. A Pakeha Maori is a European (or 'pakeha') living as a Maori.

15. See Gell, *Wrapping*, 247.

16. Compare the mixture of fear and admiration with which Frederick Edward Maning details the 'absolutely horrible' sight, in his *Old New Zealand: A Tale of the Good Old Times. By A Pakeha Maori* (Auckland, NZ: Creighton, 1863), 60–2.

17. Smith, *Theory of Moral Sentiments*, v. 2. 13, 11, 9, 10.

18. Millar, *Origin*, 30.

19. See, for example, George Forster's comments: 'Among all savage nations the weaker sex is ill-treated, and the law of the strongest is put in force. Their women are mere drudges, who prepare raiment and provide dwellings, who cook and frequently collect their food, and are requited by blows and all kinds of severity. At New Zealand it seems they carry this tyranny to excess, and the

males are taught from their earliest age, to hold their mothers in contempt, contrary to all our principles of morality.' *Voyage*, 277.

20. Forster writes: 'and if we add to this a certain stench which announced them even from a distance, and the abundance of vermin which not only infested their hair, but also crawled on their clothes, and which they occasionally cracked between their teeth'. *Voyage*, 121, 123.

21. Smith, *Theory of Moral Sentiments*, V. 2. 9.

22. J. Forster, *Observations*, 208.

23. The more widely accepted account of the incident apportions more blame to John Rowe, the master's mate in charge of the cutter sent to Grass Cove, who is said to have shot dead a Maori who was helping himself to some bread. See for example Anderson's account, in Cook, *Journals*, iii: 798–9; and Samwell's account, iii: 998–9; as well as Cook's, iii: 63–4, 68–9. See also Ian G. Barber, 'Early contact ethnography and understanding: an evaluation of the Cook expeditionary accounts of the Grass Cove conflict', in Calder, Lamb, and Orr, eds., *Voyages and Beaches*; Thomas, *Discoveries*, 250–5; and Anne Salmond, *Cannibal Dog*, ch. 11.

24. Obeyesekere, '"British cannibals"', 641, 653 (the examples Obeyesekere has in mind here are the fate of the Marion voyage, and the Grass Cove incident).

25. Elsdon Best, 'Notes on the art of war', Part 2, *Journal of the Polynesian Society*, 11 (1902), 71, quoted in Marshall Sahlins, 'Other times, other customs: the anthropology of history', in his *Islands*, 59. I quote from pp. 58–9 of this essay.

26. For a suggestive account of the parallel relation between sexual possession and social consumption in land acquisition, see Marshall Sahlins, 'The stranger-king; or, Dumézil among the Fijians', in *Islands*, 89. The Madden Ballad collection includes, for example, 'The chieftain of Hunkyway', 'King of the cannibal islands', and 'The queen of Otaheite'. These must all have been in print by the 1830s, as they often appear juxtaposed on the same sheet as the ballad 'Our king is a true British sailor' – a loyal ditty about King William IV.

27. G. Forster, *Voyage*, 278.

28. Cook, *Journals*, iii: 61–2.

29. Cook, *Journals*, iii: 73.

30. Millar, *Origin*, 45, 3.

31. G. Forster, *Voyage*, 283.

32. Forster writes of the bay 'Between the Capes Tera-Wittee and Palliser', now the site of Wellington, the capital city of New Zealand. G. Forster, *Voyage*, 283, 127–8.

33. [Marra], *Journal*, 21.

34. Elliott, in *Journals of Elliott and Pickersgill*, 14.

35. G. Forster, *Voyage*, 79–80.

36. G. Forster, *Voyage*, 105, 106.

37. *Virgil's Aeneid, Translated by John Dryden*, ed. Frederick M. Keener (Harmondsworth: Penguin, 1997), Book 1. ll. 582–3.

38. *Aeneid*, Bk. 1. ll. 592–3.

39. Nicholas Thomas reads this passage in similar terms in his *Discoveries*, 175–6. My discussion, however, points towards different conclusions.

40. Cook, *Journal*, II: 134.

41. See Nicholas Thomas, 'Liberty and licence: the Forsters' accounts of New Zealand society', in Chloe Chard and Helen Langdon, eds., *Transports: Imaginative Geographies 1660–1800* (New Haven: Yale University Press, 1996), and *Discoveries*, 176–8; and Salmond, *Between Worlds*, chs. 3–6.

42. Cook, *Journals*, II: 133, 119.

43. G. Forster, *Voyage*, 90–1.

44. Joppien and Smith, *Art*, II: 28.

45. Gainsborough wrote, 'do you really think a regular Composition in the Landskip way should ever be fill'd with History, or any figures but such as fill a place (I won't say stop a Gap) or to create a little business for the Eye in order to be drawn from the Trees in order to return to them with more glee – I did not know you admired those *tragicomic* Pictures'. Letter to William Jackson, in Michael Rosenthal, *The Art of Thomas Gainsborough* (New Haven and London: Yale University Press, 1999), 186.

46. Joseph Addison, *The Spectator*, ed. Donald F. Bond (Oxford: Clarendon Press, 1965), 5 vols. no. 411 (21 June 1712), III: 538. See Robert Jones, *Gender and the Formation of Taste in Eighteenth-Century Britain: The Analysis of Beauty* (Cambridge: Cambridge University Press, 1998), 44–5, for an illuminating discussion of the implications of 'property' in this essay.

47. See, for example, Cowper's accounts of the waggoner, in Book 4, ll. 341–73, and the woodman engaged in his 'solitary task', in Book 5, ll. 33–62, in contrast to his judgements on less solitary figures later in Book 4. *The Task* (1785), in *The Poems of William Cowper*, II: *1782–1785*, ed. John D. Baird and Charles Ryskamp (Oxford: Clarendon Press, 1995).

48. See Joppien and Smith, *Art* II: 129.

49. G. Forster, *Voyage*, 106.

50. G. Forster, *Voyage*, 81.

51. Smith, 'Posthumous reputation', in *Imagining*, 231, 236.

52. *Morning Post*, 22 Sept. 1775. For a detailed analysis of the changing political allegiances see Lucyle Werkmeister, *The London Daily Press, 1772–1792* (Lincoln, NB: University of Nebraska Press, 1963).

53. *The Whitehall Evening-Post*, 29 Jan. – 1 Feb. 1780.

54. See Margaret Ashmun, *The Singing Swan* (New Haven: Yale University Press, 1931), 74 and n.

55. Seward, *Elegy*, 4, 5. For further discussion of this poem, see Harriet Guest, *Small Change: Women, Learning, Patriotism, 1750–1810* (Chicago: Chicago University Press, 2000), ch. 10, and Chapter 6 below.

56. Helen Maria Williams, *The Morai, An Ode*, in Andrew Kippis, *The Life of Captain James Cook* (London: G. Nicol, 1783), Appendix 2, 525. Kippis notes that the poem was written at his request, 511.

57. *Expostulation*, ll. 364–5, 369, 372, in Cowper, *Poems*, i. The editors note that the poem was begun before 25 Feb. and finished before 8 Apr. 1781, see i: 520.

58. *Charity*, ll. 27–34, 83–4, 139, in Cowper, *Poems*, i. The editors note that the poem was written between late June and 12 July 1781.

59. Kathleen Wilson, *The Sense of the People: Politics, Culture and Imperialism in England, 1715–1785* (Cambridge: Cambridge University Press, 1995; paperback edn 1998), 277.

60. Sea Officer, *An Ode to the Memory of Captain James Cook, of his Majesty's Navy. By a Sea Officer* (Dublin: Hallhead, 1780), 9, 20.

61. W. Fitzgerald, of Gray's Inn, *An Ode to the Memory of the Late Captain James Cook* (London: Robinson, Flexney, Sewell and Faulder, 1780), 8, 13–16.

62. *A Poem on a Voyage of Discovery, Undertaken by a Brother of the Author's, with Other Sonnets, &c* (London: C. & G. Kearsley, 1792), 33, 29.

63. Letter from Cowper to Joseph Hill, Sunday, 13 July, 1777, in William Cowper, *The Letters and Prose Writings of William Cowper*, i: *Adelphi and Letters 1750–1781*, ed. James King and Charles Ryskamp (Oxford: Clarendon Press, 1979), 271–2. The poems do mention both navigation and astronomy, but it is natural history they particularly praise.

64. *Task*, Bk 1, ll. 672–4, 634–5.

65. [Gerald Fitzgerald], *The Injured Islanders; or, The Influence of Art upon the Happiness of Nature* (London: J. Murray, 1779), Preface, 5–6.

6 Ornament and use in London

1. Momus: or The Laughing Philosopher, no. xx, in *Westminster Magazine*, July 1774, 348, 346. This chapter draws extensively on McCormick, *Omai*. Lichtenberg comments that we here see the Viscount [Earl in Paulson] 'in the consulting room of a certain Monsieur de la Pillule, a French doctor' specialising in VD. He adds that 'the success of his practice can be inferred from the whole appearance of the elegant room with its vaulted window overlooking the street, and from what is loudly proclaimed not by the architecture alone but by all the realms of art and nature on the walls . . . there will hardly be a soul except the owner who will understand all the little object lessons hanging up there . . . Whether Hogarth had a purpose in displaying just these relics is difficult to decide; but it is quite possible, even if we regard the whole cabinet as a perfect general satire upon certain collectors of all the rubbish of Nature and Art.' Georg Christoph Lichtenberg, *Lichtenberg's Commentaries on Hogarth's Engravings*, trans. and intro., Innes and Gustav Herdan (London: Cresset Press, 1966), 103–4, 110. This chapter was first published as 'Ornament and use: Mai and Cook in London', in Kathleen Wilson, ed., *A New Imperial History: Culture, Identity and Modernity in Britain and the Empire, 1660–1840* (Cambridge: Cambridge University Press, 2004).

2. Smith, *Theory of Moral Sentiments* iv. 1. 6, 8.

3. Letter from Revd Michael Tyson to Revd Sir John Cullum, 4 Jan. 1775, and Sarah S. Banks 'Memorandums', [15]–[17], cited in McCormick, *Omai*, pp. 130, 113.

4. 'Authentic particulars relating to OMIAH', *Westminster Magazine; Or, The Pantheon of Taste*, Aug. 1774, 427.

5. Smith, *Theory of Moral Sentiments*, IV. 1. 9, 183.

6. Nigel Leask writes that 'It may not be an exaggeration to claim that the accumulation of knowledge in the travel *narrative* (usually based on the redaction of field journals) was seen to provide the sole philosophical justification for the moral and physical risks of distant travel.' In his *Curiosity*, 22. While this is less obviously the case with voyages, including Cook's, than with the land-based travels Leask focuses on, there is a clear sense that the published accounts of voyages were an important form of justification. Prior to the publication of those accounts, however, the curiosities collected by the voyagers were the main focus of public interest.

7. Boswell, *Johnson*, Wednesday, 3 Apr. 1776, 723; McCormick, *Omai*, 169; Burney, *Early Diary*, letter to Mr Crisp, 1 Dec. 1774, I: 337.

8. Burney, *Memoirs of Doctor Burney* (1832), I: 270–1, quoted in Beaglehole, *Life*, 289.

9. Burney, *Early Diary*, 14 Dec. 1775, II: 130–1.

10. Ferguson, *Civil Society*, 251, 253.

11. *London Chronicle*, 22–4 June 1775, 389.

12. William Gardiner, *Music and Friends; or Pleasant Recollections of a Dilettante* (London, 1838), 2 vols., I: 4–5, cited in McCormick, *Omai*, p. 114.

13. *The General Evening Post (London)*, 10–13 June 1775.

14. *Gentleman's Magazine*, Historical Chronicle for 1 Sept. 1774.

15. Reynolds, *Discourses*, 138–9.

16. G. Forster, *Voyage*, 11.

17. Cook, *Journals*, III: 1514–15. Samwell was first appointed as surgeon's mate on the *Resolution*, but was promoted to surgeon on the *Discovery* following the death of Anderson.

18. Douglas Oliver, *Return to Tahiti: Bligh's Second Breadfruit Voyage* (Honolulu: University of Hawai'i Press, 1988), 227.

19. Cook, *Journals*, III: 1073, 1386.

20. G. Forster, *Voyage*, 765.

21. G. Forster, *Voyage*, 11.

22. Hester Thrale Piozzi to Samuel Lysons, 8 July 1789, in Hester Lynch Piozzi, *The Piozzi Letters: Correspondence of Hester Lynch Piozzi, 1784–1821 (formerly Mrs. Thrale)*, ed. Edward A. Bloom and Lillian D. Bloom (Newark: University of Delaware Press, 1989), 6 vols., I: 298. Thrale seems to have heard a version of the report from the *Lady Penrhyn*. See McCormick, *Omai*, 267.

23. The astronomer William Bayly commented on Mai's outfitting for his return that 'Omi being a man of pleasure neglected to inspect into his own Affairs but

left it entirely to other people.' Those other people, Bayly thought, 'used him exceeding ill'. Cook, *Journals*, III: 193 n. 2.

24. For an example, see the photograph of 'Bowles's new travelling map of England and Wales', in Mary Schoeser, *Printed Handkerchiefs*, The London Connection: Number Fourteen (London: Museum of London, 1988), fig. 8.

25. William Ellis, *An Authentic Narrative of a Voyage Performed by Captain Cook and Captain Clerke, in His Majesty's Ships Resolution and Discovery* (London: Robinson, 1782), 2 vols., I: 147. See McCormick, *Omai*, 180, 255.

26. Leask, *Curiosity*, 62.

27. See Seward, *Elegy*, 9: 'To these the Hero leads his living store, / And pours new wonders on th'uncultur'd shore; / The silky fleece, fair fruit, and golden grain; / And future herds and harvests bless the plain.' Seward refers specifically to New Zealand.

28. [Kearsly], *Omiah's Farewell*, Preface, iv.

29. G. Forster, *Voyage*, 12.

30. Boswell, *Boswell: The Ominous Years*, London, 2 Apr. 1776, 310–11.

31. G. Forster, *Voyage*, 11.

32. Smith, *Theory of Moral Sentiments*, IV. 1. 10, 184; 9, 183.

33. Oliver, *Return*, 228.

34. William Ellis, *Polynesian Researches, during a Residence of nearly Eight Years in the Society and Sandwich Islands* (1829; 2nd rev. enl. edn, London: Fisher, Son & Jackson, 1831–2), 4 vols., II: 370. On Ellis see Rod Edmond, 'Translating cultures: William Ellis and missionary writing', in Lincoln, ed., *Science and Exploration*; Rod Edmond, *Representing the South Pacific: Colonial Discourse from Cook to Gauguin* (Cambridge: Cambridge University Press, 1997), ch. 4; Rod Edmond, 'Missionaries on Tahiti, 1797–1840', in Calder, Lamb, and Orr, eds., *Voyages and Beaches*; and Andrew Porter, 'The career of William Ellis: British missions, the Pacific, and the American connection', in Alan Frost and Jane Samson, eds., *Pacific Empires: Essays in Honour of Glyndwr Williams* (Melbourne: Melbourne University Press, 1999).

35. Cook, *Journals*, III: 193. The Europeans only seem to see the degree of interest and sentiment which they had clearly expected to be widespread in the reunion of Mai with his sister. See Cook's account, III: 192–3, 213, and Samwell's journal, III: 1052–3. On value created by association, see Thomas, *Entangled Objects*, ch. 3.

36. See McCormick, *Omai*, 180.

37. [? John Townshend], 'Omiah: an ode', in *The New Foundling Hospital for Wit* (London, 1784), 6 vols., II: 132–6, quoted in McCormick, *Omai*, 186.

38. [Rickman], *Journal*, 133–4.

39. *Gentleman's Magazine*, review of Cook, *Voyage* (1777). See also Smith, 'Posthumous reputation', in *Imagining*, 227.

40. Smith, *Theory of Moral Sentiments*, IV, 1. 10, 183.

41. Prince Hoare, *Memoirs of Granville Sharpe, Esq. Composed from his Own Manuscripts, and Other Authentic Documents in the Possession of his Family and of the African Institution* (London: Colburn, 1820), 249.
42. See Obeyesekere, *Apotheosis*; and Marshall Sahlins, *How 'Natives' Think: About Captain Cook, for Example* (Chicago: Chicago University Press, 1996).
43. Smith, 'Posthumous reputation', in *Imagining*, 231.
44. Boswell, *Ominous Years*, London, 2 Apr. 1776, 309, 308.
45. On Mai's attention to dress, see McCormick, *Omai*, 115, 125.
46. Kippis, *Cook*, ch. 7, 482.
47. Kippis, *Cook*, Preface, ix.
48. Letter from Molesworth Phillips to William Brockenden, 5 Apr. 1826, quoted in Rüdiger Joppien and Bernard Smith, *The Art of Captain Cook's Voyages*, III: *catalogue, The Voyage of the Resolution and Discovery, 1776–1780* (New Haven: Yale University Press, 1988), cat. 3.453, p. 648.
49. Jane Austen, *Persuasion*, intro. Forrest Reid (London: Oxford University Press, 1930), 22–3, 20.
50. *St. James's Chronicle; or, British Evening-Post*, no. 2946, for 27–9 Jan. 1780.
51. *Westminster Magazine*, Jan. 1780, 7.
52. Marie Sophie von La Roche, *Sophie in London, 1786: Being the Diary of Sophie von La Roche*, trans. and intro. Clare Williams (London: Jonathan Cape, 1933), 277.

Epilogue: *the Effects of Peace* and *The Consequences of War* in 1794–1795

1. Farington, *Diary*, I: 248, 5 Oct. 5 1794. See also I: 265–7, 29 and 30 Nov. 1794. See also, for example, the *Oracle*, 29 Nov. 1794. For a fuller account, see Stuebe, *Hodges*. The exhibition is also discussed briefly in Holger Hoock, *The King's Artists: The Royal Academy of Arts and the Politics of British Culture, 1760–1840* (Oxford: Clarendon Press, 2003), 191–2; see also Stephen Deuchar, *Sporting Art in Eighteenth-Century England: A Social and Political History* (New Haven: Yale University Press, 1988), 157–9. This chapter is a substantially revised version of the essay first published as '"The consequences of war" in the winter of 1794–95', in Quilley and Bonehill, eds., *Hodges*.
2. Extracts from Hodges's Catalogue appear in Edwards, *Anecdotes*. I quote from 247–8.
3. See Farington, *Diary*, I: 271, 275, 1794 Dec. 7 and 14, and II: 296, 26 Jan. 1795.
4. Farington, *Diary*, II: 296, 25 Jan. 1795.
5. I quote from the advertisement for Loutherbourg's exhibition which appeared, for example, in the *Morning Chronicle*, 3 Dec. 1794.
6. Farington, *Diary*, II: 302, 7 Feb. 1795.
7. Hayley reported on Hodges's state to Nathaniel Marchant, who was Farington's principle source of news about the painter. Farington recorded Hayley's remarks on 3 Feb. 1795, II: 301. Farington reports, on 20 June 1796 (II: 587), that Hodges

intends to exhibit the following year, but on 2 Mar. 1797 (III: 783), he records that 'Hodges is likely to do very well at Dartmouth; He has bought a House there in a beautiful situation. He has never painted since He went there.'

8. See Stuebe, *Hodges*, 350, 352–3.

9. Hodges's Catalogue, in Edwards, *Anecdotes*, 248.

10. 'Biographical anecdotes of William Hodges, Esq. with an elegant portrait', *Literary and Biographical Magazine, and British Review*, 8 (May 1792). On Hotham and Fawkes see Stuebe, *Hodges*, 68, and *DNB*. Farington on Hayley, *Diary*, II: 289, 6 Jan. 1795. For the date of publication of Hayley's *The National Advocates*, see *Memoirs of the Life and Writings of William Hayley, Esq.*, ed. John Johnson (London: Henry Colburn, 1823), 2 vols. I: 467.

11. In his earlier *Essay on Painting*, Hayley had endorsed the unrivalled status of history painting, and praised the more limited social utility of portraiture in representing for emulation the 'inspiring forms of ancient days', and dispelling 'the cloud, with melancholy fraught, / That absence throws', but had not commented on landscape painting. William Hayley, *An Essay on Painting, in A Poetical Epistle to an Eminent Painter. With Notes* (2nd edn., Dublin: P. Byrne, 1781), First Part, ll. 111, 116–17.

12. William Hodges, letter to William Hayley from London, dated 19 Aug. 1794, from a copy held in the Mitchell Library, State Library of New South Wales. I am grateful to Michael Rosenthal, who generously alerted me to this letter. I have reproduced the letter at some length because as far as I am aware it has not been reproduced elsewhere.

13. Farington, *Diary*, II: 301, 3 Feb. 1795. Hodges participated in the dinner celebrating the twenty-fifth anniversary of the Royal Academy held in December 1793, at which toasts were proposed to the Dukes of York and Clarence and the army and navy. Hodges approved the loyal address Farington produced for the occasion. See Simon MacDonald, 'William Hodges's *The Effects of Peace* and *The Consequences of War* (1794–95)', MA dissertation, Courtauld Institute of Art, University of London, 2005, 4 n. 8; and Farington, *Diary*, I: 126, 31 Dec. 1793, and I: 123, 23 Dec. 1793.

14. *PH*, XXXI: 959.

15. See John Barrell, *Imagining the King's Death: Figurative Treason, Fantasies of Regicide, 1793–1796* (Oxford: Oxford University Press, 2000), 191.

16. *Morning Post*, 28 Nov. 1794.

17. I quote from Guildford's amendment, *PH*, XXXI: 970.

18. *PH*, XXXI: 1231.

19. *Oracle*, 22 July 1794.

20. *Oracle*, 22 Oct. 1794. The report noted that 'The sketches, which are finely worked up, are finished; the large canvasses begun upon.'

21. *Times*, 28 Nov. 1794.

22. Sir Edward Knatchbull's speech, *PH*, XXXI: 1008.

23. *PH*, XXXI: 984.

24. *PH*, xxxi: 1029.

25. *PH*, xxxi: 1031.

26. Earl of Lauderdale's speech, *PH*, xxxi: 988.

27. C. J. Fox, *PH*, xxxi: 1052–3.

28. Duke of Bedford's speech, *PH*, xxxi: 993.

29. *PH*, xxxi: 1047.

30. *Morning Post*, 2 Feb. 1795.

31. *Courier*, 12 Jan. 1795.

32. Hodges's Catalogue in Edwards, *Anecdotes*, 248–50. *Oracle*, 22 Oct. 1794.

33. Edwards, *Anecdotes*, 251.

34. Edwards, *Anecdotes*, 249–50.

35. Farington, *Diary*, i: 266–67, 30 Nov. 1794.

36. *Oracle*, 22 Oct. 1794.

37. Farington, *Diary*, ii: 302, 5 Feb. 1795.

38. [A. L. Barbauld], *Sins of Government, Sins of the Nation; or, A Discourse for the Fast, Appointed on April 19, 1793. By a Volunteer* (4th edn, London: J. Johnson, 1793), 27, 28, 36–7.

39. 'Religious musings: a desultory poem, written on the Christmas Eve of 1794', ll. 163–7, in Samuel Taylor Coleridge, *Poetical Works*, ed. Ernest Hartley Coleridge (Oxford: Oxford University Press, 1969). See Coleridge's note to l. 159 on the parliamentary debates on peace of 1794.

40. Joseph Fawcet, *The Art of War. A Poem* (London: J. Johnson, 1795), 36, 37.

41. *Morning Chronicle*, 5 Jan. 1795. See Anne Stott, *Hannah More: The First Victorian* (Oxford: Oxford University Press, 2003), 199, and for Dartmouth's connections with Wilberforce's circle, 82, 87, 177. *DNB* notes that Walter Ramsden Fawkes later spoke for Wilberforce's Abolition Bill.

42. In Stuebe, *Hodges*, 354.

43. *Oracle*, 22 July 1794.

44. In Steube, *Hodges*, 354.

45. Farington, *Diary*, i: 266–7, 30 Nov. 1794.

46. *Oracle*, 22 Oct. 1794.

47. Farington, *Diary*, i: 266–7, 30 Nov. 1794.

48. See *Oracle*, 23 Dec. 1793.

49. *Times*, 30 Jan. 1795; *Morning Post*, 29 Jan. 1795, and 30 Jan. 1795. See also *Oracle*, 4 Jan. 1794, 7 Jan. 1794, 8 Jan. 1794.

50. *Annual Register, or a View of the History, Politics, and Literature, for the Year 1795* (2nd edn, London: for the proprietors of Dodsley's Annual Register, 1807), The History of Europe, ch. 2, 31. Letter from 'A friend to peace and humanity', in *Courier*, 2 Jan. 1795. *Annual Register, or a View of the History, Politics, and Literature for the Year 1794* (2nd edn, London: for the proprietors of Dodsley's Annual Register, 1806), The History of Europe, ch. 12, 221. See Ian R. Christie, *Wars and Revolutions: Britain, 1760–1815* (Cambridge, MA: Harvard University Press, 1982), 197; and Stephen Pope, *The Cassell Dictionary of the Napoleonic Wars*

(London: Cassell, 1999), 'Poland', 'Ottoman Empire', 'Russia'. One of Gillray's series of prints on *The Consequences of a Successful French Invasion* (1798) shows Turkish mutes supporting the French, in allusion to French/Turkish friendship.

51. *Courier*, 23 Jan. 1795. See also S. T. Coleridge, 'Ode to the departing year' (1796), ll. 38–61, and nn, in Coleridge, *Poetical Works*.

52. On the treaty, see John T. Alexander, *Catherine the Great: Life and Legend* (Oxford: Oxford University Press, 1989), 318.

53. Letter from 'A friend to peace and humanity', in *Courier*, 2 Jan. 1795. On Turkish links with the Polish rebels, see Alexander, *Catherine the Great*, 315.

54. William T. Whitley, *Artists and their Friends in England, 1700–1799* (New York: B. Blom, 1928; reissue 1968), 2 vols. II: 99. See Dorinda Evans, *Mather Brown: Early American Artist in England* (Middletown, CT: Wesleyan University Press, 1982), 61. The *Morning Post*'s contempt for Brown was enduring. On 13 Oct. 1794, for example, he is alluded to as 'The Historical and Portrait Artist famous for painting likenesses of persons whom he never saw'.

55. Evans, *Brown*, 87, 115.

56. Farington, *Diary*, II: 312, 3 Mar. 1795, and I: 251, 7 Oct. 1794.

57. The W. T. Whitley Papers, II: 'Mather Brown'.

58. Evans, *Brown*, 114.

59. See, for example, *Oracle*, 29 Nov. 2, 3, 4, 5, 9, 13, 27 Dec. 1794; *Morning Chronicle*, 15, 17, 23, 25 Dec. 1794; *Morning Post*, 13, 15 Dec. 1794, and *Times*, 13, 16 Dec. 1794. I quote from the advertisements that appeared in the *Oracle* and the *Times*. See, for example, the petition announced in the *Courier*, 12 Jan. 1795, under the headline 'WAR OR PEACE'.

60. *Courier*, 8 Jan. 1795.

61. Farington, *Diary*, II, 270, 6 Dec. 1794.

62. Victoria and Albert Museum Library, Press Cuttings, III: 638 (September 1793), quoted in Stuebe, *Hodges*, 68. *Morning Post*, 24 May 1794.

63. *True Briton*, 2 Feb. 1795.

64. Sir William Henry Dillon, K. C. H., Vice-Amiral of the Red, *A Narrative of my Professional Adventures (1790–1839)*, ed. Michael A. Lewis (Navy Records Society, 1953), 2 vols. I: 158. See Pieter van der Merwe, 'The Glorious First of June: a battle of art and theatre', in Michael Duffy and Roger Morriss, eds. *The Glorious First of June 1794: A Naval Battle and its Aftermath* (Exeter: University of Exeter Press, 2001), 142–6; and Evans, *Brown*, 128.

65. *True Briton*, 2 Feb. 1795; *Times*, 8 Jan. 1795.

66. *Key to the Print from the Great Picture* (London: Orme, 1795).

67. Howe was reported to have remarked to the Master of the *Queen Charlotte*: 'Pray, my good fellow, do give over that eternal my Lord, my Lord; don't you know I am called Black Dick in the fleet?' In Oliver Warner, *The Glorious First of June* (London: Batsford, 1961), 53.

68. Roger Morriss, 'The Glorious First of June: The British view of the actions of 28, 29 May and 1 June 1794', in Duffy and Morriss, eds., *Glorious First*, 51.

69. London, I. Cruikshank, published by S. W. Fores, BMC no. 8469.

70. The *True Briton* roundly rebuked Loutherbourg, and the '*Jacobin Prints*' that recommended his painting of Howe's victory, for making 'the memorial of British Honour only operate to create astonishment at the exploits of his own countrymen, whom he has falsely represented as braving *Heaven* and *Man*, in the very moment of their destruction', 22 Apr. 1795. See Farington, *Diary*, II: 307, 21 Feb. 1795. Farington reported on 5 May 1795 that Poggi worried that 'if the Prints of the naval engagement do not answer He shall be ruined' (II: 339).

71. *Oracle*, 8 Dec. 1794.

72. See Gillian Russell, *The Theatres of War: Performance, Politics and Society, 1793–1815* (Oxford: Clarendon Press, 1995), 59–66.

73. Draper Hill, *Mr. Gillray the Caricaturist: A Biography* (London: Phaidon Press, 1965), 38–9.

74. *Oracle*, 22 July 1794.

75. Diana Donald, *The Age of Caricature: Satirical Prints in the Reign of George III* (New Haven: Yale University Press, 1996), 156, 157. My discussion of Gillray is indebted to Donald's chapter on '"John Bull bother'd": the French Revolution and the propaganda war of the 1790s', 142–83.

76. Marquis of Lansdown's speech, *PH*, XXXI 1272.

77. See Hill, *Mr. Gillray*, 54–5.

78. Barrell, *Imagining*, 640–1. Barrell identifies the line as from the first scene of Addison's *Cato*, I, i. 24.

79. See, for example, the *Morning Post*, 10 Dec. 1794, which reported that 'The profligate prints, in the pay of the Treasury, are opening the batteries of calumny against the Duke of YORK. To him they attribute all the misfortunes and blunders of the Campaign, when it is well known that the Duke acted strictly agreeable to plans of the Cabinet.'

80. Henry Angelo's report on Gillray's visit to St James's Palace, cited in Hill, *Mr. Gillray*, 52, and see 49–53. Gillray also visited Portsmouth in the summer of 1794 to collect material for Loutherbourg's companion piece on Howe's victory; see Hill, *Mr. Gillray*, 53, and Richard Godfrey, with an essay by Mark Hallett, *James Gillray: The Art of Caricature* (London: Tate Publishing, 2001), 109–11.

81. See Evans, *Brown*, 126.

Bibliography

Abbreviations

DNB   *Oxford Dictionary of National Biography Online Edition*
OED   *Oxford English Dictionary Online Edition*
PH   *The Parliamentary History of England*, (London: R. Bagshaw,
        T. Longman, 1806–20), 36 vols.

Primary sources

Addison, Joseph, *The Spectator*, ed. Donald F. Bond (Oxford: Clarendon Press, 1965),
    5 vols.
Austen, Jane, *Persuasion*, intro. Forrest Reid (London: Oxford University Press, 1930)
Banks, Joseph, *The Endeavour Journal of Joseph Banks, 1768–1771*, ed. J. C. Beaglehole
    (Sydney: Trustees of the Public Library of New South Wales with Angus and
    Robertson, 1962; rev. edn, 1963), 2 vols.
[Barbauld, A. L.], *Sins of Government, Sins of the Nation; or, A Discourse for the Fast,*
    Appointed on April 19, 1793. By a Volunteer (4th edn, London: J. Johnson, 1793)
Barry, James, *The Works of James Barry, Esq.* (London: T. Cadell and W. Davies,
    1809), 2 vols.
Blake, William, 'Annotations to Reynolds' *Discourses*', in Sir Joshua Reynolds, *Dis-*
    courses on Art, ed. Robert R. Wark (1959; New Haven: Yale University Press,
    1975), appendix I
Bligh, William, *The Bligh Notebook: Rough Account - 'Lieutenant Wm Bligh's Voyage*
    in the Bounty's Launch from the Ship to Tofua & from thence to Timor', 28
    April to 14 June 1789, with a Draft List of the Bounty Mutineers, facsimile and
    transcription, ed. John Bach (North Sydney: Allen & Unwin with National
    Library of Australia, 1987)
Boswell, James, *Boswell: The Ominous Years, 1774–1776*, ed. Charles Ryskamp and
    Frederick Pottle (Melbourne: Heineman, 1963)
Boswell, James, *Life of Johnson*, ed. R. W. Chapman, intro. Pat Rogers (Oxford:
    Oxford University Press, 1980)
Burney, Frances, *The Early Diary of Frances Burney, 1768–1778*, ed. Annie Raine
    Ellis (London: G. Bell, 1913), 2 vols.
Burney, James, *With Captain James Cook in the Antarctic and Pacific*, ed. Beverley
    Hooper (Canberra: National Library of Australia, 1975)

Coleridge, Samuel Taylor, *Poetical Works*, ed. Ernest Hartley Coleridge (Oxford: Oxford University Press, 1969).

[?Combe, William], *Letters of the Late Lord Lyttelton* (London: J. Bew, 1785), 2 vols.

Cook, James, *A Voyage towards the South Pole, and round the World. Performed in His Majesty's Ships the Resolution and Adventure, in the years 1772, 1773, 1774, and 1775* (London: Strahan and Cadell, 1777), 2 vols.

Cook, James, *The Journals of Captain James Cook on his Voyages of Discovery*, i: *The Voyage of the Endeavour, 1768–1771*, ed. J. C. Beaglehole, Hakluyt Society Extra Series xxxiv (Cambridge: Cambridge University Press for the Hakluyt Society, 1968)

Cook, James, *The Journals of Captain James Cook on his Voyages of Discovery*, ii: *The Voyage of the Resolution and Adventure, 1772–1775*, ed., J. C. Beaglehole, Hakluyt Society Extra Series xxxv (Cambridge: Cambridge University Press for the Hakluyt Society, 1969)

Cook, James, *The Journals of Captain James Cook on his Voyages of Discovery*, iii: *The Voyage of the Resolution and Discovery, 1776–1780*, Parts 1 and 2, ed. J. C. Beaglehole, Hakluyt Society Extra Series xxxvi (Cambridge: Cambridge University Press, 1967)

Cowper, William, *The Letters and Prose Writings of William Cowper*, ii: *Adelphi and Letters 1750–1781*, ed. James King and Charles Ryskamp (Oxford: Clarendon Press, 1979)

Cowper, William, *The Poems of William Cowper*, i: *1748–1782*, ed. John D. Baird and Charles Ryskamp (Oxford: Oxford University Press, 1980)

Cowper, William, *The Poems of William Cowper*, ii: *1782–1785*, ed. John D. Baird and Charles Ryskamp (Oxford: Clarendon Press, 1995)

Craik, G. L., *The New Zealanders*, The Library of Entertaining Knowledge (London: Knight, 1830)

Dayes, Edward, *The Works of the Late Edward Dayes: Containing an Excursion through the Principal Parts of Derbyshire and Yorkshire . . . ; Essays on Painting; Instructions for Drawing and Colouring Landscapes; and Professional Sketches of Modern Artists* (London: Davies, Vernor & Hood, 1805)

Dillon, Sir William Henry, K. C. H., Vice-Amiral of the Red, *A Narrative of my Professional Adventures (1790–1839)*, ed. Michael A. Lewis (Navy Records Society, 1953), 2 vols.

Duff, William, *Letters, on the Intellectual and Moral Character of Women* (Aberdeen: J. Chalmers, 1807)

Edwards, Edward, *Anecdotes of Painters Who Have Resided or Been Born in England: With Critical Remarks on their Productions* (London: Leigh and Sotheby, et al., 1808)

Edwards, Edward, Captain, R. N., and George Hamilton, *Voyage of the H. M. S. 'Pandora' Despatched to Arrest the Mutineers of the 'Bounty' in the South Seas, 1790–91: Being the Narratives of Captain Edward Edwards, R. N., the*

Commander, and George Hamilton, the Surgeon, with intro. and notes by Basil Thomson (London: F. Edwards, 1915)

Elliott, John, and Richard Pickersgill, *Captain Cook's Second Voyage: The Journals of Lieutenants Elliott and Pickersgill*, ed. Christine Holmes (London: Caliban Books, 1984)

Ellis, William, *An Authentic Narrative of a Voyage Performed by Captain Cook and Captain Clerke, in His Majesty's Ships Resolution and Discovery* (London: Robinson, 1782), 2 vols.

Ellis, William, *Polynesian Researches, during a Residence of nearly Eight Years in the Society and Sandwich Islands* (1829; 2nd rev. enl. edn, London: Fisher, Son & Jackson, 1831–2), 4 vols.

Farington, Joseph, *The Diary of Joseph Farington*, ed. Kenneth Garlick and Angus Macintyre (London: Yale University Press for the Paul Mellon Centre, 1978–98), 17 vols.

Fawcet, Joseph, *The Art of War. A Poem* (London: J. Johnson, 1795)

Ferguson, Adam, *An Essay on the History of Civil Society*, intro. Louis Schneider (1767; New Brunswick, NJ: Transaction, 1980)

[Fitzgerald, Gerald], *The Injured Islanders; or, The Influence of Art upon the Happiness of Nature* (London: J. Murray, 1779)

Fitzgerald, W., of Gray's Inn, *An Ode to the Memory of the Late Captain James Cook* (London: Robinson, Flexney, Sewell and Faulder, 1780)

Forster, George, *A Voyage round the World, in His Britannic Majesty Sloop, Resolution, Commanded by Capt. James Cook, during the years 1772, 3, 4, and 5* (London: B. White, J. Elmsly, and G. Robinson, 1777), 2 vols.

Forster, George, *A Voyage round the World*, ed. Nicholas Thomas and Oliver Berghof, assisted by Jennifer Newell (Honolulu: Hawai'i University Press, 2000), 2 vols., continuously paginated

Forster, Johann Reinhold, *Observations Made during a Voyage round the World, on Physical Geography, Natural History, and Ethic Philosophy* (London: G. Robinson, 1778)

Forster, Johann Reinhold, *History of the Voyages and Discoveries Made in the North. Translated from the German of John Reinhold Forster* (London: G. G. J. and J. Robinson, 1786)

Forster, John Reinhold, 'An essay on India, its boundaries, climate, soil, and sea', trans. from the Latin by John Aikin, in Thomas Pennant, ed., *Indian Zoology* (2nd edn, London: R. Faulder, 1790)

Forster, Johann Reinhold, *The Resolution Journal of Johann Reinhold Forster, 1772–1775*, ed. Michael Hoare (London: Hakluyt Society, 1982), 4 vols., continuously paginated

Forster, Johann Reinhold, *Observations Made during a Voyage round the World*, ed. Nicholas Thomas, Harriet Guest, and Michael Dettelbach, with a linguistic appendix by Karl H. Rensch (Honolulu: Hawai'i University Press, 1996)

Gregory, George, *Essays Historical and Moral* (London: J. Johnson, 1785)

Hawkesworth, John, *An Account of the Voyages Undertaken by the Order of his Present Majesty for Making Discoveries in the Southern Hemisphere, and Successively Performed by Commodore Byron, Captain Cartaret, Captain Wallis, and Captain Cook, in the Dolphin, the Swallow, and the Endeavour: Drawn up from the Journals which Were Kept by the Several Commanders, and from the Papers of Joseph Banks, Esq.* (London: W. Strahan, 1773), 3 vols.

Hayley, William, *An Essay on Painting, in A Poetical Epistle to an Eminent Painter. With Notes* (2nd edn, Dublin: P. Byrne, 1781)

Hayley, William, *The National Advocates, A Poem. Affectionately Inscribed to the Honourable Thomas Erskine, and Vicary Gibbs, Esquire* (London: J. Debrett, 1795)

Hayley, William, *Memoirs of the Life and Writings of William Hayley, Esq.*, ed. John Johnson (London: Henry Colburn, 1823), 2 vols.

Hoare, Prince, *Memoirs of Granville Sharpe, Esq. Composed from his Own Manuscripts, and Other Authentic Documents in the Possession of his Family and of the African Institution* (London: Colburn, 1820)

Hodges, William, *A Dissertation on the Prototypes of Architecture, Hindoo, Moorish, and Gothic* (London: [s.n.], 1787)

[Hodges, William], 'An account of Richard Wilson, Esq. landscape painter, F. R. A.', *European Magazine, and London Review*, June 1790, 404

Hodges, William, *Travels in India, during the Years 1780, 1781, 1782, & 1783* (London: author, 1793)

Hodges, William, 'A letter sent to William Hayley, from London, 19 August 1794', copy held in Mitchell Library, State Library of New South Wales, Doc. 2998a.b.c.

Home, Henry, Lord Kames, *Sketches of the History of Man. Considerably Enlarged by the Last Additions and Corrections of the Author* (Edinburgh: A. Strahan and T. Cadell, 1788), 4 vols.

Jones, Sir William, 'An essay on the poetry of the eastern nations', in *Poems Consisting Chiefly of Translations from the Asiatick Languages. To Which Are Added Two Essays* (Oxford: Clarendon Press, 1772)

Jones, Sir William, 'The third anniversary discourse, on the Hindus, delivered 2d of February, 1786', in *The Works of Sir William Jones* (London: G. G. and J. Robinson, 1799), 6 vols.

[? Kearsly, G.], *Omiah's Farewell; Inscribed to the Ladies of London* (London: G. Kearsly, 1776).

Kippis, Andrew, *The Life of Captain James Cook* (London: G. Nicol, 1783)

Knox, Vicesimus, *Winter Evenings: Or, Lucubrations on Life and Letters* (London: C. Dilly, 1788), 3 vols.

La Roche, Marie Sophie von, *Sophie in London, 1786: Being the Diary of Sophie von La Roche*, trans. and intro. Clare Williams (London: Jonathan Cape, 1933)

Ledyard, John, *John Ledyard's Journey through Russia and Siberia, 1787–1788: The Journal and Selected Letters*, ed. Stephen D. Watrous (Madison: University of Wisconsin Press, 1966)

Lichtenberg, Georg Christoph, *Lichtenberg's Commentaries on Hogarth's Engravings*, trans. and intro. Innes and Gustav Herdan (London: Cresset Press, 1966)

Mariner, William, *An Account of the Natives of the Tonga Islands, in the South Pacific Ocean. Compiled and Arranged from the Extensive Communications of Mr. William Mariner, Several Years Resident in those Islands. By John Martin, M. D.* (1st UK edn, 1817; 1st North American edn, Boston: Charles Ewer, 1820)

[Marra, John] *Journal of the Resolution's Voyage* (London: F. Newbury, 1775)

Millar, John, *The Origin of the Distinction of Ranks: Or, an Inquiry into the Circumstances Which Give Rise to Influence and Authority, in the Different Members of Society* (3rd edn, London: J. Murray, 1779)

Murray, Hugh, *Historical Account of Discoveries and Travels in Asia, from the Earliest Ages to the Present Time* (Edinburgh: Archibald Constable & Co., 1820), 3 vols.

Niehof, Johan, *Voyages and Travels to the East Indies 1653–1670*, intro. Anthony Reid, Oxford in Asia Hardback Reprints (Singapore: Oxford University Press, 1988)

O'Keeffe, John, *A Short Account of the New Pantomime Called Omai, or, A Trip round the World; Performed at the Theatre-Royal in Covent-Garden* (London: Cadell, 1785)

Parkinson, Sydney, *A Journal of a Voyage to the South Seas* (London: Caliban Books, 1984)

Pilkington, Matthew, and Henry Fuseli, *A Dictionary of Painters, from the Revival of the Art to the Present Period; by the Rev. M. Pilkington, A. M. A New Edition, with Considerable Alterations, Additions, an Appendix, and an Index, by Henry Fuseli, R. A.* (London: J. Johnson et al., 1805)

Piozzi, Hester Lynch, *The Piozzi Letters: Correspondence of Hester Lynch Piozzi, 1784–1821 (Formerly Mrs. Thrale)*, ed. Edward A. Bloom and Lillian D. Bloom (Newark: University of Delaware Press, 1989), 6 vols.

Pope, Alexander, *The Poems of Alexander Pope: A One-Volume Edition of the Twickenham Text*, ed. John Butt (London: Routledge, 1968)

Pott, J. H., *An Essay on Landscape Painting. With Remarks General and Critical, in the Different Schools and Masters, Ancient and Modern* (London: J. Johnson, 1782)

Reynolds, Sir Joshua, *Discourses on Art*, ed. Robert R. Wark (1959; New Haven: Yale University Press, 1975)

[Rickman, John], *Journal of Captain Cook's Last Voyage to the Pacific Ocean, on Discovery, Performed in the Years 1776, 1777, 1778, 1779* (London: Newbery, 1781)

Robertson, George, *An Account of the Discovery of Tahiti: From the Journal of George Robertson, Master of H. M. S. Dolphin*, ed. Oliver Warner (London: Folio Society, 1955)

Robertson, William, *An Historical Disquisition concerning the Knowledge which the Ancients Had of India* (London: A. Strahan and T. Cadell, 1791)

Robley, H. G., *Moko; or Maori Tattooing* (London: Chapman and Hall, 1896)

Samwell, David, *A Narrative of the Death of Captain James Cook, to Which Are Added Some Particulars concerning his Life and Character, and Observations respecting the Introduction of the Venereal Disease into the Sandwich Isles* (London: Robinson, 1786).

Savage, John, *Some Account of New Zealand; Particularly the Bay of Islands* (1807), in A. D. McKinley, ed., *Savage's Account of New Zealand in 1805, together with Schemes of 1771 and 1824 for Commerce and Colonization* (Wellington, NZ: Watkins, 1939)

Sea Officer, *An Ode to the Memory of Captain James Cook, of his Majesty's Navy. By a Sea Officer* (Dublin: Hallhead, 1780)

Seward, Anna, *An Elegy on Captain Cook, to Which Is Added, An Ode on the Sun* (2nd edn, London: Dodsley, 1780)

Smith, Adam, *The Theory of Moral Sentiments*, ed. D. D. Raphael and A. L. Macfie (Oxford: Clarendon Press, 1976)

Smith, Adam, 'Of the nature of that imitation which takes place in what are called the imitative arts', in W. P. D. Wightman and J. C. Bryce, and I. S. Ross, eds., *Essays on Philosophical Subjects* (Oxford: Clarendon Press, 1980)

Sparrman, Andrew [Anders], *A Voyage to the Cape of Good Hope, towards the Antarctic Polar Circle, and round the World: But Chiefly into the Country of the Hottentots and Caffres, from the Year 1772, to 1776* (London: G. G. J. and J. Robinson, 1785), 2 vols.

Thomson, James, *The Seasons*, ed. James Sambrook (Oxford: Oxford University Press, 1981).

Virgil's Aeneid, Translated by John Dryden, ed. Frederick M. Keener (Harmondsworth: Penguin, 1997)

Wales, William, *Remarks on Mr. Forster's Account of Captain Cook's Last Voyage round the World, in the Years 1772, 1773, 1774, and 1775* (London: J. Nourse, 1778)

Wesley, John, *An Extract of the Rev. John Wesley's Journal, from September 13, 1773, to January 2, 1776. No. XVII* (London: G. Whitfield, 1797)

West, Jane, *Letters to a Young Lady, in Which the Duties and Character of Women Are Considered, Chiefly with a Reference to Prevailing Opinions* (1806; 3rd edn, London: Longman, Hurst, Rees, and Orme, 1806), 3 vols.

Williams, Helen Maria, *The Morai, An Ode*, in Andrew Kippis, *The Life of Captain James Cook* (London: G. Nicol, 1783)

Wollstonecraft, Mary, *The Works of Mary Wollstonecraft*, ed. Janet Todd and Marilyn Butler (London: Pickering, 1989), 7 vols.

Newspapers and periodicals

Analytical Review, or History of Literature, Domestic and Foreign
Annual Register, or a View of the History, Politics, and Literature for the year 1794
Annual Register, or a View of the History, Politics, and Literature, for the year 1795
Courier and Evening Gazette
Drewry's Derby Mercury
European Magazine, and London Review

The General Evening Post (London)
Gentleman's Magazine
Literary and Biographical Magazine, and British Review
London Chronicle
London Packet or Lloyd's New Evening Post
The Mirror
Morning Chronicle
Morning Post
Oracle and Public Advertiser
Oxford Magazine
St. James's Chronicle; or, British Evening-Post
The Times
True Briton
The Westminster Magazine; or The Pantheon of Taste
Whitehall Evening-Post

Secondary Sources

Alexander, John T., *Catherine the Great: Life and Legend* (Oxford: Oxford University Press, 1989)

Alexander, Michael, *Omai: Noble Savage* (London: Collins and Harvill Press, 1977)

Archer, Mildred, *Company Drawings in the India Office Library* (London: H. M. Stationery Office, 1972)

Archer, Mildred, *Early Views on India: The Picturesque Journeys of Thomas and William Daniell, 1786–1794* (London: Thames & Hudson, 1980)

Archer, Mildred, and Ronald Lightbown, *India Observed: India as Viewed by British Artists, 1761–1860* (London: Victoria & Albert Museum, 1982)

Archer, W. G., 'Benares through the eyes of British artists', *Apollo*, 92 (Aug. 1970), 96–103

Ashmun, Margaret, *The Singing Swan* (New Haven: Yale University Press, 1931)

Barber, Ian G., 'Early contact ethnography and understanding: an evaluation of the Cook expeditionary accounts of the Grass Cove conflict', in Alex Calder, Jonathan Lamb, and Bridget Orr, eds., *Voyages and Beaches: Pacific Encounters, 1769–1840* (Honolulu: University of Hawai'i Press, 1999)

Barrell, John, *The Political Theory of Painting from Reynolds to Hazlitt: The Body of the Public* (New Haven: Yale University Press, 1986)

Barrell, John, ed., *Painting and the Politics of Culture: New Essays on British Art, 1700–1850* (Oxford: Oxford University Press, 1992)

Barrell, John, *Imagining the King's Death: Figurative Treason, Fantasies of Regicide, 1793–1796* (Oxford: Oxford University Press, 2000)

Barrow, Terence, *The Art of Tahiti and the Neighbouring Society, Austral and Cook Islands* (London: Thames & Hudson, 1979)

Baugh, Daniel A., 'Seapower and science: the motives for Pacific exploration', in Derek Howse, ed., *Background to Discovery: Pacific Exploration from Dampier to Cook* (Berkeley: University of California Press, 1990)

Bayly, C. A., *Imperial Meridian: The British Empire and the World, 1780–1830* (London: Longman, 1989)

Beaglehole, J. C., *The Life of Captain James Cook* (London: Hakluyt Society, 1974)

Bell, Leonard, *The Maori in European Art* (Wellington: Reed, 1980)

Bender, John, *Imagining the Penitentiary: Fiction and the Architecture of Mind in Eighteenth-Century England* (Chicago: Chicago University Press, 1987)

Bindman, David, *Ape to Apollo: Aesthetics and the Idea of Race in the 18th Century* (London: Reaktion, 2002)

de Bolla, Peter, *The Discourse of the Sublime: Readings in History, Aesthetics and the Subject* (Oxford: Oxford University Press, 1989)

Bonehill, John, '"This hapless adventurer": William Hodges and the London art world', in Geoff Quilley and John Bonehill, eds., *William Hodges 1744–1797: The Art of Exploration* (New Haven: Yale University Press, 2004)

Brewer, John, *The Sinews of Power: War, Money and the English State, 1688–1783* (London: Unwin Hyman, 1989).

Bryson, Norman, ed., *Calligram: Essays in New Art History from France* (Cambridge: Cambridge University Press, 1988)

Calder, Alex, Jonathan Lamb, and Bridget Orr, eds., *Voyages and Beaches: Pacific Encounters, 1769–1840* (Honolulu: University of Hawai'i Press, 1999)

Caplan, Jane, ed., *Written on the Body: The Tattoo in European and American History* (London: Reaktion, 2000)

Carter, Paul, *The Road to Botany Bay: An Essay in Spatial History* (London: Faber, 1987)

Chard, Chloe, and Helen Langdon, eds., *Transports: Imaginative Geographies 1660–1800* (New Haven: Yale University Press, 1996)

Christie, Ian R., *Wars and Revolutions: Britain, 1760–1815* (Cambridge, MA: Harvard University Press, 1982)

Cobbe, Hugh, ed., *Cook's Voyages and the Peoples of the Pacific* (London, British Museum Publications, 1979)

Colley, Linda, *Britons: Forging the Nation, 1707–1837* (New Haven: Yale University Press, 1992)

Cooper, Nicholas, 'Indian architecture in England, 1781–1830', *Apollo*, 92 (Aug. 1970), 124–33

Coote, Jeremy, Peter Gathercole, and Nicolette Meister, with contributions from Tim Rogers and Frieda Midgley, 'Curiosities sent to Oxford: the original documentation of the Forster collection at the Pitt Rivers Museum', *Journal of the History of Collections*, 12, 2 (2000), 177–92

Copley, Stephen, ed., *Literature and the Social Order in Eighteenth-Century England* (London: Croom Helm, 1984)

Dening, Greg, 'Ethnohistory in Polynesia: the value of ethnohistorical evidence', in Barrie Macdonald, comp., *Essays from the Journal of Pacific History* (Palmerston North, NZ: Journal of Pacific History, 1979)

Dening, Greg, *Mr Bligh's Bad Language: Passion, Power and Theatre on the Bounty* (Cambridge: Cambridge University Press, 1992)

Deuchar, Stephen, *Sporting Art in Eighteenth-Century England: A Social and Political History* (New Haven: Yale University Press, 1988)

Donald, Diana, *The Age of Caricature: Satirical Prints in the Reign of George III* (New Haven: Yale University Press, 1996)

Douglas, Bronwen, 'Art as ethno-historical text: science, representations and indigenous presence in eighteenth and nineteenth century oceanic voyage literature', in Nicholas Thomas and Diane Losch, eds., Jennifer Newell, ass. ed., *Double Vision: Art Histories and Colonial Histories in the Pacific* (Cambridge: Cambridge University Press, 1999)

Douglas, Bronwen, '"Cureous figures": European voyagers and *tatau*/tattoo in Polynesia, 1595–1800', in Nicholas Thomas, Anna Cole, and Bronwen Douglas, eds., *Tattoo: Bodies, Art and Exchange in the Pacific and the West* (London: Reaktion, 2005)

Drummond, James, ed., *John Rutherford, The White Chief: A Story of Adventure in New Zealand* (Christchurch, NZ: Whitcombe and Tombs, 1908)

Duffy, Michael, and Roger Morriss, eds., *The Glorious First of June 1794: A Naval Battle and its Aftermath* (Exeter: University of Exeter Press, 2001)

Eaton, Natasha, 'Hodges's visual genealogy for colonial India, 1780–1795', in Geoff Quilley and John Bonehill, eds., *William Hodges 1744–1797: the Art of Exploration* (New Haven: Yale University Press, 2004)

Edmond, Rod, *Representing the South Pacific: Colonial Discourse from Cook to Gauguin* (Cambridge: Cambridge University Press, 1997)

Edmond, Rod, 'Translating cultures: William Ellis and missionary writing', in Margarette Lincoln, ed., *Science and Exploration in the Pacific: European Voyages to the Southern Oceans in the Eighteenth Century* (Woodbridge: Boydell Press and National Maritime Museum, 1998)

Edmond, Rod, 'Missionaries on Tahiti, 1797–1840', in Alex Calder, Jonathan Lamb, and Bridget Orr, eds., *Voyages and Beaches: Pacific Encounters, 1769–1840* (Honolulu: University of Hawai'i Press, 1999)

Edmond, Rod, and Vanessa Smith, eds., *Islands in History and Representation* (London: Routledge, 2003)

Eisler, William, and Bernard Smith, eds., *Terra Australis: The Furthest Shore* (Sydney: International Cultural Corporation of Australia, 1988)

Ellis, Markman, *The Politics of Sensibility: Race, Gender and Commerce in the Sentimental Novel* (Cambridge: Cambridge University Press, 1996)

Evans, Dorinda, *Mather Brown: Early American Artist in England* (Middletown, CT: Wesleyan University Press, 1982).

Fara, Patricia, *Sex, Botany and Empire: The Story of Carl Linnaeus and Joseph Banks* (Cambridge: Icon, 2003)

Fliegelman, Jay, *Prodigals and Pilgrims: The American Revolution against Patriarchal Authority, 1750–1800* (Cambridge: Cambridge University Press, 1982)

Frost, Alan, and Jane Samson, eds., *Pacific Empires: Essays in Honour of Glyndwr Williams* (Melbourne: Melbourne University Press, 1999)

Gascoigne, John, *Joseph Banks and the English Enlightenment: Useful Knowledge and Polite Culture* (Cambridge: Cambridge University Press, 1994)

Gathercole, Peter, 'Contexts of Maori *moko*', in Arnold Rubin, ed., *Marks of Civilization: Artistic Transformations of the Human Body* (Los Angeles: Museum of Cultural History, 1988)

Gathercole, Peter, 'Lord Sandwich's collection of Polynesian Artefacts', in Margarette Lincoln, ed., *Science and Exploration in the Pacific: European Voyages to the Southern Oceans in the Eighteenth Century* (Woodbridge: Boydell Press and National Maritime Museum, 1998)

Gell, Alfred, *Wrapping in Images: Tattooing in Polynesia* (Oxford: Clarendon Press, 1993)

Gilroy, Paul, *The Black Atlantic: Modernity and Double Consciousness* (London: Verso, 1993)

Godfrey, Richard, with an essay by Mark Hallett, *James Gillray: The Art of Caricature* (London: Tate Publishing, 2001)

Guest, Harriet, 'The great distinction: figures of the exotic in the work of William Hodges', *Oxford Art Journal*, 12, 2 (1989), 36–58

Guest, Harriet, 'Curiously marked: tattooing, masculinity, and nationality in eighteenth-century British perceptions of the South Pacific', in John Barrell, ed., *Painting and the Politics of Culture: New Essays on British Art, 1700–1850* (Oxford: Oxford University Press, 1992)

Guest, Harriet, *Small Change: Women, Learning, Patriotism, 1750–1810* (Chicago: Chicago University Press, 2000)

Guest, Harriet, 'Cook in Tonga: terms of trade', in Rod Edmond and Vanessa Smith, eds., *Islands in History and Representation* (London: Routledge, 2003)

Guest, Harriet, '"The consequences of war" in the winter of 1794–95', in Geoff Quilley and John Bonehill, eds., *William Hodges 1744–1797: The Art of Exploration* (New Haven: Yale University Press, 2004)

Guest, Harriet, 'Ornament and use: Mai and Cook in London', in Kathleen Wilson, ed., *A New Imperial History: Culture, Identity and Modernity in Britain and the Empire, 1660–1840* (Cambridge: Cambridge University Press, 2004)

Hill, Draper, *Mr. Gillray the Caricaturist: A Biography* (London: Phaidon Press, 1965)

Hoare, Michael, *The Tactless Philosopher: Johann Reinhold Forster (1729–1798)* (Melbourne: Hawthorn Press, 1977)

Hoock, Holger, *The King's Artists: The Royal Academy of Arts and the Politics of British Culture, 1760–1840* (Oxford: Clarendon Press, 2003)

Howse, Derek, ed., *Background to Discovery: Pacific Exploration from Dampier to Cook* (Berkeley: University of California Press, 1990)

Hulme, Peter, *Colonial Encounters: Europe and the Native Caribbean, 1492–1797* (London: Routledge, 1986)

Jolly, Margaret, 'Illnatured comparisons: racism and relativism in European representations of Ni-Vanuatu from Cook's second voyage', *History and Anthropology*, 5 (1990), 331–64

Jones, Robert, *Gender and the Formation of Taste in Eighteenth-Century Britain: The Analysis of Beauty* (Cambridge: Cambridge University Press, 1998)

Joppien, Rüdiger, *Philippe Jacques de Loutherbourg, R. A.: 1740–1812* (London: Greater London Council, 1973)

Joppien, Rüdiger, and Bernard Smith, *The Art of Captain Cook's Voyages*, i: *The Voyage of the Endeavour, 1768–1771* (New Haven: Yale University Press, 1985)

Joppien, Rüdiger, and Bernard Smith, *The Art of Captain Cook's Voyages*, ii: *The Voyage of the Resolution and Adventure, 1772–1775* (New Haven: Yale University Press, 1985)

Joppien, Rüdiger, and Bernard Smith, *The Art of Captain Cook's Voyages*, iii: *Catalogue, The Voyage of the Resolution and Discovery, 1776–1780* (New Haven: Yale University Press, 1988)

Joppien, Rüdiger, and Bernard Smith, *The Art of Captain Cook's Voyages*, iii: *Text, The Voyage of the Resolution and Discovery, 1776–1780* (New Haven: Yale University Press, 1988)

Kaeppler, Adrienne L., *'Artificial Curiosities', Being and Exposition of Native Manufactures Collected on the Three Pacific Voyages of Captain James Cook, R. N.*, Bernice P. Bishop Museum Special Publications 65 (Honolulu: Bishop Museum Press, 1978)

Kaeppler, Adrienne L., 'Pacific culture history and European voyages', in William Eisler and Bernard Smith, eds., *Terra Australis: The Furthest Shore* (Sydney: International Cultural Corporation of Australia, 1988)

Lamb, Jonathan, *Preserving the Self in the South Seas, 1680–1840* (Chicago: Chicago University Press, 2001)

Lamb, Jonathan, Vanessa Smith, and Nicholas Thomas, eds., *Exploration and Exchange: A South Seas Anthology, 1680–1900* (Chicago: Chicago University Press, 2000)

Leask, Nigel, *Curiosity and the Aesthetics of Travel Writing, 1770–1840: 'From an Antique Land'* (Oxford: Oxford University Press, 2002)

Lincoln, Margarette, ed., *Science and Exploration in the Pacific: European Voyages to the Southern Oceans in the Eighteenth Century* (Woodbridge: Boydell Press and National Maritime Museum, 1998)

Lyte, Charles, *Sir Joseph Banks: 18th Century Explorer, Botanist and Entrepreneur* (Newton Abbot: David and Charles, 1980)

McCormick, E. H., *Omai: Pacific Envoy* (Auckland, NZ: Auckland University Press and Oxford University Press, 1977)

MacDonald, Simon, 'William Hodges's *The Effects of Peace* and *The Consequences of War* (1794–95)', MA dissertation, Courtauld Institute of Art, University of London, 2005

Maning, Frederick Edward, *Old New Zealand: A Tale of the Good Old Times. By A Pakeha Maori* (Auckland, NZ: Creighton, 1863)

Marshall, P. J., and Glyndwr Williams, *The Great Map of Mankind: British Perceptions of the World in the Age of Enlightenment* (London: Dent, 1982)

Merwe, Pieter van der, 'The Glorious First of June: a battle of art and theatre', in Michael Duffy and Roger Morriss, eds., *The Glorious First of June 1794: A Naval Battle and its Aftermath* (Exeter: University of Exeter Press, 2001)

Mitchell, W. J. T., ed., *Landscape and Power* (Chicago: University of Chicago Press, 1994)

Mohanty, Chandra Talpade, 'Under Western eyes: feminist scholarship and colonial discourses', *Feminist Review*, 30 (Autumn 1988), 61–88

Morriss, Roger, 'The Glorious First of June: the British view of the actions of 28, 29 May and 1 June 1794', in Michael Duffy and Roger Morriss, eds., *The Glorious First of June 1794: A Naval Battle and its Aftermath* (Exeter: University of Exeter Press, 2001)

Mukherjee, Ramkrishna, *The Rise and Fall of the East India Company: A Sociological Appraisal* (rev. edn, New York: Monthly Review Press, 1974)

Newell, Jennifer, 'Irresistible objects: collecting in the Pacific and Australia in the reign of George III', in Kim Sloan with Andrew Burnett, eds., *Enlightenment: Discovering the World in the Eighteenth Century* (London: British Museum Press, 2003)

Nicholson, Adam, 'Reynolds wanted Omai to be a man of the world', *Telegraph*, 7 Jan. 2003.

Nussbaum, Felicity A., *The Autobiographical Subject: Gender and Ideology in Eighteenth-Century England* (Baltimore: Johns Hopkins University Press, 1989)

Obeyesekere, Gananeth, '"British cannibals": contemplation of an event in the death and resurrection of James Cook, explorer', *Critical Inquiry*, 18, 4 (1992), 630–54

Obeyesekere, Gannath, *The Apotheosis of Captain Cook: European Mythmaking in the Pacific*, with an new afterword by the author (Princeton: Princeton University Press, 1997)

Oetterman, Stephan, 'On display: tattooed entertainers in America and Germany', in Jane Caplan, ed., *Written on the Body: The Tattoo in European and American History* (London: Reaktion, 2000)

Oliver, Douglas, *Return to Tahiti: Bligh's Second Breadfruit Voyage* (Honolulu: University of Hawai'i Press, 1988)

Pocock, J. G. A., *The Machiavellian Moment: Florentine Political Thought and the Atlantic Republican Tradition* (Princeton: Princeton University Press, 1975)

Pocock, J. G. A., 'Nature and history, self and other: European perceptions of world history in the age of encounter', in Alex Calder, Jonathan Lamb, and Bridget Orr, eds., *Voyages and Beaches: Pacific Encounters, 1769–1840* (Honolulu: University of Hawai'i Press, 1999)

Pope, Stephen, *The Cassell Dictionary of the Napoleonic Wars* (London: Cassell, 1999)

Porter, Andrew, 'The career of William Ellis: British missions, the Pacific, and the American connection', in Alan Frost and Jane Samson, eds., *Pacific Empires: Essays in Honour of Glyndwr Williams* (Melbourne: Melbourne University Press, 1999)

Pratt, Mary Louise, *Imperial Eyes: Travel Writing and Transculturation* (London: Routledge, 1992)

Quilley, Geoff, and John Bonehill, eds., *William Hodges, 1744–1797: The Art of Exploration* (New Haven: Yale University Press, 2004)

Rennie, Neil, *Far-Fetched Facts: The Literature of Travel and the Idea of the South Seas* (Oxford: Clarendon Press, 1995)

Rodger, N. A. M., *The Wooden World: An Anatomy of the Georgian Navy* (London: Fontana, 1988)

Rosenthal, Michael, 'Gainsborough's *Diana and Actaeon*', in John Barrell, ed., *Painting and the Politics of Culture: New Essays on British Art, 1700–1850* (Oxford: Oxford University Press, 1992)

Rosenthal, Michael, *The Art of Thomas Gainsborough* (New Haven: Yale University Press, 1999)

Rudé, George, *The Crowd in History, 1730–1848* (New York: John Wiley, 1964)

Russell, Gillian, *The Theatres of War: Performance, Politics and Society, 1793–1815* (Oxford: Clarendon Press, 1995)

Sahlins, Marshall, 'Heirarchy and humanity in Polynesia', in Antony Hooper and Judith Huntsman, eds., *Transformations of Polynesian Culture* (Auckland: The Polynesian Society, 1985).

Sahlins, Marshall, *Islands of History* (Chicago: Chicago University Press, 1985)

Sahlins, Marshall, *How 'Natives' Think: About Captain Cook, for Example* (Chicago: Chicago University Press, 1996)

Said, Edward W., *Orientalism* (London: Routledge and Kegan Paul, 1978; Harmondsworth: Penguin, 1985).

Salmond, Anne, *Two Worlds: First Meetings between Maori and Europeans, 1642–1772* (Honolulu: Hawai'i University Press, 1991)

Salmond, Anne, *Between Worlds: Early Exchanges between Maori and Europeans, 1773–1815* (Honolulu: Hawai'i University Press, 1997)

Salmond, Anne, *The Trial of the Cannibal Dog: Captain Cook in the South Seas* (London: Allen Lane, 2003)

Schiebinger, Londa, *The Mind Has No Sex? Women and the Origins of Modern Science* (Cambridge MA: Harvard University Press, 1989)

Schoeser, Mary, *Printed Handkerchiefs*, The London Connection: Number Fourteen (London: Museum of London, 1988)

Sinclair, Keith, *A History of New Zealand* (Auckland: Penguin, 1959; rev. edn, 1988)

Sloan, Kim, with Andrew Burnett, eds., *Enlightenment: Discovering the World in the Eighteenth Century* (London: British Museum Press, 2003)

Smith, Bernard, *European Vision and the South Pacific* (2nd edn, New Haven: Yale University Press, 1985)

Smith, Bernard, *Imagining the Pacific in the Wake of the Cook Voyages* (London and New Haven: Yale University Press, 1992).

Smith, Vanessa, 'Give us our daily breadfruit: bread substitution in the Pacific in the eighteenth-century', *Studies in Eighteenth-Century Culture*, 35 (2006), 53–75

Solkin, David, *Richard Wilson: The Landscape of Reaction* (London: Tate Gallery, 1982)

Spate, O. H. K., *The Pacific since Magellan*, III: *Paradise Found and Lost* (Rushcutters Bay, NSW: ANU Press, 1988)

Stott, Anne, *Hannah More: The First Victorian* (Oxford: Oxford University Press, 2003)

Stuebe, Isabel, *The Life and Works of William Hodges* (New York: Garland, 1979)

Stuebe, Isabel Combs, 'William Hodges and Warren Hastings: a study in eighteenth-century patronage', *Burlington Magazine*, 115 (Oct. 1973), 659–66

Te Riria, Ko, and David Simmons, *Moko Rangatira: Maori Tattoo* (Auckland, NZ: Reed, 1989)

Thomas, Nicholas, *Entangled Objects: Exchange, Material Culture and Colonialism in the Pacific* (Cambridge, MA: Harvard University Press, 1991)

Thomas, Nicholas, 'Liberty and licence: the Forsters' accounts of New Zealand society', in Chloe Chard and Helen Langdon, eds., *Transports: Imaginative Geographies 1660–1800* (New Haven: Yale University Press, 1996)

Thomas, Nicholas, *In Oceania: Visions, Artifacts, Histories* (Durham, NC, Duke University Press, 1997)

Thomas, Nicholas, *Discoveries: The Voyages of Captain Cook* (London: Allen Lane, 2003)

Thomas, Nicholas, and Diane Losch, eds., Jennifer Newell, ass. ed., *Double Vision: Art Histories and Colonial Histories in the Pacific* (Cambridge: Cambridge University Press, 1999)

Thomas, Nicholas, Anna Cole, and Bronwen Douglas, eds., *Tattoo: Bodies, Art and Exchange in the Pacific and the West* (London: Reaktion, 2005)

Tobin, Beth Fowkes, *Picturing Imperial Power: Colonial Subjects in Eighteenth-Century British Painting* (Durham, NC: Duke University Press, 1999)

Warner, Oliver, *The Glorious First of June* (London: Batsford, 1961)

Welles Henderson, J., and Rodney P. Carlisle, *Jack Tar: A Sailor's Life, 1750–1910* (Woodbridge: Antique Collectors Club, 1999)

Werkmeister, Lucyle, *The London Daily Press, 1772–1792* (Lincoln, NB: University of Nebraska Press, 1963)

White, Joanna, 'Marks of transgression: the Tattooing of Europeans in the Pacific Islands', in Nicholas Thomas, Anna Cole, and Bronwen Douglas, eds., *Tattoo: Bodies, Art and Exchange in the Pacific and the West* (London: Reaktion, 2005)

Whitehead, P. J. P., 'Zoological specimens from Captain Cook's voyages', *Journal of the Society for the Bibliography of Natural History*, 5 (1969) 161–201

Whitley, William T., *Artists and their Friends in England, 1700–1799* (New York: B. Blom, 1928; reissue 1968), 2 vols.

Wilson, Kathleen, *The Sense of the People: Politics, Culture and Imperialism in England, 1715–1785* (Cambridge: Cambridge University Press, 1995; paperback edn 1998)

Wilson, Kathleen, *The Island Race: Englishness, Empire and Gender in the Eighteenth Century* (London: Routledge, 2003)

Wilson, Kathleen, ed., *A New Imperial History: Culture, Identity and Modernity in Britain and the Empire, 1660–1840* (Cambridge: Cambridge University Press, 2004)

Withey, Lynne, *Voyages of Discovery: Captain Cook and the Exploration of the Pacific* (London, 1987)

Index

Actaeon 36–7, 39, 63
Addison, Joseph 142
Adventure at Grass Cove 22, 79, 133–6
Aeneid 126, 140
American war 6, 7, 23, 65, 137–44, 146,
    161
    and Cook's voyages 143–5, 161
Anahe [Ghowannahe, or Ko Anahe?] 127,
    130–1, 132–3
    and Grass Cove skirmish 133–6
Anderson, William 91, 109, 110, 111–12
Antarctic Circle 1, 7
Attenborough, Sir David 68, 89
Austen, Jane, *Persuasion* 165–6

Banks, Sir Joseph 18, 38, 61, 76–9, 147,
    168
    and curiosity, curiosities 70, 76–8
    as macaroni 78
    on New Zealand 124
    and Parry's *Omai, Joseph Banks and Dr.
        Solander* 74–5
    and Reynolds's *Members of the Society of
        Dilettanti* 76, 77
    and tattooing 79, 88
    'Thoughts on the manners of Otaheite' 78–9
    and West's portrait 76–8
Barbauld, Anna Lætitia 179–80
Barrell, John 196
Barry, James 20, 42, 105
Basire, James 116
Beaglehole, J. C. 6, 118
Blake, William 33
Bligh, William 157, 160
Bonehill, John 18
Boswell, James 7, 20, 71, 153, 159, 164
Bougainville, Louis Antoine de 103,
    118
Bounty 71, 89, 160
Boydell Shakespeare Gallery 63
Brown, Mather 184, 197
    Attack on Famars 184, 185
    and *Key to the Print* 187

*Lord Howe on the Deck of the 'Queen
    Charlotte'* 184, 187–9, 193
    and print after 189
    and publicity 185–6
Burke, Edmund 89
Burney, Frances 153–4, 155, 164, 167
Burney, James 79–80

Christian, Fletcher 71
Clerke, Charles 106
Cleveley, Robert 189
Coleridge, Samuel Taylor 180
Cook, Captain James
    and agriculture 159
    and Antarctic Circle 1
    and colonialism 143–8, 163
    and his crew 1, 24–5, 34, 127, 136–7
    first voyage 68, 124
    on knowledge of islanders 7, 91–3
    in London 153–4, 163, 168
    on Mai 71, 93, 159, 160
    on Malakula 99, 116
    on Maori 54, 124, 136–7; and cannibalism
        80–1
    on New Zealand 124, 140–1
    on Rapanui 5
    on relation between islands 5
    on Tanna 116–17, 119–20
    on Tonga 91–3, 104, 107–8; landing at 109;
        sense of disadvantage at 108, 112–13;
        Tongan aptitude for trade 108–9, 110
    on Vanuatu 115, 122–3
    posthumous reputation of 9–10, 164–5,
        166–8
    relationship with islanders 24–5
    on Tahiti 15, 17
    third voyage 68; at New Zealand 124,
        136–7; at Tonga 91, 103
    Voyage towards the South Pole 10, 17, 116,
        147
Cook Strait [Raukawa-Moana] 124, 132
    Queen Charlotte Sound [Totara-nui] 54–5,
        124, 129, 136–7, 147–8

Cowper, William 20, 142, 146, 147
Cruikshank, Isaac
    British Neptune Riding Triumphant 189
    LORD HOWE they run 189
    A Peep at the Plenipo –!!! 182
curiosity, curiosities 49–51, 70, 76–8, 89, 147

Dance, Nathaniel 165, 166
Dartmouth, William Legge, second Earl of 180
Dillon, Sir William Henry 187
Donald, Diana 195
Douglas, Bronwen 117
Dryden, John 140
Dusky Bay [Tamatea] 54, 86, 138
Dyck, Sir Anthony Van 156, 161
Dyer, John 121

East India Company 6, 30, 32
Elliott, John 89, 90, 138–9
Ellis, William 160, 161
Erromango 22
    see also Hodges's *Landing at Erramanga*
Eua [Middleburgh Is.] 22, 93, 109
    see also Hodges's *Landing at Middleburgh*
Europe
    cultures of 49, 66–7
    notions of industry 51
Evans, Dorinda 184, 185
exoticism 70, 72, 76

Farington, Joseph 169–70, 173, 174, 178, 179,
    185, 186
Fawcet, Joseph 180
Fawkes, Walter Ramsden Hawkesworth 171,
    186
Ferguson, Adam 154–5, 163
Fitzgerald, Gerald 148
Fitzgerald, William 146–7
Flaxman, John 166
Forster, George
    career of 11
    on colonialism 137–8, 139–40, 142–4
    on curiosity 49
    on Dusky Bay 139, 141, 142–4; and Hodges
        141
    on Mai 69–70, 157, 158, 159–60
    on Malakula 117–18
    on Maori: and cannibalism 135; at Dusky
        Bay 86, 139–40; at Queen Charlotte
        Sound 54, 132, 137–8
    on Tahitian fleet 14, 15, 17
    on Tanna 118, 119, 120–1, 122–3; European
        violence at 121–2

    on Tierra del Fuego 49
    on Tonga 91, 121; and Hodges 95, 97,
        103
    on Tuauru valley 61
    Voyage round the World 10, 11, 17
Forster, Johann Reinhold
    on British women 53–4
    career of 11
    and curiosities 49–51, 109, 110–11
    on Europe 49, 66–7
    on history of mankind 11–12, 49
    on Hodges 95
    journals of 52, 57, 66–7
    on Malakula 12, 109
    on Marquesas 12, 56
    on New Caledonia 12
    on New Holland 12
    on New Zealand 12, 133, 140; on Maori
        cannibalism 13; on Maori women 54–6,
        58
    on North America 58, 133
    Observations 10, 11, 17, 41, 50, 57, 66–7
    and racial division of islanders 97–9
    on Raiatea 53
    on Rapanui 3
    on sailors 50, 53
    on Society Islands 12, 56
    on Tahiti 30, 32, 45–8, 60–1; on Tahitian
        families 58–9; on Tahitian women 53,
        56–7, 58–60, 65–6
    on Tanna 12, 122–3
    on Tierra del Fuego 12
    on Tonga 12, 91; Tongan industry 106–7;
        Tongan trade 109, 110–11; on Tongan
        women 53, 56; Tongans compared to
        Tahitians 104–5
    on venereal disease 55
Foucault, Michel 26
Fox, Charles James 176, 179–80, 182, 195,
    196
France, war with 24, 171, 174
Friendly Islands *see* Tonga

Gainsborough, Thomas 62, 86, 142
Gathercole, Peter 130
Gell, Alfred 129, 130
George III, King 182, 185, 187, 196
Gillray, James
    Blessings of PEACE / The Curses of WAR
        193–5, 196, 197
    Fatigues of the Campaign in Flanders 196
    Presentation of the Mahometan Credentials
        182

Gilroy, Paul 26
Goldsmith, Oliver, *Deserted Village* 178
Gray, Thomas 178

Hastings, Warren 18
Hauraki gulf 124
Hawkesworth, John 10, 103
Hayley, William 19, 173, 181
'Heroic epistle from OMIAH to the QUEEN of OTAHEITE' 155
Hill, Thomas 80, 83–4
Hoare, Prince 161
Hodges, William
  and accuracy 19–20, 22, 33, 39, 95, 186
  career of 17–19, 23, 169, 184, 197–8
  exhibition of 1794/5 169, 178, 184, 197;
    advertisements for 185; *Morning
    Chronicle* on 180; *Oracle* on 175, 179,
    181
  in India 18, 28–32
  at New Zealand 141
  at Rapanui 1
  at Tonga 95
  at Vanuatu 95
  work of 10, 13–14; *Morning Post* on 116
  Works
    Abbey, From the Romance of the Forest, the
      19
    Consequences of War, The 23, 169, 170,
      174, 175, 177–9, 180, 186, 193, 195, 196;
      European Magazine on 181; *print after*
      170–1, 181–2; *Turkish soldiers in* 181–2,
      184, 197
    Effects of Peace, The 23, 169, 170, 174, 175,
      177–9, 186, 195, 196; *print after* 170–1
    *Jaques and the Wounded Stag in the Forest of
      Arden* 63
    James Cook 165–6
    Landing at Erramanga 22, 99, 115, 116
    Landing at Mallicollo 22, 99, 115, 117
    Landing at Middleburgh 22, 91–3, 99
    Landing at Tanna 22, 99, 115
    Landscape, Ruins, and Figures 62–3
    Old Maori Man with a Grey Beard 86
    portrait of *Mai* 156–7
    Review of the War Galleys at Tahiti 14, 15
    Select Views in India 18, 34
    Tahiti Revisited 51–2, 61, 62
    Tongatabu or Amsterdam 108
    View in Dusky Bay 142
    View in Pickersgill Harbour 139
    *View in Tahiti with Waterfall and Girls
      Bathing* 61–2

View of Cape Stephens 97
*View of Maitavie Bay, [in the Island of]
  Otaheite* 51–2, 63
View of Matavai Bay 33, 51–2
View of the Monuments of Easter Island 1,
  5–6
View of the Province of Oparee 1–3
View Taken in the Bay of Otaheite Peha 21,
  33, 34–9, 48, 51–2, 61, 62, 64
War Boats of the Island of Tahiti 14, 15, 63,
  97
Waterfall in Tahiti, A 62
Waterfall in Tuauru 62–5
Writings
  catalogue to exhibition of 1794/5 170, 171,
    173, 177–8
  *Dissertation on the Prototypes of
    Architecture* 18
  letters to Hayley 173, 181
  Select Views in India 184
  Travels in India 18, 28–32
Hogarth, William 149
Hotham, Sir Richard 171
Howe, Richard, Earl Howe 185, 187–9
  see also Mather Brown, *Lord Howe on the
    Deck of the 'Queen Charlotte'*
Hulme, Peter 23, 126
Hunter, John 156

India 18, 28–32, 137–44, 145, 146

Johnson, Samuel 153
Jolly, Margaret 119
Jones, Sir William 30, 34
Joppien, Rüdiger 1, 15, 17, 34, 51, 115, 116,
  142

Kames, Henry Home, Lord 40, 60, 119
King, James 103, 111, 157
Kippis, Andrew 164–5
Knox, Vicesimus 40
Kosciusko, Thaddeus 183

La Roche, Sophie von 167
Lamb, Jonathan 25
Leask, Nigel 11, 158
Ledyard, John 88
Leslie, C. R. 185–98
Linneaus, Carolus 74
Loutherbourg, Philippe Jacques de 170, 185,
  189, 196
Lyttelton, Thomas, second Baron Lyttelton
  37

McCormick, E. H. 68
Madras 28, 29, 30–2
  Hindu merchants of 29–32
Mai 21–2, 23, 47
  and curiosity 93, 147, 150–1
  in England 68, 89, 149, 151–63, 168
  George Forster on 69–70
  as interpreter 93
  and possessions 157–63
  his views on his portraits 69
  see also Reynolds's *Omai*, and Parry's *Omai*,
    Joseph Banks and Dr. Solander
Malakula 12, 22
  see also Hodge's's *Landing at Mallicollo*
Maori
  and Grass Cove 22, 79, 127, 133–6
  moko or tattooing 81, 86–8
  response to Hodges's work 86–7
  subservience of women 132
Marchant, Nathaniel 178–9, 181
Marquesas 12
Marra, John 84, 138
Marsden, Samuel 129
masculinity 21, 29–32, 33–4, 75–9, 83, 89
  British masculine identity 68, 74
Medland, Thomas 170, 181–2, 189
Middleburgh *see* Eua
Millar, John 57, 60, 131–2, 137
  on Tahitians 131–2
Milton, John, *Paradise Lost* 46–7
Mitchell, W. J. T. 6
Monboddo, James Burnett, Lord 42, 46, 117
Monkhouse, William 81
Montagu, John, fourth Earl of Sandwich, *see*
  Sandwich
Mortimer, John Hamilton 168
Mulgrave, Constantine Phipps, second Baron
  153, 176

Newbery, Elizabeth 126
New Caledonia 12
New Hebrides *see* Vanuatu
New Zealand 12, 22–3, 124–43, 147–8
  New Zealanders (*see also* Maori) 22, 103

Obeyesekere, Gananath 134
Ode to the Memory of Captain James Cook 146
O'Keeffe, John, *Omai, Or, A Trip round the
  World, An* 78
Omai see Mai
'Omiah: an ode' 161
Omiah's Farewell 159
Orme, Daniel 185, 187

Key to the Print of the Great Picture 187
Orme's Gallery 18, 169, 184, 185

Parker, William 187–9
Parkinson, Sydney 81, 86, 88
Parry, William, *Omai, Joseph Banks and
  Dr. Solander* 74–6, 78
Pitt, William 173, 174, 182, 183, 196
Pocock, J. G. A. 25–6, 120
Poem on a Voyage of Discovery, A 147
Poggi, Anthony 189
Poland 183–4
Pope, Alexander 43, 47
Pratt, Mary Louise 23, 126, 136
Prince of Wales, George 171

Quilley, Geoff 18
Quiros, Pedro Fernandez de 118

Rapanui [Easter Island] 1–5
Reeves, John 195, 196, 197
Reynolds, Sir Joshua 20, 21, 34, 39, 42, 45
  Discourses 69, 72–4, 75–6, 78, 79, 80, 88,
    156
  Head of Omai 156–7, 161
  Members of the Society of Dilettanti 76, 77,
    78
  portrait of *Joseph Banks* 166
  portrait of *Omai* 68, 69, 70, 75–6, 78, 86;
    and national importance 68, 89
Resolution
  course of 1, 7, 20, 118
  crew of 1, 7, 10
  at New Zealand 138
  proposed alterations to 18
Rickman, John 23, 70, 81
  Gentleman's Magazine on 126
  on Mai 161–3
  on New Zealand 124, 126–31, 132–6
Robertson, William 30, 40, 42
Robley, Horatio G. 128
Roggeveen, Jacob 5
Rosenthal, Michael 62
Royal Academy 14, 17, 18, 19, 20, 33, 34, 62
  Hodges and 116, 142
  and Mather Brown 185
  Reynolds's *Omai* at 68
Russia 182–4
Rutherford, John 128

Sahlins, Marshall 134
Salmond, Anne 24–5, 86
Samwell, David 9, 157, 159

Sandwich, John Montagu, fourth Earl of 49,
    155–6, 160, 168
Savage, John 129
Scottish enlightenment 20, 21, 131, 135
Seward, Anna 145, 158, 159
Sharpe, Granville 163
Sherwin, J. K., *Landing at Middleburgh* 95
Smith, Adam 133, 161
    on gadgets 151, 152–3, 154, 155, 160
    on music 118
    on passion 131
Smith, Bernard
    Art of Captain Cook's Voyages 1, 15, 17, 34,
        51, 115, 116, 142
    'Cook's posthumous reputation' 23, 120,
        144, 146, 161, 163
    European Vision and the South Pacific 3, 5–6,
        69
Society Islands 12, 20, 21–2, 103
    status of women 21, 35–9
Solander, Daniel, in Parry's *Omai, Joseph Banks
    and Dr. Solander* 68, 74–5
Solkin, David 24, 64
Sparrman, Anders 41
Spate, O. H. K. 91
Spöring, Herman 81
Stuebe, Isabel Combs 17
Suvorov, Alexander 182–3

Tahiti 5, 21, 33
    population of 15, 17
    Tahitians compared to Tongans 103
    war boats and naval strength 14, 17
Tanna 12, 22
    and see Hodges's *Landing at Tanna*
Tasman, Abel 95
tattoos 21–2, 39, 63, 64, 72, 89
    Banks on 79
    and hand of Thomas Hill 80, 83–4
    maori tattooing or moko 81; Hodges's
        representations of 86–8; and Rickman's
        anecdote 128–30, 135–6, 137
    and men of Bora Bora 89
    and Parry's *Omai, Joseph Banks and Dr.
        Solander* 68–9
    Reynolds on 74, 78
    and Reynolds's *Omai* 68–70, 72
    and sailors 88–9, 128–30
Thomas, Nicholas
    Discoveries: The Voyages of Captain Cook
        24–5, 86

    on George Forster 122
    on Melanesians and Polynesians 97–9, 119
Thomson, James 15, 63, 121
Thrale, Hester Lynch [also Piozzi] 153, 157–8
Tierra del Fuego 1, 49
Titian 62
    Diana and Actaeon 36–7
    Venus Anadyomene 52, 63
Tonga 12, 22
    Tongans compared to Tahitians 103
    visits of Cook's ships at 91–115
Tongatapu [Tongatabu, or Amsterdam Is.]
        93
    landscape of 107–8
treason trials of 1794 170, 174
Tuauru valley 61–2, 63
Tupia [Tupaya] 42, 46, 70, 138
Turkey 182–4
Turner, J. M. W. 62

Vaitepiha 61, 62
Vanuatu 22, 95, 115
    and masculinity 103

Waihou river 124
Wales, William 119
    on J. R. Forster 50
    on Rapanui 5
Webber, John 165, 166
Wesley, John 42–4, 47
West, Benjamin 115, 184, 185, 187
    Joseph Banks 38, 76
Westall, Richard 171
Wheatley, Francis 62, 178
Wilberforce, William 175, 176, 179, 180
Williams, Helen Maria 145
Wilson, Kathleen 9, 146
Wilson, Richard 18, 19, 24, 40, 62
    Et in Arcadia Ego 3
    Solitude 64
    White Monk, The 64–5
Windham, William 176, 179, 196
Wollstonecraft, Mary 20, 60
Woollett, William 3, 14, 15
Wordsworth, William 142
    York, Prince Frederick, Duke of 18, 23, 170,
        178, 182, 184, 185, 189–93, 196

Yusuf Agah Efendi 182

Zoffany, Johann 18